IN FAVOR OF THE SAINTS

Living, Standing And Taking Possession of the Kingdom in This Evil Day

DON UPHAM

authorHOUSE

AuthorHouse™
1663 Liberty Drive
Bloomington, IN 47403
www.authorhouse.com
Phone: 833-262-8899

© 2022 Don Upham. All rights reserved.

No part of this book may be reproduced, stored in a retrieval system, or transmitted by any means without the written permission of the author.

Published by AuthorHouse 06/27/2022

ISBN: 978-1-6655-6267-6 (sc)
ISBN: 978-1-6655-6270-6 (e)

Print information available on the last page.

Any people depicted in stock imagery provided by Getty Images are models, and such images are being used for illustrative purposes only.
Certain stock imagery © Getty Images.

Scripture quotations taken from the New American Standard Bible®, Copyright © 1960, 1962, 1963, 1968, 1971, 1972, 1973, 1975, 1977, 1995 by The Lockman Foundation. Used by permission. (www.Lockman.org)

This book is printed on acid-free paper.

Because of the dynamic nature of the Internet, any web addresses or links contained in this book may have changed since publication and may no longer be valid. The views expressed in this work are solely those of the author and do not necessarily reflect the views of the publisher, and the publisher hereby disclaims any responsibility for them.

CONTENTS

ACKNOWLEDGMENTS xi
INTRODUCTION xiii

> *My preferred means of communication is face to face, for then I can see how you are receiving and reacting to the information I am presenting, and know whether you are truly interested. Face to face also gives the opportunity to modify the presentation in order to answer your specific questions at the time that they come up. But unfortunately, there may not be enough time to get this information to all of you face to face.*

Chapter 1   CALLED TO BE A MINISTER, BUT NOT A PASTOR 1

> *I know from talking with many of you over the years, that there are lots of other Christians, also sensing they have been called to and equipped for ministry. You, like I, had found no platform or encouragement to exercise that calling.*

Chapter 2   LESSONS FROM ARGENTINA 11

> *Omar began to ponder, if this was the case in this city, demonic authority over the city had to be removed before the people were able to see and respond to the Gospel, "Could it be that this is a general principal that might also apply to the other cities in Argentina?"*

Chapter 3   WHAT DO YOU MEAN THE LORD SAID…? 29

> *If you already are very familiar with how the Lord communicates with you and are tempted to skip over this chapter, I would suggest that you suppress that temptation. Read anyway, because what you read here may help you to assist and train someone else to hear the Lord or even to realize that you should help others with this skill.*

Chapter 4   MORE EXAMPLES OF HEARING THE LORD 39

I was very convicted, through the teaching of John Wimber, of the necessity to see what the Lord was doing in another person before we start praying for healing (or anything else for that matter). Also, convicted of the necessity to speak over them what we hear the Lord speaking, not what we are thinking or our desires for the person.

Chapter 5   A STOP BY THE ARMORY ON THE WAY TO THE
FRONT LINES 51

The army of the Body of Christ has gradually become accustomed to increasing difficulties in life and personal challenges that have become gradually greater and greater. They have not recognized that like the frog placed in the pot of cold water, the heat is being turned up and they are being boiled alive.

Chapter 6   THE YEAR 2001, A YEAR OF TRANSITIONS 67

By December of 2000, I had reached the spiritual low point of my entire life. I found myself crying out to the Lord and yet feeling the growing suspicion that maybe there was not really a God at all. My prayers certainly seemed to be just disappearing into a void of nothingness.

Chapter 7   DOING DAMAGE TO THE ENEMIES CAMP 71

The word I heard now from the Lord on New Year's Eve 2001 was both a rebuke and a command. He said, "For the last seven years you have been withdrawing more and more from the ministry to which I called you and as a result you have been suffering more and more hits from the enemy, it is time that you start doing some damage to the enemy's camp."

Chapter 8   "U" IS FOR UNDERSTANDING 79

The study of this two-week period of time was also unlike any of the study or research I had ever done before. I did not have to search through hours of material to find one sentence that may be relevant. The Lord seemed to direct me to every relevant page on the World Wide Web, and also in the libraries.

| Chapter 9 | THE HISTORY OF A SEAL ON KNOWLEDGE.................... 95 |

The root establishing of a spiritual authority structure by men, leads to many other events and actions by persons living in that city. The actions of persons in later generations will come into agreement with that same spirit. This is just like I described with the demonic watcher symbol in an earlier chapter.

| Chapter 10 | THE REVELATION OF THE SEAL.. 103 |

That night, at 2:30 in the morning the Lord awoke me with this phrase repeating over and over, "The key is in the crown." I knew in my head that literally, the key passes through the crown in the seal, but what I understood the Lord to be saying to me was, the key to understanding this mystery is in the crown.

| Chapter 11 | SO NOW WHAT DO I DO LORD?... 121 |

The God in Heaven who reveals mysteries had just revealed a mystery and all of the knowledge to be able to understand that mystery. So now, what do I do Lord?

| Chapter 12 | ENLARGE THE PLACE OF YOUR TENT............................. 133 |

I know house wives who do not work outside the house, who are not considered church leaders, or leaders of any organization and who have no appointed secular or religious authority, yet appear to have great spiritual authority over a region simply because of their obedience in listening to the Lord and carrying out the acts and worship of which He instructs them.

| Chapter 13 | SPIRITUAL MAPPING THIRTEEN POINTS OF UNDERSTANDING...153 |

During the month of October 2002, I was trying to get groups throughout Los Angeles to recognize and take spiritual responsibility in the territory during this demonic festival of "Sacred Music." I was also, for my own part, taking responsibility to obey the Lord to understand the meaning of the thirteen points that He had revealed to me in that prayer meeting in September.

Chapter 14   A PROTECTIVE CANOPY IS RAISED 177

I now heard from the Lord to go ahead and set a date for the Canopy prophetic act. The Lord did not give me a date and the roads were still closed in the National Forest areas, but the Lord said for me to set a date. I still did not even have thirteen people who I thought might want to be a part of this.

Chapter 15   RETALIATION? OR EVIDENCE OF VICTORY? 201

Many people, through fear, have not prepared for or entered into an offensive state of spiritual warfare out of fear of what the enemy might do to them or to others around them if they did. As a result, they have taken a very passive role in their Christian walk.

Chapter 16   SIZING UP A SPIRITUAL PROBLEM 221

The Lord went on to say, "If you will simply walk down the boardwalk and worship Me, I will draw near to you. If you will refuse to acknowledge Satan's authority over this area, he will flee as you enthrone Me on your praises."

Chapter 17   TAKING A WALK ON VENICE BEACH 237

Very shortly after entering into the city, we had our first experience of a warlock coming up out of nowhere and speaking curses in our face in tongues (nose to nose). We just kept quietly worshipping under our breath and tried to ignore that first challenge to our presence in this spiritual realm.

Chapter 18   INNOCENT BLOOD AND BREAKING THE NECK OF WITCHCRAFT 255

What I saw was a gathering of homeless, witches and warlocks numbering in the thousands all gathering on the Western edge of the death scene. They were absorbing the empowering resulting from the shedding of the blood of ten lives two days before.

Chapter 19   TIME FOR A MANDALA TO CHANGE THE LAW OF THE WORLD 273

The Chakrasamvara Mandala that was about to be built in Los Angeles is referred to as the "Law Mandala." Its purpose is to alter the law of the world by initiating the world rule of the Chakravartin.

Chapter 20	GATES OF DESTRUCTION FROM THE ABYSS 291
	Was the Lord trying to tell us that it would be the South Gate, The Water Gate that would be the next to be opened, or did our worship and the intercession over that area contain this storm to where it would do very little damage?
Chapter 21	A FOURTH KINGDOM WAGES WAR WITH THE SAINTS 311
	As "king and politician," the Chakravartin is a sovereign who reigns over all the states on earth. The leaders of the tribes and nations are subordinate to him. His epithet is "one who rules with his own will, even the kingdoms of other kings."
Chapter 22	WHEN THE SAINTS HAVE BEGUN TO TAKE POSSESSION OF THE KINGDOM.. 325
	It is the power and authority of His Kingdom. We can aim and fire the weapons, but unless those bullets, artillery shells and bombs are filled with His powder (power) they are useless.
Appendix A	Definitions 343
Appendix B	The Revelation of the Seal of the City of Pasadena, California... 345
Appendix C	Prophetic Words 367

ACKNOWLEDGMENTS

There have been many teachers in my life over the years that I would consider my mentors. I have had a personal relationship with some, but not many of them. Their teachings and life experiences have helped to shape how I look at life and how I came to a point in my life where the Lord has become my primary mentor in the past 9 years.

Those I would like to thank for the things you have added to my life through your teachings, writings, and examples are; Ed Silvoso, Mark Bubeck, Dr. Jack Hayford, Dr. Peter Wagner, Dr. Ed Murphy, John Wimber, Dr. Dutch Sheets, Bill Johnson, Lou Engle, Chuck Pierce, Cindy Jacobs, Omar Cabrerra, Omar Olier, Pastor Lorenzo, Don Paul, James Stephens, Dr. Paul L. Cox, Eddie Smith and Arthur Burke.

There is also the mother I never got to know but whom I believe was praying for me as I lived in foster homes until I was adopted at age 4 and a half. My adopted parents Con and Nelle are no longer alive, but they taught me unconditional love and gave me a secure home to grow up in out in beautiful Topanga Canyon on the West side of Los Angeles.

Of course there are hundreds of others of you out there that do not have notable names that I would also like to thank for the times of discussion, council, prayer, intercession, worship, and prophetic acts together that have poked holes in the canopy of Satan's dominion in this world and encouraged me on. Then, there are many others of you, that our brief encounter for a few minutes or a few hours, was a divine appointment that touched both of us. For those experiences, thank you Lord.

I would also like to thank a dear brother in the Lord, Loren, whose generosity and obedience made it possible to finish this project.

Finally, I wish to thank my wife Janice for her vision and encouragement that finally pulled me down into the chair before the computer keys to get this book written and into your hands. Her constant encouragement, prayer covering and urging is what has enabled me to just, "do it." Here is Janice's endorsement as she asked me to include in this publication:

To those committed Christians who read this book and follow the leading of the Holy Spirit, those who have living relationship (Matthew 7:23) with the master of all creation and have a reservation for all eternity, I say to you: It is not accidental that you have chosen this book.

Don's experiences in life and the things he went through following exactly what the Lord directed; exactly in the way He directed and with the timing He directed; are written here for your utter amazement at how God intervenes in the lives of men, and just a little example of how you can be used by God also. The book also includes cautions to not stray from God's orders and instruction on steps to take in order to not be a "needless casualty of war".

Most important also, how to break off any attachments after spiritual battle. Learn from our mistakes, and carefully cover your loved ones also, when in spiritual warfare.

This book covers how to prepare for battle; stand and above all stand to finish the good work He began in you in order to hear "well done thou good and faithful servant".

As Don's wife of 17 years, I know the man clearly and can tell you what you see is what you get. I highly recommend and endorse this book.

Don is a godly man that God gave me as a gift and I recommend this book to you as an honest and thrilling read to gain understanding of spiritual warfare and taking possession of the kingdom of God.

p.s. I wasn't particularly thrilled by Chapter 10, numbers bore me! LOL

INTRODUCTION

My preferred means of communication is face to face, for then I can see how you are receiving and reacting to the information I am presenting, and know whether you are truly interested. Face to face also gives the opportunity to modify the presentation in order to answer your specific questions at the time that they come up. Unfortunately, there may not be enough time to get this information to all of you face to face. So far in the past several years, I have only been able to meet one on one, or face to face with several hundred people and then only able to present a limited amount of the information due to time constraints. I have perhaps reached a few hundred more with a small portion of content through audio CD's of some of the teaching and experiences, and perhaps another couple of hundred through individual emails and newsletters. In all of this, I seldom have been able to fully develop and communicate the extent of downloads from the Lord and the experiences He has taken myself, and others through, over the last seven years. I have barely been able to touch on some of the boot camp, basic training and specialty schools the Lord put me through before he kicked me out of the airplane and I again parachuted into the front lines of spiritual warfare on January 4 of 2002.

In the past several years, the Lord has specifically instructed me to create a book that will be a testimony of the battles and victories the Lord has used to retrain me, and others, in Spiritual Warfare. This book also contains many of the research revelations and scriptural revelations that the Lord used to motivate, give understanding and guide through this time.

I am not going to attempt to address, in this writing, the major traditional doctrinal issues with regard to end times. I know that there are differing views among factions of the Body of Christ, many of which I have studied in depth and with which I am very familiar. I am not here to debate or speculate on any of those. The central focus of what I am presenting, is simply and primarily a walk and talk with the Lord over a period of seven years and what the Lord revealed as the important issues to understand and be dealt with right now. This is primarily a book about living, standing and taking possession of the Kingdom in this evil day. As a result of the things that are being revealed through the spiritual warfare in which you and I are engaged, this writing will by default point to some prophesies in scripture that could be interpreted as being fulfilled in this present day. I will present these in later chapters, and I am sure they will be controversial with some people, as I am not aware of very many other people who are connecting the same dots at present. It is my hope that pointing out prophetic fulfillments and their applications to this day will not take the focus off of equipping the saints for the work of the ministry, which is the primary reason for writing this book and presenting this material.

This goes for other doctrinal issues that may come up in this book. You will hear interpretations of scripture and events that you perhaps have never heard anyone else teach or which you have heard very differently in the past. Ask the Lord. Listen to the Holy Spirit and search the scriptures yourself, to see if it is so. Don't just follow and believe everything you hear or read. I have been around a bit in my sixty-eight years as a Christian, and I have been exposed to just about every use and abuse of doctrine in nearly every denomination in this country and several others. I am not writing this book to debate anyone's doctrine or to put anyone down. I am simply sharing with you what has been the reality of my walk with the Lord. The things He has revealed to me and to others that has enabled us to stand in this evil day; and not only to stand, but also to move forward in taking possession of the Kingdom.

I know there are some who will read this book that strongly believe that the Kingdom is future and we cannot take possession of it now. I hope that after reading this book the Spirit might give you a different understanding. As evidenced by those I have taught and spoken with over the last several years, the information I am about to share with you, has opened their eyes of understanding in a way that has empowered, encouraged and set them free to be about taking possession of the kingdom. It has also brought them out from the bondage of a religiosity, which had kept them hopeless and powerless for years.

I am not presenting this material as a methodology for doing spiritual warfare in any particular location throughout the world, though I will talk about some general principles for approaching spiritual warfare that seem to be common in all of the parts of the world I have visited. Please do not take any one of the examples that I will give and try to apply it to a situation that you are facing just because it seems like a similar situation. You will hear me repeat this over and over throughout this book, you must know how you hear the Lord's voice and you must hear from Him what you are to do, speak, or not do or speak, how you are to do it, with whom you are to do it and when you are to do it. Then you must obey Him exactly!

I am quite aware that when I use the statement, "The Lord showed me this" or "The Lord told me this," some people are incredulous, or equate me to one of those mass murderers who "heard god's voice telling him or her to do it." Or you are just hopeless that you will never be able to do these things because you just don't hear the Lord like I am describing. For that reason, I have included a chapter near the beginning of this book "What do you mean the Lord said," to address this with some biblical teaching and lots of practical examples.

Now, here is a brief word about the title of this book. I have titled this book, *In Favor of the Saints*, which is a portion of the passage, which has become the focus of my teaching and the Lords revelation to me for the last six years. This comes from Daniel 7:22 and I will expound on the centrality of this statement in a later Chapter.

In the interpretation of the centrality of this passage in Daniel for the present time, I will make statements about certain other religious beliefs and practices. Please hear me clearly, I am not doing this out of any animosity and do not wish to create any animosity toward the individuals who hold and practice those beliefs. I make these statements to illustrate the depth of our misunderstanding of the age in which we live, and the reality of a spiritual realm of which few people today in the United States are able to conceive. I hate the demons controlling and destroying these human vessels. I pray salvation through the blood of Jesus for the humans involved and affected by them. The fate of the demons they carry, worship and to which they give authority, is already determined. My greatest hope is that the human vessels not suffer the same end.

I have come to conclude that many in the United States, who call themselves Christians, do not know or believe the Bible. They have been too caught up in their own self-centered view of salvation and personal comfort (Monday night football or whatever); or, they have been misled, by "spiritual leaders" whose agendas are more controlled by self-preservation and perpetuation of institutions. They have not had their primary focus in "overcoming by the blood of the Lamb, the word of their testimony, and the fact that they did not love their lives even unto death."[1] They have been practicing a form of godliness, but denying or just plain oblivious to the power of it.[2] As a result, those who understand and are able to manipulate, or be manipulated by, the demonic gods of this world are very well along in their agendas. They are gaining dominion over cities, states and nations right under the noses of the disbelieving and distracted "saints of the Most High God." In some cases, "Christian" churches are even opening their doors and welcoming the human representatives of these demon gods right into the pulpit. They are being given permission and authority to establish the dominion of these demons over the church and the city, but more about this later in the book.

This is a true story. None of the events and experiences shared has been made up for the sake of example. Everything happened just as described. What cannot be proved as factual by scientific methodology are the interpretations of the events and the experiences described. I can only say, Christianity is a walk of faith and faith is the key ingredient if we are to do "righteous acts"[3] and take possession of the Kingdom.[4] Often at the time of an event and even for a time after, faith in the results of obedience, was the only thing to which to cling until some evidence of the fruit of our labors would form and give substance to our faith. Unfortunately, if action is taken to prevent physical disaster and the disaster does not occur, who will believe you? It is difficult to convince some that the disaster would have occurred if others had not acted in faith to pre-empt it. It is like changing the oil in your car every three thousand miles because you know by faith in the experiences of others, if you don't, the car will break down eventually. If the car never breaks down, however, you have no evidence that your frequent oil changes prevented it from breaking down. You just have faith that this is the case.

Some of the names of people and places where events occurred have been changed. We are still in the battle. To reveal some things would put fellow saints and accomplished work in danger.

Unless otherwise noted, scripture quotes are from the *New American Standard Bible* (NASB®), as this is the translation I have found to consistently be a most literal and accurate translation of the original Hebrew and Greek texts. Even at that, it is often necessary to use tools that are now available on computer and other reference tools to look at the original words in the Greek and Hebrew. This is to understand the derivations and the grammar structures of the word and the sentence. I make no claim to being a scholar in these original languages, even though I have had formal seminary training in both. I rely heavily upon the work of those scholars who have put together tools to probe understandings that do not translate well into our current culture. Sometimes understanding of the original use and context, of a word or phrase, is simply passed over because it does not seem important or because we have attached an understanding that fits our worldview or doctrinal stance.

I also rely heavily upon The Holy Spirit to teach both you and me, to make the scriptures relevant[5]. There are a few of these understandings, which may be overlooked using a different translation of the Bible. So, bear with me if you have a personal preference for a different translation or paraphrase of the Bible.

With the previous disclaimers and disclosures in place, fasten your seat belts and join me on the wild ride to the front lines of spiritual warfare. We will first attend some boot camp basic training and then I will describe to you some of the ways that The Ancient of Days is ruling, "In Favor of the Saints" as the saints are taking possession of the Kingdom.

Endnotes

1. Rev 12:11
2. 2 Timothy 3:5
3. Revelation 19:8
4. Daniel 7:22
5. 1 John 2:27

CHAPTER 1

CALLED TO BE A MINISTER, BUT NOT A PASTOR

In the year 2000, I became increasingly aware of my "ministry" being narrowed in definition to only the use of technical skills. Opportunities to teach and use forty-five plus years experience and study as a Christian in other areas of ministry had become non-existent. I began to wonder why had God taken me so many places, and exposed me to so many world-renowned teachers? Why had He allowed me to do three years of graduate seminary study, and allowed me to earn a master's degree in education, only to be confined in obscurity to back rooms, taping, and editing dozens of other well know peoples' teachings?

I know for one thing, I heard all of those taped teachings hundreds of times over, while editing and duplicating them for others. Through the repetition, I probably absorbed a lot more than the average conference attendee who only heard the message once on the fly. Still, I felt like I was bursting with information, council, and teaching with no place to use all that was bound up inside of me.

I know from talking with many of you over the years, that there are lots of other Christians, also sensing they have been called to and equipped for ministry. You, like I, had found no platform or encouragement to exercise that calling. You, like I, have even felt at times those in professional ministry are threatened by our gifts. They have purposely kept us suppressed, under control and "under their authority."

I remember on a number of occasions asking the Lord is this all there is, am I done with the ministry to which I was called? Should I be content with just stuffing this drive in me to teach and guide others in their growth and maturing in their Christian walk? Should I consider that all that I am to do for the rest of my life is sit in the back ground, mouth closed, making sure that other people are successfully getting their messages out?

For nine years, I tried to convince myself that this was ok, as I continually got pressure from others to keep me in this mechanical-technical mode. At times, I would share some of what the Lord was revealing to me, and teachings that were in my spirit with a few of these ministry leaders. Often the things I shared, would be incorporated into their teaching, with no credit given of the source, and I would just get calls from them about the next technical duty.

Don't get me wrong. I do have very strong technical skills, having a Bachelor's Degree in Industrial Arts, having been a Navy Helicopter Pilot and then a fireman for Twenty-four years. But, I have also been a student of the Bible since age seven and what I would consider a very strong spirit filled Christian. As I said before, I spent three years in seminary training and then another year for the Masters of Education. I have preached from the pulpit, ministered prayer for healing and seen people healed, I led a missions training and support ministry for years in the early 80's, I was a full time chaplain for a major West Coast Fire Department for five years, and have taught adult and youth Sunday Schools for many years. I had attended just about every major Christian Conference in the Los Angeles Area over a period of 20 years and been to conferences in Argentina over a period of thirteen years with the best-known Christian teachers and evangelists of the day. I was close personal friends with several of these and had traveled numerous places around the world with them. But here I was now, sitting alone in a darkened editing studio with the tapes playing as my only contact with the world outside. My spirit was burning with information and desire to touch the world more directly.

Seminary: an Experience to Remember

Let me back up a bit. Since the mid 1960's, I have known I had a call to ministry. Having entered the Navy while in college in 1966, this call was recognized shipboard, and I was often called upon to hold the Sunday morning chapel services on board the aircraft carrier to which I was assigned. I also was put into leadership positions in the civilian churches I attended in Pensacola Florida and in Lakehurst New Jersey. When I was offered an early release from the Navy as they were reducing forces in the fall of 1971, I applied for and was accepted to Seminary. I was eagerly supported by some of the Churches I had been involved with over the years and so off to seminary I went.

What a surprise it was for me to find ninety percent of those at the seminary I was attending in Louisville, Kentucky, appeared to not believe the Bible. Instead they believed mostly what other people philosophized about the Bible. In fact, in one class, I was severely scolded and threatened on several occasions for quoting the Bible in answer to questions that are clearly taught in the Bible. Instead, other texts such as the *Tibetan Book of the Dead* were given as source material for how we should understand various topics. Well after a year and a half at that school I decided to head out to California to continue my "education" at another well know evangelical seminary in Pasadena, California.

The next year and a half went a little better, though the professor that I was a teaching assistant for and really respected at the time, came out of the closet about ten years later, and left his wife. He is now one of the leading advocates in the United States for gays in ministry.

In my third and senior year of a Master of Divinity Degree at this graduate level seminary, I ran into another bump in the road. I questioned my denominational leaders as to why the denomination had just adopted a doctrine that contradicted itself. I was told that I did not understand the issues and assigned a period of study with a local Senior Pastor holding a Doctor of Theology degree. After numerous books read on the subject and several papers prepared for this Doctor of Theology, I received a diagnosis of my problem. "My theology was perfectly sound and orthodox, it just wasn't Presbyterian." When I took this diagnosis back to my candidate's committee, I was advised to not worry about it, just get ordained and then do whatever seems right to me. By the way, the very prominent minister who chaired that Candidates' Committee stepped down from his position as senior pastor of a large church some years later as the result of an "indiscretion."

Shortly after the doctrinal examination of my theology, I attended an ordination examination for some other ministry candidates at the local Presbytery of which I was a member. This was "so I would understand the process." I sat silently in disbelief when I heard a candidate's response to the question, "do you believe that Jesus is the Son of God?" The candidate's answer was NO! The candidate's sponsor, an ordained pastor, gave some excuse that "he just had a different way of understanding this." After several other such shocking answers, well, apparently I was the only one shocked, because after several more similar NO answers, the Presbytery voted to ordain the man.

My head was spinning and I talked to the Lord. I decided after council with a friend and former pastor to take some time off from seminary to pray and try to understand what I was doing there, even though I was quite certain that the Lord had brought me there. The answer came shortly. I heard, very clearly, from the Lord, "I called you to ministry; I did not call you to be a Pastor." My next question was, "what does that mean?"

My orientation up to that point was that there were only two types of ministries, being a pastor or being a missionary. At that point, I knew I had not been called to be a missionary. I also heard clearly that it was not necessary to have a degree from seminary, even though I was only about three or four courses from finishing. The Lord assured me that He had brought me to seminary, and had accomplished His purposes in doing so, now I was to get on with the ministry.

What ministry? I had done "ministry" all through seminary working as a pastor intern in a small rural church in Kentucky and a youth minister in Malibu and Pasadena. Now I found myself in 1975, working full time, in the background, editing audio tapes and radio programs of well know ministers at $5.00 an hour before taxes and wondering how I was going to feed my family that now included my first child.

Putting Out Fires of a Different Kind

I knew I needed to find a job that would support my family. Early in 1976, I saw an ad, in the *"Los Angeles Times,"* that the Los Angeles County Fire Department was accepting applications. My father, who had adopted me when I was four and a half, had been a fireman for the County. I knew he loved his job and it supported our family well enough during my growing years that we were able to take yearly vacations and lived a modest but comfortable life. I have always loved the out of doors and I care about helping people, a combination that I was told is a perfect fit for a fireman. I applied and was hired in September of 1976 just before my 30th birthday. I did love the job and progressed from Fireman to Paramedic to Apparatus Engineer and then to Captain by the spring of 1982. All this time I continued to ponder, "What does it mean to be a minister but not a pastor?"

On a Mission to Learn

Well, at the same time I was appointed Captain and assigned to a station eighty miles each way from home, I was also appointed as an elder in the non-denominational independent church I had been a part of for the previous six years. As an elder, I was assigned the responsibility of chairing and overseeing the missionary sending program of the church. This church commission was floundering at the hands of four very overworked individuals. I prayed for several weeks about how to make that ministry work. The Lord revealed a strategy of reorganization that would bring about fifty additional people into the committee overseeing the missions program, thus spreading the workload. The implementation was near miraculous as when the concepts were shared, person after person volunteered. Within two months, the new, improved, missions program was launched. For a year, that ministry flourished and touched many lives. Just about one year later, something very strange happened. The co-chair with me who was working on a Doctorate in Psychology at the same seminary I had left eight years prior, suddenly notified me, through a letter in the mail while I was out of town, that he was no longer available to assist. I learned shortly after, he had left his wife and children and was seeing another woman "more attuned to his status and education." I would not see or hear from this man again for more than ten years. The same week another one of my co-chairs called and asked to meet with me for breakfast. At the breakfast meeting, he informed me that he had suffered a nervous breakdown some years before and was feeling the same symptoms coming on again. He asked to be relieved of his leadership position in the missions program, which I did immediately on the condition he would meet with me weekly so that I could stand with him in his struggle. This we did and he never did manifest another breakdown.

Welcome to spiritual warfare 101! I had not known much about spiritual warfare up to that point, but losing two ministry leaders out of the blue in one week caught my attention. I prayed and met with the rest of the committee. We decided that if we were to be equipping and counseling missionaries on the foreign field, where we knew they faced spiritual warfare, maybe we in the church back home had better start learning more about spiritual warfare. For the next nine months, we spent the majority of our meetings together praying and learning how to put on the armor and more importantly how to stand! Stand! Stand in the midst of this evil day as Ephesians 6 tells us.

Face to Face with Spiritual Warfare

For me, the spiritual warfare was not just confined to the missions program at church. All of a sudden, spiritual warfare was also cropping up at home, and on the job. A relative became very hostile and verbally abusive, sometimes for hours at a time. I became convinced that there was need for deliverance, so I read everything I could find and tried to cast the demon out. I would learn later that this is very difficult to do if the person you are trying to help does not want to be helped and you don't understand the concept of spiritual authority.

On the job, spiritual warfare was even harder to deal with. I remember one incident very clearly. We had just gone out on a medical call to a mobile home. The lady there was life threateningly ill from several advanced chronic conditions. As the paramedics struggled to get an IV and establish medications, I glanced at the wall above her couch bed. There was a black velvet painting of Satan smiling down at her. "Whoa lady, now I understand why you are so sick," I almost said out loud. She was so out of it she probably would not have heard me. I did not have time anyway, for just then the alarm went off on my radio. My crew and I left the paramedics to load her in the ambulance as we rushed off to another incident a few blocks away.

As we arrived, we found a young man in his late teens cowering next to a fence on the corner of the block. The story I got from a neighbor was that he had started acting "really weird" earlier in the afternoon and then had locked himself in the bathroom. After hours of family members pleading with him through the bathroom door, he had burst out, shattering the still locked wooden bathroom door and run out of the house. As I looked down at him there on the street corner, a demon glared from his eyes and he began cursing me. But in the next moment, the demon disappeared and tears came to his eyes and he whispered to me, "please help me, please help me, he's hurting me." With that, the demon glare returned and a guttural laughter came out of his mouth.

By this time the Sheriffs, an ambulance and another paramedic squad had showed up on scene. I was in charge of the scene and I struggled, as the only Christian in that crowd, to know what to do. I did not fully understand my spiritual authority at that time, but I did know that I was an official representative of the County and the authority charged with caring for this person for which the system only had one solution. It was my duty to turn him over to the Sheriffs and ambulance for transport to a facility for a 72 Hour Hold, and psychological evaluation. I knew that this was not what he needed. What he needed was deliverance, but what could I do in my official position as a Fire Captain? I would learn some time later, the very troubling news, that three days after release from the 72 Hold, this young man killed another person and then himself.

That was a heavy weight on my spirit for months along with all of the other warfare I was facing only somewhat successfully.

A short time later, I was on a family vacation in the fall of 1983 with my friend Ed Silvoso and his family. As we were driving along the road near Monterey California, I was telling Ed about these various encounters and asking him, "Was this spiritual warfare?" He assured me that it was. He recommended that I read and use *The Adversary* by a Baptist Pastor Mark Bubeck[1], to learn more about praying through spiritual warfare by praying doctrinal prayers. Ed also told me I needed to go to Argentina to learn more about spiritual warfare and how to deal with it. I was able to arrange to go with him for three weeks in February 1984. For the fourteen hour flight to Argentina, I had been assigned to sit next to Dr. Ed Murphy, then President of Overseas Crusades, who had written the *Handbook for Spiritual Warfare*[2] and whose spiritual warfare curriculum I would teach as a nine month Sunday School Course a number of years later.

Dr. Murphy never showed for the flight. We learned several days later that he had suffered a near nervous breakdown and had been isolated, the night before the trip, from contact with all others by his doctors. He had just returned from two exhausting trips. One was to Africa where he and a ministry associate had been stranded in a coup. Severely dehydrated, they had to escape from the county on foot with only the clothes on their back. They went right from there to ministering at "high places" in Columbia, South America and being challenged by high-level demonic principalities that were controlling much of the drug trade in Columbia. When I did speak with Dr. Murphy a couple of years later, he would tell me what he learned from that trip; "Travel light with what you can easily carry on your back when on spiritual assignment in foreign countries, and to never again travel without his wife." "She would never have allowed me to go into such intense warfare in such an exhausted and weakened condition." I would learn that lesson about warring when exhausted for myself many years later, but we will get to that in another chapter.

Well the trip to Argentina in 1984 was a major turning point in my life. I finally got the answer after nine years of asking, "What does it mean to be a minister but not a pastor?

Endnotes

1 Bubeck, Mark I. The Adversary. Chicago: The Moody Bible Institute, 1975.
2 Murphy, Dr. Ed. The Handbook for Spiritual Warfare. Nashville: Thomas Nelson Publishers, Inc. 1992, 1996

CHAPTER 2

LESSONS FROM ARGENTINA

I spent three weeks in Argentina in February 1984, just two months into the elected presidency of Alfonsin. This was just after the "dirty war" where thousands of women and young people disappeared at the hands of a corrupt military dictatorship. This dictatorship also plundered the people of the country of their jewelry, silver and gold, ostensibly to finance the war over the Falkland Islands with the British. Americans were still not too popular in Argentina because of our support of the British. Argentina is a country whose government was still Catholic by constitution, meaning you could not hold public office unless you were a practicing Catholic. Yet two years before the ending of the "dirty war" and while there was still strong Catholic control in the government, an incredible thing had happened. I was able to see some of the fruit of what was happening right as it was beginning to spread across that nation. In fact, this move of God being advanced by the actions of a single man beginning to take possession of the Kingdom, is probably what caused the Ancient of Days to start ruling in favor of the Saints in Argentina[1]. This may have been among the righteous acts of the saints, bringing an end to the "dirty war" by the military dictatorship, and starting one of the greatest revivals in the history of the world.

The Priestly Anointing of Unity

The small group of people with whom I traveled to Argentina, began our three weeks there participating in a weeklong conference at the Harvest Evangelism Training Center near the town of San Nicolas. At this conference, there were pastors and leaders from protestant churches all over that area of Argentina. What struck me first was the friendship and fellowship of this group of people from a number of different mainline denominations as well as from independent churches and house churches. I remember one afternoon, singing worship hymns knowing there was a Baptist pastor on my right, a Nazarene pastor on my left, a Pentecostal in front of me, and a Presbyterian behind me. They were all in one accord and enjoying one another's company with no competition and no doctrinal issues between them. I had never experienced that in the United States up to that point, and it is still pretty rare here. In part, I believe that this was because the Protestant groups were by far still the minority in Argentina, so they had to work together to some extent. The other amazing thing was there was also no issue that some spoke in tongues and were more active in manifestation of gifts than others. This just seemed accepted as a non-issue. A passage that is often quoted in Argentina is Ps 133.

> Behold, how good and how pleasant it is
> For brothers to dwell together in unity!
> It is like the precious oil upon the head,
> Coming down upon the beard,
> Even Aaron's beard,
> Coming down upon the edge of his robes.
> It is like the dew of Hermon,
> Coming down upon the mountains of Zion;
> For there the LORD commanded the blessing-- life forever.

The significance of this passage is that it was the oil that was poured over Aaron that was the seal of the anointing on the priesthood. It was the oil poured down his robe and that soaked the fabric of the garment all the way to the hem or "edge" that carried the anointing. When the priesthood was passed on from Aaron there was no new robe constructed. The new priest wore the same robe that Aaron had worn because this oil soaked garment carried the anointing of Aaron or the mantle of the priesthood that rested on him. Just before Aaron dies on the top of Mount Hor, Moses strips off his anointed priestly garment and puts it on Aaron's son Eleazar at God's direction.[2]

In this Song of Ascents (Psalm 133) by David, we see that, these brothers dwelling in "unity" is equated to the anointing of the priesthood that rested on Aaron and his garment. Throughout chapters 39 and 40 of the book of Exodus there is a strong emphasis on the anointed garments created for Aaron in order for him to be a priest to God. So too in Revelation 5:10 we are now told that we have been made to be priests of God. We carry that anointing when we dwell in unity. The unity between the brothers of different denominations in Argentina carried a significant anointing of the priesthood. It was such that several years later, when Carlos Anacondia would be called forth as an evangelist who drew crowds of over one hundred thousand to various public locations, he would not enter a town or city to hold a meeting unless all of the pastors of the town agreed that he should come. They all were required to be at all of the meetings, sitting right up front signifying their unity over what was occurring. This is why, I believe, such power and anointing would rest on those meetings with tens of thousands being delivered of demons and receiving Jesus the Christ into their lives.

From San Nicolas, my traveling companions and I went to the city of Santa Fe. There, various gatherings were set up and hosted to share with groups of people that were in similar occupations. I was given the opportunity to meet with about thirty members of the city Fire Department including the Fire Chief. Having shared a number of statistics about my own Los Angeles County Fire Department, I went on to talk about the importance of my faith and trust in the Lord when faced with the hazards of the job as a fireman. At the end of my talk, the Fire Chief asked me if I have opportunities to share these things in training sessions with the members of my department. When I explained that the government structure here in the United States would not allow that, he was very upset and said, "Well, these are life and death issues, you should be teaching them to all of your firemen." Several firemen in that meeting which was in a public building, not in a church, gave their lives to Christ that night. This was much to the pleasure of their Fire Chief who now knew their fear would be under control in dangerous situations they would face, as they now knew who had control over their life.

Next on the trip was one of the most influential meetings that I would have in my life and the lesson that became a turning point in my life. It was the meeting where I heard the piece of information that answered my question for all time about what it means to be a minister and not a Pastor.

Finally the Answer

Our group traveled to the City of Rosario, where several in our group were assisting in a one-week training conference for the elders and deacons of the churches of Omar and Marfa Cabrerra. Omar and Marfa, husband and wife, were Protestant Evangelists who traveled throughout Argentina holding evangelistic meetings. Now remember I said that Argentina was still Catholic by Constitution. As a result of their teachings and laying hands on for healing, Omar had been arrested on several occasions for practicing medicine without a license. They had been held up by highway robbers and had been persecuted by the priests in a number of locations. Despite this, through the 1970's they were still seeing moderate crowds of a thousand or more show up for their meetings and were seeing conversions to Christ both from Catholics and from non-believers.

Omar would relate to me as we sat and talked over afternoon tea there in Rosario, that in 1982, something changed in his approach that transformed their ministry. This has since affected the entire country of Argentina and would also greatly affect my life as I came to understand the implications of the story.

In 1982, he was pondering why one particular city was so closed to the Gospel. He had been there several times and found there were no Protestant ministries in the city and even many of the Catholic Churches were without a priest. Yet, spiritism and occult healers were rampant throughout the city. He had held evangelistic meetings there before, but always very small crowds and almost no response of those coming to Christ. This was totally out of proportion with results in other cities. So Omar decided to rent a hotel room in the city to pray and fast as he asked the Lord why was this city so closed to the Gospel? The Lord's response to him was to reveal the demonic principalities that controlled the city through a canopy of authority or a "dominion" over the city. The Lord then led him through a process of taking authority over the city and driving out the demonic principalities. Omar knew, by the end of five days in the hotel, this had been accomplished. He then went out and rented a basketball stadium, put up signs around town and held an evangelist meeting. The results were phenomenal. Over five thousand people showed up the first night and over forty-five hundred received Christ. A church was planted in one night in a basketball stadium. Omar would return twice a week to pastor this huge church in a basketball stadium.

Omar began to ponder if this was the case in this city, demonic authority over the city had to be removed before the people were able to see and respond to the Gospel, "Could it be that this is a general principal that might also apply to the other cities in Argentina?" He decided to test the principal. Over the next two years, Omar went to ten other cities in Argentina, prayed and fasted in each city until he was able to sense a break in the demonic authority over the city. He then held an evangelistic meeting and saw results similar to the first city.

So then, in 1984, there I was sitting, talking to him as the elders and deacons of these eleven new churches were being trained and discipled. There were eleven hundred elders and deacons at that training session. They were all new believers within the past two years and just a portion of the one hundred thirty-eight thousand new believers who had come to Christ in these eleven cities in the previous two years. This was simply as a result of removing the demonic canopy of principalities over the cities and then inviting the people to Christ. The Argentine revival was born out of this act of spiritual warfare and would expand over the next several years as God also called forth other evangelists. Carlos Anacondia and Claudio Friedzon would draw crowds of more than 100,000 people to individual events. At one point Friedzon's church Rey de Reyes (King of Kings) in Buenos Aires, would have people lined up for blocks to attend the services being held Twenty-three hours as day, seven days a week (They closed for an hour in the middle of the night to clean).

Understanding the Christian Life

What did I learn through this that would transform my life and understanding? Up to that point, I had pretty much thought that the Christian life was just about coming into a relationship with Christ, with the promise of salvation through having received Him as my savior. The rest of my life was pretty much just trying to live a good and relatively sinless life until I died and went to heaven. Sure, I understood the imperative to share Christ with others and teaching them everything the Lord had commanded[3], but I had a pretty shallow view of what comprised "everything." I believe many today in the United States still hold that shallow understanding as they simply wait for the Lord's return. Even though it is right there in scripture, it never occurred to me that there are spiritual forces that keep the people of this world in blindness and darkness. That I might have to get their eyes open and remove the darkness covering eyes before they could be able to see the light of Christ[4].

Scripture tells us; "And He gave some as apostles, and some as prophets, and some as evangelists, and some as pastors and teachers, for the equipping of the saints for the work of service, to the building up of the body of Christ."[5] The word "service" in this scripture is also translated as "ministry" which, in the Greek can mean an appointment in an official office under authority. My concept of ministry up to this point was only those who served in the office of pastor or missionary, but if this were true why would this passage in Ephesians say that the purpose of pastors and teachers, apostles, prophets and evangelists was to equip the "saints" for the work of the ministry. This would imply that at some point the saints become equipped and were to be released into the ministry. This was not what I saw happening in the United States, where those holding the professional, salaried jobs as pastors and teachers seemed to be bent on endless equipping, but never releasing anyone who was not seminary trained and ordained to do "ministry" other than being an usher, Sunday school worker, or church committee member.

The Lord opened my eyes in Argentina to understand that ministry was what was supposed to happen after you have been equipped. Like a parent teaching and equipping a child until they become an adult, at some point the parent must release the child to function as an adult. The parent must release their child to at some point to become a parent who will train their own child. I came to realize I had been very well equipped by the many teachers and pastors in my life. Now as the Lord had told me nine years prior it was time to get about the ministry to which I was called, and which according to the Lord, was not to be a pastor.

I now understood that my "ministry" was that of a spiritual warrior, an enforcer of the Lord's authority. It was to be involved in removing the demonic hindrances and bondages over peoples' lives, so that they could see and hear, and as a result respond to the good news through the process we call evangelism.

I had never felt particularly gifted as an evangelist, so I was amazed at how easy it was to share the "good news" of Christ when I first dealt with those things that were holding these people in darkness and deafness. Much to my surprise, I would discover that this is exactly what Jesus had told Paul on the road to Damascus. Here is Paul's account to King Agrippa using Jesus words as recorded in Acts 26:15-19

> "I am Jesus whom you are persecuting. 'But arise, and stand on your feet; for this purpose I have appeared to you, to appoint you a minister and a witness not only to the things which you have seen, but also to the things

in which I will appear to you; delivering you from the Jewish people and from the Gentiles, to whom I am sending you, to open their eyes so that they may turn from darkness to light and from the dominion of Satan to God, in order that they may receive forgiveness of sins and an inheritance among those who have been sanctified by faith in Me."

One of the first things to strike me about this passage is Jesus begins by telling Paul, "For this purpose I have appeared to you." How would you respond if today Jesus appeared to you and said, "For this purpose I have appeared to you?" After you picked yourself up off the ground, would you be all ears if the Lord of the Universe prefaced what He was about to say to you with the words, "For this purpose I have appeared to you?" So then let's listen very carefully to what the Lord has to say. I believe the intention of the inclusion of this passage in the Bible, is that it also applies to us in this day.

What is a Minister?

Jesus says…I have appeared to you, to "appoint you a minister and witness not only to the things you have seen but also to the things in which I will appear to you." Let's deal with the word "minister" first, as this had been my question for the previous nine years. We quite commonly equate the word minister with the word pastor, but in the Greek they are two completely different words and positions. The word minister here is "huperetes," which might commonly be translated as servant, or an officer of the military or police. Derived from the words for "under" and "oarsman," it means someone serving under the authority of another. Since Jesus is the one making the appointment here, it is under His authority, Paul is being placed. As an officer under authority, that officer has the responsibility of enforcing the authority of the one who appointed him.

Since I have the spiritual gift of "servant" and I have served both as a military officer and as a public safety officer, both positions under authority, I now understood very well what the Lord had said to me back in 1975, when he told me that he had called me to be a minister, not a pastor. I was being appointed, under his authority to enforce His authority, not to be ordained by men.

A Witness to What You have Seen and Heard

Let's continue as we look at the word "witness." The Greek "mártura," can mean a "witness" in the same manner in which we use it in the judicial system today as a person called to testify to the events, which they have seen or heard. It can also mean "martyr," one who testifies to a particular belief by holding that belief even unto death. Paul in his life and death fulfilled both of these meanings.

This takes us also to Revelation 12:11, where we learn that the "they" who overcame the accuser of the brethren who was cast down to the earth, did so by the blood of the Lamb, by the word of their "mártura," testimony or witness and by the fact that they did not love their lives even unto death. Again, the double meanings of witness and martyr appear here.

So back to Acts 26, "…I have appeared to you, to appoint you a minister and witness, not only of the things you have seen." Paul had been present to see the martyrdom of Stephen, and had seen the effect the knowledge of Jesus was having on many of the Jews. Jesus continues, "…but also to the things in which I will appear to you." So here is the resurrected and ascended Jesus, appearing to Paul and telling him, I am not done appearing to you, as you will see me through the things you will see in the future. You might ask; how can this be? Well, Jesus regularly in the Book of John says that He only does what He sees the Father doing and only speaks what the Father commands or speaks to Him. Now no one could see the Father and in fact, Phillip said to Him, "Show us the Father and that will be good enough for us"[6]. Jesus had this connection to the unseen Father such that He was continually looking to see what the Father was doing and constantly listening to hear what the Father was saying so that He would know what He was to do here on earth. Jesus then tells us,

> "I will not leave you as orphans; I will come to you." After a little while the world will behold Me no more; but you will behold Me; because I live, you shall live also. "In that day you shall know that I am in My Father, and you in Me, and I in you[7].

And then,

> "...when He, the Spirit of truth, comes, He will guide you into all the truth; for He will not speak on His own initiative, but whatever He hears, He will speak; and He will disclose to you what is to come. "He shall glorify Me; for He shall take of Mine, and shall disclose it to you. "All things that the Father has are Mine; therefore I said, that He takes of Mine, and will disclose it to you." [8]

So, we see that Jesus left in place a mechanism by which He would be there for us through the Holy Spirit in the same way that the Father was there for Him to show Him how to deal with the things going on around Him. He tells Paul and us, that as ministers and witnesses the Holy Spirit will continue to disclose Jesus also in the future.

Witness Protection Program

But now the best part (in my opinion), Jesus tells Paul, "I am protecting you from both the Jews and Gentiles to who I am sending you," (a promise of protection and covering because you are serving under His authority), "to open their eyes so that they may turn from darkness to light and from the dominion of Satan to God." Again, we have a purpose statement, "to open their eyes." Paul will later expound on this concept of opening eyes in 2 Corinthians.

> And even if our gospel is veiled, it is veiled to those who are perishing, in whose case the god of this world has blinded the minds of the unbelieving, that they might not see the light of the gospel of the glory of Christ, who is the image of God[9].

Paul, having taken his understanding from Jesus, recognizes that if eyes are blinded and in darkness, in need to be opened, it is because of the veil, the blinding that had been put in place by the "god of this world." Jesus tells Paul I am sending you to these ones "to open their eyes."

Now how does one open the eyes of an unbelieving person who has been blinded by the "god of this world"? Jesus very literally went about healing the blind and every kind of sickness and disease, and delivering all who were oppressed by the devil, proclaiming to them the Gospel (good news) of the Kingdom.[10] The Kingdom, (the king's domain, the authority of the king) has come near to you today.

> "And as you go, preach, saying, 'The kingdom of heaven is at hand.' "Heal the sick, raise the dead, cleanse the lepers, cast out demons; freely you received, freely give."[11]

Now let me ask you, if you had been blind all your life, and others around you know that this had been your situation in life, and a man walks up to you, heals your eyes, and you open them for the first time, do you think that this act would also open a few eyes and minds of those standing nearby?

One way in which we open eyes and bring people out of the darkness into the Light, is through bringing the power and the authority of the Kingdom near to them. In our role as ministers, servants, officers under authority, we demonstrate that power and authority by releasing healing in their body, or driving the demonic oppression and/or demonically induced sickness off them. We have just lifted the veil of darkness off them and allowed the light of the glory of Christ's Kingdom to penetrate their minds.

Turning Toward the Light

More purpose statements follow the "opening their eyes." It is for the purpose, "so that they might turn from the darkness to the light." Just like a plant in a dark room that is now been placed near a sunlit window, the plant will turn and bend toward the light. An additional purpose stated, is for turning from the dominion of Satan, to God. So, Jesus was telling Paul, get their eyes open so that they will bend toward me, away from the authority of Satan, towards the authority of God.

Omar Cabrerra, as the Lord disclosed to him during his time of prayer and fasting, went one better by removing the authorities that were holding the people of the city in darkness and blindness. He got their eyes open by removing the dominion of Satan over the city. Now people could see the signs for the evangelistic meetings. Their minds, freed from the dark veil that had been over them, were able to accept the light and truth of the message.

There is one more step in the methodology that Jesus is laying out to Paul, a final purpose statement that is preceded by all the rest. You are going to open their eyes, get them out of the darkness into the light, out of Satan's dominion and into Gods Kingdom (dominion, authority), "in order that they may receive forgiveness of sins and an inheritance among those who have been sanctified by faith in Me."

No Forgiveness in that Place

We must understand there is no forgiveness of sins in the dominion of Satan. The explanation in the book of Hebrews, Chapter 2, Verse 15, tells us Satan has held them in slavery to the fear of death all the days of their lives. You have to get them out of that authority structure before there is even an opportunity for the forgiveness of sins, let alone the inheritance of eternal life. Unfortunately, in this country and many others, this last purpose statement is the only one that is preached or dealt with. Preachers and evangelists will say, "Repent of your sins, and be saved." But people are unable to do so, because they do not understand what is being said. They are still in darkness, held by an authority structure that is holding them in slavery through the threat of death, and the keeping of their mind under a veil of darkness.

A Purpose for Ministry

This is what I learned in Argentina in 1984 as I sat and talked with Omar Cabrerra. I had a ministry, an appointment under authority to get peoples' eyes open, and to get them out from under the dominion of the "ruler of this world,"[12] the "god of this world."[13]

Suddenly there was purpose back in my life. I understood that the Christian life was not just living good and righteous until death. I had been assigned as an officer in God's army to invade the darkness and rescue the prisoners from the enemies holding cells on death row. I was to get them out of the territory under the authority or dominion of the enemies' commander, Satan. To overthrow that rule, so that they would have the opportunity within the King's domain (the Kingdom of God) of receiving forgiveness of their sins and an inheritance of eternal life among those who were being cleansed by the washing work of Jesus as a result of their faith in Him.

The Kings Domain

I suddenly understood the Kingdom of God as not just some future place where Jesus sits on a throne, but as the dominion, domain or authority structure that is established whenever a person, a city or a territory, is removed from the authority structure of Satan. That person, city or territory now is instead, brought under or placed in subjection to, the dominion or authority structure of God. It does not necessarily have anything to do with the physical, human governmental or religious structure that is in place, but instead refers to the spiritual authority structure to which that person, city, or territory is subject. Revelation 5:9-10 tells us, "for Thou [The Lamb] wast slain, and didst purchase for God with Thy blood men from every tribe and tongue and people and nation. And Thou hast made them to be a kingdom and priests to our God; and they will reign upon the earth." We were purchased through the redemption price paid in the Lord's blood and made to be a part of His Kingdom.

In the dark ages, there were men who laid claim to large tracts of land in the European Continent. In order for them to hold that land against other rulers and commanders of invading army's, they needed people to occupy the land and create a "kingdom," a dominion under the authority of that land owner. Only then would they have sufficient resources to stand against the invaders. These landowners, in addition to giving portions of land to those living on it, would purchase or "redeem" slaves, give them a small portion of the land or dominion, and some seed and livestock with which to make that land fruitful. The landowner became their king, the authority over the dominion, and in exchange for a portion of the fruit of the land, which he owned, provided protection and means of life to those who had been set free from slavery. He also now had people with a stake in the land who could be trained as an army to defend the land from invaders.

One King One Kingdom Many Priests

With all due respect to those who translate this passage[14] (including the translators of the A.D. 1620 King James Version[15]) as having been made to be "kings" and "priests" in order to justify our "reigning" on the earth, there can only be one king of a kingdom, though there can be many priests as we will come to understand in a later chapter. The Greek word "basileia," can be translated as "king", but more often understood as the realm of the king, or his Kingdom, dominion, the place where the king's authority is in existence. This translation of having been made to be "kings" is used, in recent years, to justify a position that sets apart certain ones (as kings) in the Body of Christ who have an elevated role above the common person who has just received salvation (laypersons) but is not a pastor (clergy or priests). It tries to create a spiritual leadership office among those who earn their living at the top of the business world, but who are not in a full time position of leadership as a pastor of a church. There is no such distinction as "kings" in Ephesians 4 (though some have tried to argue for that understanding) where we are told of the types of offices given by the Lord for the equipping of the saints for the "work of the ministry." These offices are for the equipping of the saints for the work of the ministry, not titles of the only ones doing the ministry. Otherwise, why were not these offices listed with kings and priests in Revelation 5:10? It is because these offices were given to "some" by the Lord, and were not to be equated to being made to be a kingdom and priests, which is for "all" who have been purchased by the blood.

Reigning Here on Earth

I believe that the misunderstanding comes from the use of the word "reign" in the end of verse 10 of Revelation Chapter 5. In our understanding of the English language, we generally only equate reign as having to do with the position of a king or the top official of a dominion or authority structure. Even with this definition, how, do we then understand the role of a priest which is not usually a reigning position, but who serves at the pleasure of and under the king's authority? I think we can clear up this misunderstanding through another definition of the word "reign." *The American Heritage Dictionary* gives, as another definition, "dominance or widespread influence" or "to be predominant or prevalent." To paraphrase Revelation 5:10 with this definition in mind; Having been made to be a kingdom or having been purchased to be under the authority and in the domain of the king, we have been given the office of a priest to the King, God, and we shall have widespread influence in or prevail on the earth.

This is the ministry to which we have all been called. Everyone who has been purchased with the blood of Jesus and made to be a part of His

Kingdom, through our role as priests to God (to be further expounded later in this book), are to have widespread influence (just like the "super power" that the United States has become), and to prevail over the "ruler of this world." We are to be taking possession of, and occupying the Kingdom.

Much of this I believe will become clearer in the following chapters, but it is important at this point to see a distinction that a call to ministry is not necessarily a call to be a pastor and attending theological seminary is not the only way to train for ministry. Everyone who has been purchased by the blood, redeemed from his or her slavery under the dominion of Satan, has been made to be a part of the Kingdom. They may need training and equipping in order take back and hold the land from invading foes of the king and to rescue those held in bondage under the sentence of death by those enemies, but as a part of the Kingdom, they all have a role to carry out.

Revival in the Prisoner of War Camp

I now understood I had been called to ministry, and trained and assigned as an officer in the army under the authority of Jesus. It was time to get into the battle. I understood just by looking around me, that the enemy had already overrun much of the Kingdom, and was holding many of those who refused to fight, in prisoner of war camps. They were still rejoicing that they were alive, but continually crying out to the Lord to "revive us again."

In *The American Heritage Dictionary,* revive means:

1. To bring back to life or consciousness; resuscitate.
2. To impart new health, vigor, or spirit to.
3. To restore to use, currency, activity, or notice.
4. To restore the validity or effectiveness of.
5. To renew in the mind; recall.
6. To present (an old play, for example) again.

Yes, it was evident that these people were in fact in prisoner of war camps because they were wounded, overwhelmed, did not have their weapons or armor with them, and did not have the freedom to join in the battle going on all around them. Many did not even know that there was a battle still going on, as they were listening to the enemy twisting the truth, proclaiming the battle was already won, and they should just wait there in the camps until the king comes and air lifts them out.

Retreat!

When I looked around, others who had been made to be a part of the Kingdom, were not in the prisoner of war camps because they had retreated. They had gone on retreat to get away from the noise of the battle so that they could contemplate the future when there would be no more war and they could just rest in the Lord's arms. However, when they came back down the mountain the battle was still going on, so they retreated again. Every time they heard the Lord issue the command to charge or advance, they thought it had to do with using their credit cards. They would charge it or get a cash advance in order to go on another retreat. (Come on friend, lighten up a bit, even though we are talking about very serious things here, we've got to be able to see the humor in some of the language we use. God created humor also:>)

So, now as an officer in the army about to enter the battle, it was time to check the radios and other communication gear. I understood that if I was to carry out this assignment as an officer, I better have my communications links well established, so that I can get my orders clearly from the one under whose authority I have been assigned.

The next chapter of this book will deal with what does it mean to hear the Lord and how you do it.

Endnotes

1. Numbers 20:26
2. Numbers 20:28
3. Mathew 28:19-20
4. 2 Corinthians 4:3-4
5. Eph 4:11-12
6. Acts 14:8
7. John 14:18-21
8. John 16:13-15
9. 2 Corinthians 4:3-4
10. See for example Matt 4:23 and 9:35
11. Matt 10:7-8
12. John 12:31, 14:30, 16:11
13. 2 Corinthians 4:4
14. Revelation 5:9-10
15. Though the King James Version is a very good translation of the original Greek and Hebrew, it was a translation commissioned by a king for kings and priests. It is very understandable that this particular verse would be translated as it was, because the translators did not understand the nature of the kingdom, so their translation favored a line of thinking that God had made there to be Kings and Priests, to reign in all the earth. The kings were to rule over the secular affairs of the people and the priests to reign over the spiritual aspects. As compared to the Geneva Bible the King James reflects a bias that avoids any translation that would imply overthrow or supplanting of earthly kingdoms and supports the divine establishment of human kings.

CHAPTER 3

WHAT DO YOU MEAN THE LORD SAID…?

If you already are very familiar with how the Lord communicates with you and are tempted to skip over this chapter, I would suggest that you suppress that temptation. Read anyway, because what you read here may help you to assist and train someone else to hear the Lord or even to realize that you should help others with this skill.

I suspect, as a result of many of the conversations that I have had with other Christians over the years, that there are many of you out there who have been afraid that if you asked this question, you would just get a knowing glance and the person would say something like, "you mean you don't hear the Lord?" So rather than expose yourself as some freak of nature that is missing the piece that is supposed to "hear the Lord," you just keep quiet and act like, yah, sure, I hear the Lord all the time, in fact He told me the exact same thing just last week.

Well, maybe you just were never trained to hear the Lord, or maybe you have been hearing Him all along, but you did not recognize Him because you were expecting something different.

Samuel Learns to Hear God

So let's first talk about being trained to hear the Lord. Perhaps you will recall the story in 1 Samuel Chapter 3 about the young man Samuel being trained to hear the Lord's voice. Here is that story to refresh your memory:

> Now the boy Samuel was ministering to the LORD before Eli. And word from the LORD was rare in those days, visions were infrequent. And it happened at that time as Eli was lying down in his place (now his eyesight had begun to grow dim and he could not see well), and the lamp of God had not yet gone out, and Samuel was lying down in the temple of the LORD where the ark of God was, that the LORD called Samuel; and he said, "Here I am." Then he ran to Eli and said, "Here I am, for you called me." But he said, "I did not call, lie down again." So he went and lay down. And the LORD called yet again, "Samuel!" So Samuel arose and went to Eli, and said, "Here I am, for you called me." But he answered, "I did not call, my son, lie down again." Now Samuel did not yet know the LORD, nor had the word of the LORD yet been revealed to him. So the LORD called Samuel again for the third time. And he arose and went to Eli, and said, "Here I am, for you called me." Then Eli discerned that the LORD was calling the boy. And Eli said to Samuel, "Go lie down, and it shall be if He calls you, that you shall say, 'Speak, LORD, for Thy servant is listening.'" So Samuel went and lay down in his place. Then the LORD came and stood and called as at other times, "Samuel! Samuel!" And Samuel said, "Speak, for Thy servant is listening." And the LORD said to Samuel, "Behold, I am about to do a thing in Israel at which both ears of everyone who hears it will tingle.[1]

Note that this story starts with the explanation that the word of the Lord was rare and visions were infrequent in those days. Basically, the people had become dull of hearing and were not looking for any input from the Lord, so He looked for someone who would hear Him and respond. Samuel was responsive, but he did not yet have his senses trained to discern that he was hearing from the Lord. He did not "yada" the Lord. Yada is a Hebrew word that is often translated, "to know". This word is used nine hundred forty-four times in the Old Testament. This term is also used to indicate something that is discerned or learned through the use of the five physical senses or through intuition.

That brings us to the other point, which I stated, some people may actually be hearing the Lord, but they do not have their senses trained to discern that it is actually the Lord they are hearing.

I must clarify here also that hearing is not the only way in which the Lord discloses Himself to us. I will get to that in a minute, but first, I also want to clear up another point.

Can I Really Do That?

Some pastors and whole groupings of churches, will tell you that you should not expect to hear from the Lord. They will say this is the job of the clergy, or that this just does not happen anymore, it was just for the apostles. Both those positions are pretty hard to justify without purposely distorting scripture, or claiming that the average person should not believe that the scriptures are speaking to them just as much as they did to the early church. It is absurd to claim that the words recorded in the New Testament were only for the apostles, as most of the apostles were dead by the time the words were written down and accepted by the church. Paul specifically instructs Timothy,

> "All Scripture is inspired by God and profitable for teaching, for reproof, for correction, for training in righteousness; that the man of God may be adequate, equipped for every good work."[2]

Since scripture is profitable for teaching, for training in righteousness, that we may be adequate, equipped for every good work, let's continue and see what scripture has to say about hearing or discerning, the Lord.

Jesus made it very clear in the book of John that He was completely dependent upon the Father in order to do the things that He did:

> Truly, truly, I say to you, the Son can do nothing of Himself, unless it is something He sees the Father doing; for whatever the Father does, these things the Son also does in like manner. For the Father loves the Son, and shows Him all things that He Himself is doing; and greater works than these will He show Him, that you may marvel.[3]
>
> I can do nothing on My own initiative. As I hear, I judge; and My judgment is just, because I do not seek My own will, but the will of Him who sent Me.[4]
>
> When you lift up the Son of Man, then you will know that I am He, and I do nothing on My own initiative, but I speak these things as the Father taught Me. And He who sent Me is with Me; He has not left Me alone, for I always do the things that are pleasing to Him.[5]
>
> If I do not do the works of My Father, do not believe Me; but if I do them, though you do not believe Me, believe the works, that you may know and understand that the Father is in Me, and I in the Father."[6]
>
> For I did not speak on My own initiative, but the Father Himself who sent Me has given Me commandment, what to say, and what to speak. And I know that His commandment is eternal life; therefore the things I speak, I speak just as the Father has told Me.[7]
>
> Do you not believe that I am in the Father, and the Father is in Me? The words that I say to you I do not speak on My own initiative, but the Father abiding in Me does His works. Believe Me that I am in the Father, and the Father in Me; otherwise believe on account of the works themselves. Truly, truly, I say to you, he who

believes in Me, the works that I do shall he do also; and greater works than these shall he do; because I go to the Father.[8]

With all of these repeated instances of the statement made by Jesus that He can do nothing of His own initiative, and yet being told that we will do greater works than He did because He is going away to the Father, it seems very important that we get the communications connection understood so that what we do, will also be what the Father is showing.

Jesus clarifies this a bit in the passages I shared in the last Chapter from John 14 and 16:

> After a little while the world will behold Me no more; but you will behold Me; because I live, you shall live also. In that day you shall know that I am in My Father, and you in Me, and I in you. He who has My commandments and keeps them, he it is who loves Me; and he who loves Me shall be loved by My Father, and I will love him, and will disclose Myself to him.[9]
>
> These things I have spoken to you, while abiding with you. But the Helper, the Holy Spirit, whom the Father will send in My name, He will teach you all things, and bring to your remembrance all that I said to you.[10]
>
> But when He, the Spirit of truth, comes, He will guide you into all the truth; for He will not speak on His own initiative, but whatever He hears, He will speak; and He will disclose to you what is to come. He shall glorify Me; for He shall take of Mine, and shall disclose it to you. All things that the Father has are Mine; therefore I said, that He takes of Mine, and will disclose it to you.[11]

Full Disclosure

If then as Jesus has promised, the Holy Spirit will become the means by which we are to be taught and reminded, and also the agent through which the Father will continue to be disclosed to us, so that we can do the "greater works than these," we must be able to discern by some means what is being disclosed. The question becomes what does that look, sound, feel, smell, or taste like? We are all aware that we were created with at least six senses (the sixth being something that we often label as intuition). Various scriptures of which you might be aware, describe God, Jesus or an angel appearing to men. All illustrate instances of hearing, seeing, feeling or intuition. It could very well be that smell and taste were also involved when instances of fire, smoke or other manifestations were described. In particular, when the Lord appeared to Paul on the road to Damascus, there was a light that blinded Paul but not those around him. There was a voice, which Paul and those around him heard, but they saw no one. We learn in Acts 26 that the Lord told him that he is going to be a witness of both the things which he has seen and of the things that he will see in the future of the Lord. This becomes evident in Paul's later writings and he distinguishes in a few instances that what he is saying he has "not received from the Lord."

Ananias, in Acts Chapter 9 sees and hears in a vision one whom he clearly identifies as the Lord and responds to Him by replying simply "Behold, here am I, Lord."[12] Note that in this instance there is no fear involved. Ananias feels at perfect liberty to question the Lord regarding the instruction he just received to go find Paul, and lay hands on him for the healing of the blindness from the light. Ananias answers, "Lord, I have heard from many about this man, how much harm he did to Thy saints at Jerusalem; and here he has authority from the chief priests to bind all who call upon Thy name."[13]

The Lord was not offended by his response and did not rebuke him, but simply clarifies the instructions after which Ananias quickly goes about obeying the Lords instruction.

There are too many other examples in scripture of the Lord communicating with people through various means for me to include them all or even a lot of them. But that would be a good study for you if you were still struggling to believe that God communicates with mere men and women and that He does not always speak though a voice booming out of the sky.

Equip the Saints

It is also evident in scripture that there are some purposes for which He gave some as apostles, and some as prophets, and some as evangelists, and some as pastors and teachers, for the equipping of the saints for the work of service, to the building up of the body of Christ.[14] These are ones the Lord has specially equipped in order to get the saints equipped for the work of the ministry or service (Remember the definition of ministry? If not, go back and look at it again in Chapter 2). It is very clear in scripture that these are not the only ones doing ministry, they are simply some of the ones to whom giftings have been given to help equip and make adequate the saints to do ministry. Jesus makes it very clear He must see or hear from the Father in order to do the works He does, and we are to be doing greater works. It then seems that one of the jobs of those given to equip the saints for the work of the ministry should be to train them how to discern when the Lord is being disclosed to them by the Holy Spirit. The problem is that many of those who lead our churches today were never trained themselves, because many never had a course in seminary that covered this area, or they do not feel it important to pursue. They stick with the basics of baptism, repentance, loving one another, and doing good works. They never get down to talking about some of the more mature understandings and training that you will need if you are going to open peoples' eyes, get them out of the darkness into the light, out of the dominion of Satan to God, so that they can receive the forgiveness of sins.

In Hebrews, Paul addresses this malady of the Church, which was apparently an issue even before seminaries came into being:

"It is hard to explain, since you have become dull of hearing. For though by this time you ought to be teachers, you have need again for someone to teach you the elementary principles of the oracles of God, and you have come to need milk and not solid food. For everyone who partakes only of milk is not accustomed to the word of righteousness, for he is a babe. But solid food is for the mature, which because of practice have their senses trained to discern good and evil. Therefore leaving the elementary teaching about the Christ, let us press on to maturity, not laying again a foundation of repentance from dead works and of faith toward God, of instruction about washings, and laying on of hands, and the resurrection of the dead, and eternal judgment. And this we shall do, if God permits."[15]

Practice Helps!

I want you to take particular note of the verse, "But solid food" (or we might say, the ability to understand deeper things and more complicated teachings) "is for the mature, who because of practice have their senses trained to discern good and evil." See particularly the words "practice" and "senses." Though a musician may have a certain amount of talent and genetic ability to play an instrument, in order to consistently produce good notes and not sour ones, they still need someone to teach them certain skills and they need lots of practice. They have to train their senses of touch and hearing. So also, all of our senses have been given to us but we need to train them in order to discern between good and bad.

Let's look at the sense of taste. We train our taste through a combination of practice, tasting different things, and hearing others warn or encourage us that something tastes either bad or good. We perhaps all have experienced seeing babies putting just about everything in their mouths, but occasionally spitting something out because it tastes bad. Through practice, they have been training their "taste" to discern between good and bad. In the same way, we train our senses through a combination of practice and the words and teaching of others. We learn to use the senses to discern between good and evil.

Let me give an example of this in my own life. My friend, Dr. Paul L. Cox has a ministry that among other things helps people become more discerning of what their senses are telling them. He became aware that he would feel different kinds of pains, pressures and other sensations in his body in the presence of angels, demons, or witchcraft. After being with him on a number of occasions when he announced the presence of one of these entities which he had come to recognize by sensations in his body, I became aware that I was consistently feeling a pain or pressure in the front or back of my head just before and during the times Paul announced their presence. I would get a pain(s) and/or pressure in the forehead when demons were present, and pain and/or pressure in the back occipital area of my head when angels were present. The intensity and the size of the area that was covered also seemed to relate to the numbers and power of the angels or demons present. On occasions, I would also see just wispy glimpses of either the angels or demons. On rare occasions, I would clearly see their presence. Through the practice of equating my senses with the experience of another who had more practice than I, I was able to train my senses to discern between good and evil appearances of angels or fallen angels. These sensations are still present and I continue to practice at that discernment as I have been in meetings with other people who are able to discern the presence of demons and angels. I consistently have the same feelings in the head before they say anything about the presence they are discerning or seeing.

Let's go on to talk about some other ways that the Lord might disclose Himself through the Holy Spirit. Turn to the next Chapter and I will give you some concrete examples.

Endnotes

1. 1 Samuel 3:1-12
2. 2 Timothy 3:16-17
3. John 5:19-20
4. John 5:30
5. John 8:28-30
6. John 10:37-39
7. John 12:49-50
8. John 14:10-13
9. John 14:19-22
10. John 14:25-26
11. John 16:13-15
12. Acts 9:10-16
13. Acts 9:13-14
14. Ephesians 4:11-12
15. Hebrews 5: 11-6:3

CHAPTER 4

MORE EXAMPLES OF HEARING THE LORD

In 1985, I attended a conference at the Anaheim Vineyard on praying over others for healing. I was very convicted, through the teaching of John Wimber, of the necessity to see what the Lord was doing in another person before we start praying for healing (or anything else for that matter). Also, convicted of the necessity to speak over them what we hear the Lord speaking and not what we are thinking or our desires for the person. I realized I needed something more than what I had experienced of the Lord's communication to me up to that point for this type of ministry. I was not having those kinds of enlightening disclosures from the Lord, but I determined to ask for them so that I could be more mature in my prayers for others and not just speak out my desires or best counsel. I came to realize, if this person was truly to be healed, it had to come from the Lord, as I am not able to cause the healing to happen.

The conference teaching had encouraged as a first step, to ask the Lord to start disclosing to us individually and that we would come to recognize the things that the Lord was disclosing. Secondly, that when we were praying for others, we would always ask the Lord first what He was doing in this person's life, tuning down our own thoughts and intentions just like turning down the radio, so that we could hear the Lord. We were not to pray anything until we saw what the Lord was doing and the Lord had showed or spoken how to proceed. For two weeks, I prayed that the Lord would begin showing me what He was doing and that I would hear what He was speaking. I am not aware of having heard or seen anything during the two weeks, though I just might not have recognized it as being from the Lord, like Samuel.

One day near the end of the two weeks, I was meeting with Ted (not his real name), a missionary candidate who I had under a mentoring relationship in my role as an elder of the church. As we started talking that day, I asked Ted how things were going and he said his wife was still sick after about three weeks and he did not know what to do about it. I asked him if he had laid hands on her and prayed for her healing. Much to my surprise, Ted responded angrily that, "he was pretty sick of people asking him if he had prayed for her." Even more to my surprise, I responded back to him in a manner totally uncharacteristic to my personality and normal approach toward people. I said, "Well, do you want to pray about that attitude?"

That really caught Ted off guard and he looked at me hard and then said, "ok." The prayer that followed was labored and grudging as he recounted to me and to the Lord that he knew that he should not have that attitude, but tried to justify his feeling that way.

As he was dragging his feet along a path of repentance, suddenly I saw a glimpse of something, wispy, transparent but appearing somewhere at an undetermined distance directly in front of my eyes. The image I saw, I "knew in my head" was my hand with my forefinger sticking in his ear. My first response was the thought, "well, that is pretty weird." "Where did that come from and why did I just make up this brief glimpse somewhere in my mind?" Then I remembered that I had been praying for the past two weeks that the Lord would disclose things to me so I would know what to do and say when praying with and for others. I made the conscious decision that I would have faith that this was an answer to my prayer and that I needed to act on what I had seen. I chose to believe that my finger in his ear was something that the Lord was disclosing for a purpose about which I had not a clue.

Well, yes I decided to act on what I had seen. However, I felt too foolish to actually stick my finger in his ear, so I kind of brushed my hand past his ear without actually touching it. It was then that I learned a second way in which the Lord was capable of disclosing Himself through my senses. The first thing I had sort of seen, but now a very firm and loud voice came into my head saying, "I said in his ear." There was no doubt in my mind now that this was from the Lord and I had better obey Him exactly as I had seen. I still felt foolish, but I stuck my forefinger in his ear just as I had seen.

I was not prepared for what happened. I was fully expecting this man who was already somewhat upset with me and with God, to turn around and say something like, "what in the name of Jesus do you think you are doing, get your finger out of my ear." That is not what happened. Instead, the whole tone of his prayer changed and he instantly became humbly repentant and began calling out to the Lord for the healing of his wife and for a heart in him that would be more attentive to his wife.

When Ted finished praying after a little while, I asked him what was going on in this time of prayer. He confessed to having been angry with me and grudging as he started praying. But then he acknowledged the finger in the ear, and said, "When you stuck your finger in my ear, I heard a voice that I knew to be the Lord, ask me, 'Is this the way you want to live the rest of your life'?" He knew in an instant that he did not want to continue living with that attitude and immediately humbled himself before the Lord.

Obedience is Essential and Quickly is Better

While we are on the subject of obeying what we hear or see, I want to tell you about another experience. This one brought tears to my eyes when I realized how long it took the Lord to get me to obey and how important it was that I do so.

I talked in the first chapter about being a Fireman. In one station where I was Captain for several years, I was sitting in the dormitory one evening, talking with another man who was a Christian about my experiences in Argentina. At one point, the man I was talking to turned to Dean (not his real name) and asked him what he thought of the stories that the Captain was sharing. Dean, who was sitting on his bed at the other end of the dorm reading the latest best seller novel, looked up from his book and said, "that Christian stuff is just a crutch for those who need one," and quickly turned back to his book. I responded inside of myself, "Well, now I know where he stands."

Dean was not assigned to my crew but worked a lot of overtime to fill in for people who were sick or on vacation. Over the next several months there were a number of times when he was working on my shift as part of my crew. About two weeks after the dorm incident, I was in the locker room in the morning at shift change when Dean walked in. The strangest thought occurred to me, that I should ask him, "What would have to happen in your life for you to know that there is a God and that He loves you and desires you for His own?" I call it a thought more than words because I didn't really hear it, but it just sort of crossed my mind. My mental response was to immediately dismiss the thought because, after all, "I knew where Dean stood with regard to spiritual things" and I was not going to make a fool of myself saying such a thing to him. I dismissed the thought and went on about my responsibilities over the station.

The next morning, when I saw Dean in the locker room, the thought was back there again. Over the next several weeks, this occurred over and over again every time I saw Dean in the locker room. By this point, I was sure that I was hearing from God, but equally sure that there was no way I was going to make a fool of myself and actually ask him such a question. After about two weeks, I was not troubled by the thought any more when I saw Dean in the locker room and I was relieved.

About a month later as I entered the locker room in the morning, there was Dean and this time it was not just a thought in my head, but I was hearing a voice that said, "When, are you going to tell him?" I still did not have the courage to act, so I quickly left the locker room. The next morning we met again in the locker room, and now the voice was shouting in my head, "WHEN, ARE YOU GOING TO TELL HIM?" I knew I could not avoid this any longer, as I also knew that this had to be more important than my feeling foolish for the Lord to become so forceful with me.

I walked up to Dean and said, "I know this may sound a bit strange, but I have had this question swirling in my head for weeks and I believe it is for you from God." Then I just blurted out, "What would have to happen in your life for you to know there is a God and that He loves you and desires you for His own?" Tears welled up in Dean's eyes as I spoke and he said, "I already know that there is a God, but I am afraid to give up what I have to give up, to come to Him." "But don't stop talking to me." That response was a real shock to me. (I continue to be surprised, when people respond to God's word to them in a different way than I think they might respond based upon my understanding. So was Jonah!)

Over the next several weeks, we were able to sit and talk on several occasions and I came to realize what a tender and caring person Dean was. I learned also that he had put in for a transfer to a station in a remote area that was closer to his home. He was now having second thoughts about the transfer, because he really liked the guys that he was working with now at our station. We didn't talk about God; we just talked as men about the things going on in our lives.

Dean transferred to the remote station. The first week he was in the new station his crew and he went on a rescue where they were required to do CPR and other life support measures that covered them with the two victims' blood. Several hours later they would learn that both of the victims were in late stages of Aids and the entire crew had been exposed to HIV as well as to a number of other blood born diseases. Well news of the exposure got back to the tiny community where Dean and his family lived and the next year became a living hell for them as he waited for tests to be done to determine if he also would develop HIV. The entire community shunned both he and his wife. She would go into the grocery store and other shoppers would leave their baskets and leave the store. The kids would sit in their seats at school and the other kids would move their desks to the other side of the room. Dean was of Catholic background and fortunately, in that year, a young Catholic priest, whom I believe really knew and loves Jesus, came along side Dean and his wife and just loved them both back into relationship with Jesus and with one another. I would learn later that the thing that Dean had not wanted to give up to come to the Lord was removed from him as a result of the exposure to HIV. By the way, Dean never became HIV Positive.

Several years later I would run into Dean on a brush fire and asked him, "How are things going?" His response, "Great, now that I know what had to happen in my life before I would know that God loves me."

I tell this story, because I am not proud of how long it took me to obey the Lord. I still weep remembering the lengths He had to go to with me, shouting at me, to get me to obey so that this man would know that what was about to happen in his life had to do with his relationship with God. I learned a tremendous lesson about obedience. See it is not about our thoughts, pride, or feelings of foolishness. This is serious business and if we are going to carry out our role as priests to God, then we had better be obedient to do things His way. Remember that they used to tie a rope to the leg of the priest when he went into the Holy of Holies once a year least he should be stuck dead through over looking some procedure or lack of obedience. The other priests would be able to drag the corpse out of the presence of God without taking a chance of losing the life of another priest by sending them in to retrieve the corpse.

In the years since this incident with Dean, I have continued to learn more and more how absolutely essential it is, particularly in doing spiritual warfare, to hear the Lord clearly. We must do exactly what He shows, in exactly the way He shows, with the people who know that the Lord called them to participate in this exact act, and at the exact time that the Lord reveals. I would learn years later, as I will share in another chapter, that to vary and not do what the Lord shows at the exact time we are to do it can be dangerous and costly. It can lead to *"Needless Casualties of War,"* as John Paul Jackson has written about.[1]

Other Ways of Discerning

So far, you have heard me talk about feeling pain or pressure to discern the presence of demons or angels, seeing things and hearing things, but I also have had experiences where smell was the means of discerning between good and evil.

MORE EXAMPLES OF HEARING THE LORD

One time in Argentina as I was working late and alone on the production of a television program to be broadcast the next day, I suddenly began smelling the scent of vomit strongly in the room. As I became aware of the smell, the video edits I had been working on all evening on a computer suddenly scrambled themselves in random order all over the time line on the screen. My heart sank as I realized that it would take hours to correct and unscramble what had just happened in an instant. Recognizing this smell and visible scrambling of the editing screen as a demonic spiritual attack, I immediately put on a CD of worship music that I have found particularly powerful in warfare situations. I also got on the phone to some intercessors. They immediately came down to the studio where I was working. Some of them also smelled the vomit smell upon entering the studio and quickly set about their work of intercession and warfare while I set about the work of unscrambling the time line on the computer. Because of their warfare and clearing the spiritual atmosphere of the room, I was able to put the program back together and finish it in less than an hour.

I have also encountered nauseating smells and tastes while prayer walking in a particularly demon infested territory which it did not take much practice to discern as evil. Lest you think that smell only indicates an evil presence, I have also smelled roses and other sweet aromas during circumstances where the presence of the Lord was very strong. In one instance, of walking out of a restaurant where I and another person had been teaching a group, there was a husband and wife walking out with us. The husband, a mason (That's another whole book) remarked, "What is that stench I smell?" The wife who is a spirit filled Christian, along with the rest of us that were with them, smelled a sweet aroma of flower blossoms. In this case, the discernment of the sense of smell revealed the spirit that was over each person.

As for intuition, on a number of occasions when I have asked the Lord for understanding or wisdom about something specific, the answer has come within a few minutes with what I can only describe as "just knowing" coming over my mind and being able to describe in detail, understanding that I did not have a few minutes before.

Another way that I have experienced the Lords disclosing to me has been in the form of a ticker tape like message moving in front of my mind somewhere just behind my forehead or a single word or object flashing up faintly and briefly in that same location.

In a later chapter, I will also describe things that the Lord has revealed by focusing me on a scene in the real world and then explaining what that scene represents.

In talking to other people who are fairly confident in the ways that they hear or sense what the Lord is disclosing, there seems to be an infinite range of ways in which various people experience this communication. Generally, there will be only a few specific ways which, individual persons consistently identify as coming from the Lord. They are able to quickly distinguish these from the unfamiliar approaches of spirits that are not of God. Jesus speaks of this also in the book of John "…the sheep follow him because they know his voice. And a stranger they simply will not follow, but will flee from him, because they do not know the voice of strangers."[2]

Be Careful Little Ears Who You Listen Too

Now I want to share with you just a few words of caution about learning to hear the Lord. Many in this world, both Christians and non-Christians, desire to experience the super natural. Therefore, when they have had their first experience of hearing a voice or of seeing something in the spirit they immediately jump to the assumption that this is God speaking to them. However, other voices also speak. Therefore, you must understand this world is occupied by fallen angels and they also have the capacity to communicate with us. Though they possess many of the attributes of the angels who did not get cast out of the heavens as recorded in Revelation 12, they are no longer under the same authority structure of God. Therefore, they have very little ability to function in this world unless they usurp the authority or gain the worship of the men and women whom God created and gave authority to on this earth. These demons also know that their time here is short so they cannot wait around for us to seek them out. While God generally waits for us to approach Him, these demonic beings are desperate to make contact with the men of this world and to function through them. It is not unusual for them to approach men and speak to them through their spirit and expect them to believe and treat them as a god. That is another reason why it is absolutely essential that we learn to recognize God's voice and His spirit so that we will recognize when a stranger is speaking to us. We do this through training with people who are clearly walking in God's spirit, and by checking our experiences with the Bible and with others.

I questioned the Lord once how I would be able to discern between the working of the spirit of God and the cults who manifest counterfeit gifts of the spirit. The Lord's answer, which He delivered to me in several different ways over several days and then confirmed from the mouth of a few close friends during those days was, "know me and know my ways and you will know the difference." I understood then and still know that this meant intimate familiarity with the Bible, His word, as well as with the Holy Spirit and His word, both of which are disclosures that enable us to know Him and His ways.

A Word About That

I have been very concerned with many in the prophetic movement of the last decade who in the attempt to train others have encouraged a speaking out of the first thing that comes to mind without first testing the spirits. Many of us have had a bad experience or two if we have been around that movement. For example, someone would speak out a word over us that did not seem to make sense or was contrary to something that the Lord had already showed us. That is ok, as long as it is done in a controlled setting and clearly understood as practice along side of someone more mature in their discernment.

Sam was constantly doing this, speaking out words over other people, until one night, he came to me for counsel about a relationship in his life. I asked him what the Lord was saying to him about this relationship. He admitted that he had never actually heard the Lord say anything, ever! I asked him, "Why are you speaking words over the lives of other people constantly, never having actually heard the Lord." He stopped immediately speaking over others. He began seeking the Lord about issues in his own life.

I personally, do not receive words spoken over me as from the Lord, unless I really know and trust the person speaking, and their words are simply a confirmation of something the Lord has already shown me. (This actually happens quite often, that the Lord will use the words of another to confirm and grow my faith that I have heard Him correctly.)

When I hear from the Lord something that is about another person, I am very careful to ask the Lord what I am to do with that word. Sometimes I am to do nothing. It is just something for me to hold and may affect my understanding so that I will know how I am to minister to that person. If I receive a word that I know I am to deliver to a person, I am generally still very cautious about saying, "The Lord says!" I again take a cue from John Wimber, who suggested that we might approach the person with something like this. "I have been having this re-occurring thought (or vision, or word) that I think may be for you and which I believe is from the Lord. I wanted to share it with you to see if it makes any sense to you or might apply to something in your life. I may just be imagining this, but I thought I would check it out with you anyway, is that all right with you?" Generally, the person will be enthusiastic about participating in the processing of determining if the Lord is speaking to them. If the word is negative or revealing of something that they are not yet ready to deal with, it also gives them the graceful out to say that they do not think that it is applicable to them. Nevertheless, we have accomplished what the Lord has asked us to do by delivering it and we have not come across as judging or condemning of something that may actually be going on in their life. The Lord will deal with them from that point.

MORE EXAMPLES OF HEARING THE LORD

Orders From the Commander

I have spent a good deal of time in this chapter and yet I know that I have but just scratched the surface of all that could be said and taught from the Bible and from experience about hearing God's voice. There are a number of good books on this topic, but I am not attempting to duplicate them here, so you may want to look at other sources also and find someone who can help you practice training your senses.

I feel that the aspect of hearing God's voice is so absolutely crucial to spiritual warfare that I needed to give it a strong emphasis here and not make the assumption that everybody that is entering into spiritual warfare understands this. On the battlefield, you must be able to discern between the voices of the enemy and the voice of your commander, no matter by which means He is communicating with you. In the modern military, orders may come in hand written notes, type written pages, over a wireless radio, over a wired telephone, on a computer screen, by a hand signal, or through some other communication channel to our senses. Through practice, you must have had your senses trained to discern that the orders are from the proper authority. This you must do by whatever means they arrive no matter what noise or other distractions the enemy is surrounding you with, in the midst of the battle. This is also the case in spiritual warfare.

I also wanted to emphasize the need for those who have more experience in this area to take serious their responsibility and actually the command from the Lord to teach those younger in the faith and newer to the battlefront, everything that the Lord has commanded us.[3]

I will talk some more about training our senses and how they come into play in battle in the next chapter, which is about "putting on the armor."

Endnotes

1. Jackson, John Paul, *Needless Casualties of War*, Fort Worth, TX: Streams Publications, 1999
2. John 10:4-5
3. Matthew 28:20

CHAPTER 5

A STOP BY THE ARMORY ON THE WAY TO THE FRONT LINES

This chapter is also one that you may be tempted to skip over because "you know all about putting on the armor." I would ask you to maintain a teachable spirit, not let the pride of the position you may have attained in the Body of Christ expose you to a gap in your armor. I have attended dozens of conferences in my sixty-eight years as a Christian, and have never heard anyone teach what I received from the Lord and am about to share here. This is also the witness of the several hundred people I have shared this within the past twenty years.

The Battle is Getting Fierce

It is my personal belief, as I will further expand upon in the chapters following, that we are in the middle of a devastating spiritual war right now (I am not talking about Iraq or Afghanistan). The army of the Body of Christ has gradually become accustomed to increasing difficulties in life and personal challenges that have become gradually greater and greater. They have not recognized that, like the frog placed in a pot of cold water, when the heat is turned up, they are being boiled alive. Many went through some basic training in warfare, and "have that armor around in a closet somewhere." They are beginning to understand that maybe they should get it out and try to remember how to put it on.

But like some of the reserves sent to Iraq, they find that the armor they were given years ago is not sufficient for the current type of battle, or that they just never were trained with or received the pieces necessary to protect them in the current battle. They may even be wearing their red, white and blue dress uniform and standing out as a distinct target amid the desert tans and beiges all around them. They also may have their bright brass or silver rank insignias proudly shinning from their uniform, instead of the olive drab or dull black battle dress insignias, making them a very likely target for being the first one picked by the enemy to shoot.

I believe that most Christians have received at least one and probably more lecture(s) (sermon or bible study) on Ephesians 6:10-17. However, few have really thought through the significance of these pieces. Even fewer have actually put them on with an understanding other than simply saying something like I am putting on my helmet of Salvation, my breastplate of righteousness, my belt of truth, etc.

Understanding the Armor

I began to understand a more complete function of the armor many years ago through praying the "doctrinal" prayers, contained in Mark Bubeck's book *The Adversary*.[1] I also owe some of my understanding of verses 10-12 to Ed Silvoso and his teachings on unity of the body and standing in this evil day. It was not until a few years ago though, when I started engaging in heavier warfare than I had ever encountered before, that the Lord began to give me a more complete understanding of this process of putting on the armor.

When I put on the armor, which for me starts with verse 10 and runs through verse 19 of Ephesians 6, I do so by first preparing my mind for the battle ahead even as modern day soldiers do as they are putting on their armor and moving into battle. I do this by understanding that it is not just the pieces of armor that I need to put on. I must put on a whole mind-set of understanding the army I am with in this battle, how we relate as soldiers to one another and to the Lord, the layout of the battlefield, and the resources at hand in addition to the actual armor.

I also do not put on the armor in the order given in Ephesians 6 simply because it is easier for me to remember and be complete moving in this process from head to toe. The Lord has not instructed that I need to do otherwise or I would. As I go through this process, I go through it describing what I am doing and why, as a dialogue with the Lord and with myself. I am physically acting out putting on the various pieces. I encourage others when we are doing this in a group, to stand, close their eyes, visualize the process and act out putting on the pieces. My experience has been, that the more I fix in my mind the understanding of what the armor is doing to protect me and the more real the process is of putting it on, the less the chance I and those with me in specific battles are likely to suffer wounds.

So now, let me put on the armor along with you just as I would whether in a battle on my own or with a group. I will have more to comment about the process and examples of how this works after we have been through this process.

His Strength

Ephesians 6:10: Be strong in the Lord and the strength of His might. Thank you Lord for the constant reminder, that it is your strength, in which I must be strong. I know that I can do nothing in my own strength as regard to the spiritual realm that is carrying out the attack I am facing in this warfare. Lord, I realize that it is not just strength as one might think of physical strength, but I am to be strong in you. I understand that to mean, as you spoke to me many years ago, that I am to be strong in my knowledge of you and of your ways. This means that part of my strength in this battle is the knowledge and understanding of the scriptures by which I can know you and know your ways. Thank you my Lord for this physical, tangible piece of weaponry by which I have been equipped for this day. Also, Lord I am to be strong in the strength of your might. To me, this means I need to rely on the Holy Spirit to bring Your power, Your "powder" if you will, into this battle. Holy Spirit, I know that I can aim the gun of prayer, but unless the weapon actually fires powerful bullets and artillery shells, which will hit and destroy the enemy, I am of no use in this battle. Fill my ammunition boxes with the strength of Your might. I will be strong both in the knowledge of You Lord, and in the strength of Your might.

I also recognize there are various ones in the Body of Christ who are stronger in one or the other aspects of this verse. I recognize that some of our denominational brothers are stronger in their knowledge of the Bible, of the Lord and of His ways, because of their stronger emphasis on the study and teaching of scripture. They may be more reliant upon this understanding than they are in their reliance upon, experience with, and understanding of the work of the Holy Spirit. On the other hand, there are other segments of the Body which function powerfully in signs and wonders because of their reliance upon the Holy Spirit. However, sometimes they are missing some important understandings to go along with that work because they may not have taken as much time to know, understand and teach the scriptures. Father as there may be those together here today whose walk with you has been more strongly guided by one or the other of these parts of the body, I pray that all the parts of the body today would come together to function as one body and one spirit. That we all would recognize the need for all the parts and how all of the parts must function together in order to accomplish the task before us.

Forgive One Another

We come together to put on the full armor of God that we may be able to stand firm, supporting one another in the midst of the battle. Standing firm against the schemes of the devil who is our adversary and not scheming against one another. We are told in 2 Corinthians 2:10-11 that we are not to be ignorant of the schemes of Satan in order that no advantage be taken of us. We first recognize that the context of this statement is forgiveness. This is the means by which no advantage be taken of us.[2] So let us begin to, as we put on this armor, first forgive one another of any differences or previous wounds, which we have inflicted upon one another. We want and need to stand as brothers together in this battle, caring for and protecting one another so that the enemy is not able to divide us or to catch us from behind because our fellow warrior is not watching our backside. We must remember that the enemy in this battle is not the flesh and blood that stands next to us. Our enemies are the rulers, the powers, the world forces of this darkness, and the spiritual forces of wickedness in the heavenly places.[3] Even as Jesus told Paul, He was protecting him from the Jews and Gentiles to whom He was sending him, it was not his job to fight with them.[4] The job to be done was to remove the blindness, the veil over the eyes put in place by the god of this world, so that their eyes would be opened, they would come out of the darkness into the light, out of the dominion of Satan.[5] We understand that these rulers, powers and world forces are those who make up and hold in place the dominion of Satan, and not the human beings of this world even though the enemy may use and abuse humans to carry out his work. We realize even as we put on this armor, our enemy has for a short time, been given authority to make war with and overcome the saints.[6] The armor, was given to us to be able to stand in the midst of this battle, and even to begin to take possession of the Kingdom.[7] Therefore, we will resist the enemy in this evil day and having done everything, which you are disclosing to us Lord, we will continue to stand firm, having taken up the full armor that you have provided.

Armor for the Central Processing Unit

I therefore put on the Helmet of Salvation. I recognize that this helmet is a covering over my head. My head is where most of my senses receive their input and it is the location of the central processing unit (CPU). That CPU takes all of the input of my senses and distributes them throughout the body to stimulate the muscles, the glands, the internal organs, and the emotions. Since the enemy is able to affect my body through my senses including my sight, my hearing, my intuition, and even through my smell, taste and touch, I thank you Lord that I have through practice trained my senses to discern between good and evil.[8] Further, through putting on this helmet, I place the filter and protection of my knowledge of salvation between the input to my senses and my mind. This is so that my mind will see these inputs through the filter of the work of the Lord on my behalf. This work includes healing, rescue, and deliverance, all aspects of the single word salvation. Because of this helmet, I am also able to reject all thoughts and threats of death and wounding. Salvation is the gift through the blood of the lamb whereby the enemy can no longer hold me in slavery all the days of my life through the threat of death.[9] So now through the blood of the Lamb, and the witness of my testimony in Christ, and because death no longer holds me in its slavery I will overcome the enemy.[10] Thank you Lord for this helmet as I put it firmly and carefully in place as a covering over my head.

In His Righteousness

I now take the Breastplate of Righteousness and put it on over my torso. I am reminded that the emotions are not thoughts in my head, but are feelings that reside in my torso. Because in and of myself I have no righteousness, the enemy is often able to grab a hold of my gut and twist it. He is able to point a finger to a knot of anger in my stomach, or he is able to stab my heart with pain. But right now, I take this Breastplate of Righteousness and put it on as a covering over my torso. I recognize that the righteousness that I am putting on is that of Christ and not mine. Jesus said that the ruler of this world was coming, but that he had nothing in Him.[11] What did the enemy not have in Christ? In Him was found no unrighteousness.[12] The enemy, knowing that this is not the case with my life, loves to enter in and point out my lack of forgiveness, my hate, my anger and my anxiety, and all of the other emotional indicators of my lack of righteousness. But now having taken up the Breastplate of Righteousness, I am able to withstand the accusations of the enemy of my soul and point out to him that yes, that is who I am. I am covered by Christ's righteousness, and since I am hidden in Him and His righteousness, the ruler of this world has nothing in Christ including me as I am in Him. Thank you Lord, for this complete and perfect covering over my emotions, over my innermost feelings, by the breastplate of your righteousness.

Don't Let this Belt Slip

I now gird my loins with the belt of Your truth. The truth is that You love me, You died for me, and nothing can separate me from Your love.[13] This truth is just like a belt that holds up a pair of pants or a skirt. Without the belt to hold them in place, I might suffer embarrassment or exposure. So also, Your truth sets me free from the fear of embarrassment or exposure.[14] Your truth binds me tightly in covenant with You and with others in the Body of Christ.[15] As we enter into this battle today, we will remember that we are of one spirit in You.[16] With that truth wrapped tightly around us, we will not allow the enemy to separate us from one another. We will recognize all discord, disagreement, or other things that the enemy would try to set between us as the schemes of the enemy, and to be disregarded in the light of the truth of who we are in You. We will instead cover over these lies with deference, patience and forgiveness for one another. We understand that Your truth is also the belt which binds all of our armor together and on which we can fasten our weapons. We will listen carefully to the Spirit of Truth as He guides us into all truth and does not speak of His own initiative.[17] Thank You Lord for the truth that the enemy has been a murderer and liar from the beginning[18] and as a result of Your truth, we can recognize his lies and resist him.[19] Thank You for this belt of truth as we wrap it tightly around us.

Shalom Shoes

The shoes of the gospel of peace are a very special part of our armor, because they not only guide us down the path, but they also protect our understanding of who You are, like the leather sole of a shoe. It protects our feet from rocks and sharp objects trying to penetrate, and smoothes out the path on which You are leading us. They become an important implement of our armor in taking possession of the Kingdom. Peace is the Hebrew word Shalom. I thank You for giving us an understanding of this word from the ancient Hebrew, which is not evident in our cultural understanding of the word today. In the ancient Hebrew, the word Shalom consisted of four pictures or characters that represented a set of teeth, a shepherds crook, a nail and the sea. The meanings of these pictures or characters were: The picture of the teeth, meant to destroy, or the destroyer. The shepherds crook is the symbol of authority and thus represents both good and bad authority. The nail, meant to build or establish, and the sea was the bath or washing basin before the temple where the world was washed off before entering the Holy of Holies and means chaos. Very literally, the word shalom from the ancient Hebrew means, "destroys the authority that builds or establishes chaos.[20]

So Lord I rejoice at the powerful meaning and good news of these shoes that are not only made for walking, but that every place where I walk in them, I am destroying the authority that has built or established chaos in that place. That means that when I put on these shoes and walk next door to the neighbors house, every place I set the sole of these shoes, I am destroying the chaos that was established there and like Joshua I am taking possession of every place I set the sole of my feet to establish instead the Kingdom of God.[21] That means that when I enter the grocery store, a city council meeting, a PTA meeting or any other place I go with these shoes on, I am destroying every spiritual authority in that place which has built or established their own brand of chaos. I am instead taking possession and establishing Christ's authority over that place, bringing all things into subjection to Him.[22] So Lord, I thank You, for these shoes as I now put them on to destroy the authority of Satan and have my feet securely grounded and protected in Your authority.

A Willing Shield

Lord, I understand the shield that I must take up by faith to be Your very flesh and blood standing between the enemy and me. As I hold you up by faith on my right and on my left, in front of me and behind me, above me and beneath me, I see you standing there looking into my face. I see You demonstrating all of your love and compassion for me. Seeing You standing there before me, it is hard to hold You in that position, knowing that You are taking all of the blows intended for me. I know I must place you in that position by faith even though I deserve the blows, because you chose to put yourself in that position between the enemy and myself. You showed your mercy and obedience in becoming the worthy sacrifice by which the enemy is to be defeated. Lord thank you for being my shield, my rock, and my hiding place.[23] Thank you for protecting me from and extinguishing all of the fiery darts and arrows of the enemy by this shield of faith.[24]

This Sword Cuts Precisely

I now take the sword of the spirit, Your word in my hands. This sword is sharper than any two edged sword which man is able to construct, for it is able to cut off the strongest chains and bondages by which Satan has been able to hold men in slavery to the fear of death all the days of their lives.[25] It is able to penetrate, piercing as far as the division of soul and spirit, of both joints and marrow, and able to judge the thoughts and intentions of the heart.[26] Lord train my hands for war and my fingers for battle[27] that I might skillfully use this sword[28] not in a way that might wound the innocent, but which will destroy the working of the enemy. I thank You Lord that You have equipped me with and trusted me with such a powerful weapon with which to cut away the veil of blindness and destroy the dominion of Satan over the lives of those whom You created and love. I know that it is Your desire that none of these should perish and I ask Your guidance to use this sword skillfully for their rescue, healing, deliverance and salvation.[29]

All Kinds of Holy Spirit Fired Prayers

Now, we take up the weapon of prayer, fired by the Holy Spirit.[30] We will lift all kinds of prayers and petitions at all times for all of the saints. All kinds of prayers and petitions, by my mind, or by my spirit, both can and must be in the spirit,[31] whether by songs, and psalms or words of scripture still set on fire by the Holy Spirit. I will lift all kinds of prayers and petitions, at all times. I will pray in times of focused prayer in my place of prayer, I will lift up prayers while I walk in the way, while I sit, while driving in the car and while shopping in the market place. If You should wake me in the night hours, I will lift all kinds of prayers and petitions, just as I shall also do at all times through the day.[32] I will lift all kinds of prayers and petitions, at all times, for all of the saints, and Lord, even for all of those ones who do not yet know that they also have been called as saints of the Most High God.[33]

And now I and we ask for prayers of our behalf, that every utterance may be given to us in the opening of our mouth, to make known with boldness the mystery of the good news of the Kingdom of God.[34] Thank you Lord and Amen.

This is what putting on the armor has come to mean to me. I would like to illustrate through several examples how this might function in battle.

Slight Adjustments May be Necessary for Better Protection

Several years ago, in a story I will illustrate in greater depth in a later chapter in this book, I was engaged in a battle under the instruction of the Lord to remove the dominion of Satan over the area of Los Angeles City known as Venice Beach. This very popular tourist destination draws crowds of forty to sixty thousand visitors on a typical Saturday or Sunday during the summer. Yet, the demonic influence is blatant and obvious throughout the shops and public access vendors that represent just about every religious, secular, humanistic, and occult belief openly along the boardwalk. The Lord gave me the instruction to cause the dominion of Satan to flee from over the city. This was to be done by taking small teams to, quietly and unobtrusively, walk down the boardwalk every Saturday morning for seven weeks. We were silently worshiping the Lord, so as to establish His presence there and enthrone Him on the praises of His people.[35] We were aware that we were entering territory ruled by the enemy. We also knew that many of the humans practicing witchcraft and other occult crafts through the demons that empowered them, would be able to see in their spirit who we were by the very different spirit empowering us. Therefore, we very carefully put on the armor each week before entering the territory.

For the first several weeks, I had one person in the group who acted as an armor bearer. It was this person's sole assignment to keep watch over how the enemy might attempt to penetrate our armor. The rest of us were to be totally focused, not on the enemy, but upon worshiping the Lord in the midst of this battle zone. We had received from the Lord and all agreed that our focus was to be on the worship and we were not to engage individuals along the way in conversation, evangelism, or any other interaction. We were not to be distracted by the obvious signs of demonic activity that included a number of warlocks walking up to us out of nowhere and cursing us, in "tongues," nose to nose. At one point in the walk down the boardwalk, I saw off to my right, a woman and a young boy in his early teens talking with a tattoo artist. The woman, perhaps in her late forties, was helping the young boy pick out a satanic tattoo to be permanently embedded in his forearm. That scene and the words I heard spoken by them slipped in through my eye gates and my ear gates. These inputs of the senses that were trained to discern this as evil, were processed in my mind in such a way that a very strong emotion grabbed me in the pit of my stomach. I quietly spoke to those with me, "it really gets to me to see an older person like that leading this young boy into the occult." That is all that I said, but it was obvious that my focus on worship had been broken and the enemy had been able to grab my emotions. My armor bearer, doing his job, tapped me on the shoulder and told me, "Readjust your Breastplate and Helmet, the enemy has been able to penetrate your armor." I consciously took a moment to realign and reaffirm the armor that was meant to protect me from those intrusions. In spite of the armor that we wore that morning, the shear mass of the demonic assault upon us through sight, sound, smell, taste, touch and intuition left all of us struggling to stand by the end of the walk. We found ourselves nauseated and weighed down by demonic "kligons" that pestered several of the team until we were able to command them to break off their assignments and go to the feet of Jesus for Him to deal with them. But we had been able to keep standing because of the effectiveness of the armor. As we continued the worship in the following weeks, the authority of the dominion of Satan that was empowering the ground level demonic forces began to fade away. The attacks became less and less intense as we also became more confident and skilled at wearing our armor.

More about Armor Bearers

By the way, the concept of an armor bearer or gatekeeper is something that should also be considered inside the walls of churches. Witchcraft organizations regularly infiltrate the church. If we are not aware of this and do nothing about it, we will find ourselves suffering from the curses placed while we have our armor down thinking we are in the safety of God's house. If the spirit of God is not there or no one discerning through the spirit of God is standing watch, people are going to get hurt. I know, because I once had a curse placed on me while I was speaking before a group of mostly spirit filled Christians. It was not until an hour after I had been suddenly hit with an extremely sore throat just as I walked off the platform, that one of the discerning intercessors at that meeting told me that they were aware of two people in the audience who were practicing witches and who seemed to be placing curses. I thanked the person for their revelation, but suggested that they should have taken some action or let other warriors know of this sooner. I fought that sore throat for several weeks. The regular staff of the church, those who normally take care of these situations by discerning and countering in the power of the Holy Spirit the witches present, had not been at this special gathering. On other occasions, during regular services of the church when the gatekeeper staff has been on duty, we have seen witches come under the conviction of the Holy Spirit and crawl or slither to the front of the church to repent and receive Christ. (I am not making this up folks!)

Keeping Covenant in Battle

With regard to the Belt of Truth, this piece is as indicated above, is very important in maintaining covenant with one another during the battle. It has been my experience and that of others, that the enemy will generally try to get at least one person in a group to start dissenting, accusing others in the group or manifesting some form of unforgiveness that disrupts the unity. This happened so often in the early days of our doing spiritual warfare in groups, that we realized that we needed to point this out and prepare everyone beforehand that this was going to happen. They needed to understand that it is one way in which the enemy is able to harass and break down our anointing as a group. Therefore, we asked everyone participating in a particular battle to covenant with one another that when this manifestation would occur we would again tighten the belt of the truth. We would reaffirm who we all are in Christ and that we are of one spirit, and so we would reject any manifestation of division or discord among us as contrary to the truth. When doing prophetic acts[36] that involved a number of people, we also designated one person or two persons functioning jointly, as having the ultimate decision making authority as to what should happen during the prophetic act. This was generally the person who received the original direction from the Lord. We asked all who were participating to agree ahead of time to honor this person or persons as having the ultimate authority during the performance of the prophetic act. If any person participating did not feel they would be able to honor this covenant, they were asked not to participate and instead to intercede through prayer for the group from a different location.

A Little Late but Still Effective

One last example of putting on the armor, this time in the middle of an attack, will also illustrate the effectiveness of these pieces provided by the Lord. I came home from a church seminar late one evening only to find myself engaged immediately in a heated argument with a family member. It was late and I was tired, but as I tried to go to sleep, my mind was spinning wildly and my gut was churning as a result of the interchange. I lay sleepless and churning for what seemed like hours before, finally and briefly, falling asleep out of pure exhaustion. The sleep did not last long. I awoke about twenty minutes later with the mind still spinning out of control and the stomach tied in knots. Since I could not sleep, I got up and went down to the family room where I often prayed while pacing in circles.

This night I could not even get into prayer so intense was the upset in both my mind and my gut. As I struggled, unable to pray, I heard a quiet voice in my head say, "put on the armor." I stopped immediately and put on the Helmet of Salvation as I have described above, and immediately the spinning and racing of my mind stopped, but the gut was still tied in knots. So then, I put on the Breastplate of Righteousness, and what do you know, but the authority that had established chaos over my body was destroyed and this quiet calm and joy penetrated into the depths that had been chaos and pain a few minutes before. (Remember the word Shalom?)

I then did something that I had rarely done because I am not really a very good pianist, I went into the living room and quietly sat at the piano for four hours through the rest of the night making up and singing worship to the Lord.

I hope that you have found these explanations of the armor helpful and will be more aware of the absolute necessity of putting it on before engaging the enemy. I find that it is a step that is often trivialized or overlooked even by those who are supposedly seasoned warriors. I guess it is the same syndrome as the seasoned firefighters I used to work with that were too "tough" to put on their breathing apparatus during the cleanup stages of a fire and while there was still a bit of smoke in the

A STOP BY THE ARMORY ON THE WAY TO THE FRONT LINES

building. Yes, it was inconvenient and heavy and hindered the work to some degree. When we begin bringing HAZMAT squads out to the fire scene and their instruments proved to the doubting and proud firemen that the level of toxins still present in the wisps of smoke far exceeded the levels that could lead to early death or life long disability, the fireman were more willing to wear the masks.

This is the case also with the armor in spiritual warfare. You might think that you can get by without it, but the enemy may be able to penetrate your pride with a fatal blow.

In the first two chapters, I shared with you how I came to understand my call to ministry. Now let's take a look at a year of transition when the Lord updated my armor and sent be back to the front lines.

IN FAVOR OF THE SAINTS

Endnotes

1. "The Adversary" by Mark Bubeck,
2. 2 Corinthians 2:10-11
3. Ephesians 6:12
4. Acts 26:17
5. Acts 26:18
6. Daniel 7:21, Revelation 12:12, Revelation 13:7
7. Daniel 7:22, Ephesians 6:13
8. Hebrews 5:14
9. Hebrews 2:14-15
10. Revelation 12:11
11. John 14:30
12. John 7:18
13. Rom 8:38-39
14. Ephesians 5:6-21,
15. Hebrews 7:25
16. 1 Corinthians 12:12-31,
17. John 16:13
18. John 8:44
19. Ephesians 6:13, James 4:7
20. Seekins, Dr. Frank T. <u>Hebrew Word Pictures.</u> 1994, 2002
21. Deuteronomy 11:24-25, Joshua 1:2-4,14:6-9
22. Hebrews 2:8
23. Psalm 32:7, Psalm 119:114
24. Ephesians 6:16
25. Hebrews 2:15
26. Hebrews 4:12
27. Psalm 144:1
28. 2 Timothy 2:15
29. 2 Peter 3:9
30. Numbers 16:46 (this will be expanded upon in a later chapter), Revelation 5:8
31. Romans 8:26-27, 1 Corinthians 14:14-15
32. Deuteronomy 11:18-25
33. Ephesians 6:18, Psalm 57:2-3, Daniel 7:22
34. Ephesians 6:19
35. Psalm 22:3,
36. A Prophetic act is the acting out symbolically of a Biblical truth that may have been given to one by a vision or word from the Lord. These actions are taken to alter or remove a spiritual influence that has become entrenched over a place through the sinful action of some person or group in the past. More examples of these type actions will be given in following chapters.

CHAPTER 6

THE YEAR 2001, A YEAR OF TRANSITIONS

Sitting in my home editing studio early in the year 2000, I was at a point of decision. If this technical, video and television production ministry was the extent of where I was going to be ministering for as long as I was able to do so, I guessed I had better get used to the fact and settle in, and do the best I could with it. For the previous six years, because of issues going on with various family members, I had withdrawn more and more from any other form of ministry other than the video in order to take care of my home situation. Yet the more I withdrew, the more difficult things in life became. Since the video ministry was also taking up more and more time, and I was still working a full time job with the fire department, I didn't really have time to give to anything else anyway. So I thought, if this was the only door that seemed open, then so be it.

In September of 1999, I was put off duty with the fire department because of a job related deterioration of my left hip. This condition had come to the place in 1997 where I had been required to undergo a hip replacement operation. Now the workers compensation policy of the department made the determination that I no longer met the physical qualifications for my job classification. I was officially retired from the department in November of 2000. Part of my retirement settlement provided for retraining for another occupation, or a small amount of capital for equipment and start up expenses to establish my own business.

In April of 2000, I transitioned from doing video and television production on a purely voluntary basis to establishing my own company. This was a better situation for tax purposes and out of pocket expenses and allowed me to be able to set up a studio space. Now I was also able to take on some additional ministries as well as some secular clients. My technical skills were growing and I was able to help a number of small ministries launch into much more exposure through producing their teaching on video and audiocassettes.

Are You There God?

Personally, emotionally, and spiritually however, I was rapidly approaching one of the lowest points in my life. No matter what I seemed to do beyond the video, it just dragged me down more and more. By December of 2000, I had reached the spiritual low point of my entire life. I found myself crying out to the Lord and yet feeling the growing suspicion that maybe there was not really a God at all. My prayers certainly seemed to be just disappearing into a void of nothingness. Though I purposed to keep bringing back to remembrance the times of the past when I sensed the Lord so close, I began to question whether or not those times had just been my imagination.

On New Year's Eve 2000, at the encouragement of my oldest son and out of my desire, I attended the year-end prophetic service at a nearby and well-known renewal based church. As I sat in that service on New Year's Eve, and soaked in anointed worship, I reconnected with the spirit of God, and I very clearly heard Him for the first time in what seemed like years. He spoke to me, "you have faithfully been serving in another church for twenty-five years, but I brought you here tonight because this is where I want you for now; you are to become a part of this church."

Not a People Pleaser Anymore

I was filled with joy that night to have again heard my Lord and it seemed like a great weight was lifted off. Making this transition would not be easy though, because others in my life had not heard the Lord as I had, and immediately I faced opposition, a lot of opposition. This opposition came from several people in my life who felt that they had a better plan for my life than what I clearly knew was from the Lord and to be obeyed. It was difficult to deal with the opposition from the flesh of those around me, but for one of the first times in my life, I had a greater peace than I had ever experienced before. I now knew that I was obeying exactly what the Lord was telling me to do. It would be several more years before I would completely understand what and why of the Lord's work in my life. But what He was doing was absolutely necessary to prepare me for what was to come. It also caused me to stop being a people pleaser, and servant of others and to start instead pleasing Him by my exact obedience to what He would have me do. Too many times in the past, I had suppressed the Lord's instructions to me because others had insisted on my pleasing and serving their agenda's. I had gone along with them to "keep the peace."

Alive at Fifty-Five

The year 2001, though it was difficult because of the demands of others to conform to their plans and goals for my life, was also one of the best years of my life. The year of my 55th birthday would be a year of double grace as symbolized by the two fives in my age. Because of the nature of the church where the Lord had placed me for that year, I was able to immerse myself in soaking worship and prayer for the full year. I also began making friends with Christians who were actually more interested in spiritual things then in the score of the football game or what the weather looked like today. Though I had been around many Christians in my life, I now started developing deeper friendships than I had ever done before. These people were like-minded, and of the same spirit. Additionally, I was also now back among a group of Christians who considered it normal faire to experience tremendous anointing on times of worship and to expect physical healings and deliverance as "not out of the ordinary" events.

Several other significant events occurred during 2001, of which I would later come to understand the significance. A Tibetan Buddhist festival was held on the mall in Washington, D.C. that included the construction of a Sand Mandala. This Mandala when deconstructed, was poured into the Potomac River just opposite the wall of the Pentagon where an airliner under terrorist control would be crashed on 9/11. Chuck Pierce, a prophet associated with Dr. C. Peter Wagner and others, began declaring early in the year, that 2001 would be the beginning of a seven-year war in the spiritual realm and that the United States would be in a physical war by September 18 of 2001. He was greeted with a great deal of skepticism until 9/11, 2001. This seven-year period ended in the fall of 2008 with major shifts in the economy and politics of the world.

December 31, 2000, my spiritual batteries were plugged back into the charger. A former pastor of mine once described grace as the gasoline that energizes Gods moving in our life. Well, this year of double grace would certainly fill my tank back up.

Now came New Year's Eve 2001, and another very clear word from the Lord. In the following days began a series of events, I now call the best and the worst years of my life.

CHAPTER 7

DOING DAMAGE TO THE ENEMIES CAMP

The word I heard now from the Lord on New Year's Eve 2001 was both a rebuke and a command. He said, "For the last seven years you have been withdrawing more and more from the ministry to which I called you and as a result you have been suffering more and more hits from the enemy, it is time that you start doing some damage to the enemy's camp." Well, I was not sure what I was going to do to start doing damage to the enemy's camp, but I did know that my camp was certainly in pretty poor condition after the beating it had been taking for the last seven years. I was more than willing to do whatever I could do, that would turn the tables.

For a number of months in the last half of the year 2001, I had become a regular participant at a 6 a.m. prayer meeting at the church where the Lord had brought me. I really liked this prayer meeting as it was unlike any I had ever been a part of. I mean I knew that the scriptures said that we should always pray in the spirit and I knew that this did not just mean praying in tongues. Only on a few occasions before, had I been around people here in the United States that seemed to be able to pray prayers that flowed from the spirit and not from the flesh or the intellect. This prayer meeting dripped with anointing and power. It would also become the place where the Lord began my new mentoring in spiritual warfare.

Walking into the Battle

It had been decided that at this beginning of the New Year 2002, for the next forty days, those participating in the 6 a.m. prayer meeting would go out into the city of Pasadena prayer walking during that hour. The format was simple, we gathered at 6 a.m. for a brief time of worship and then out the door by 6:15 to where ever you sensed that the Lord was leading. January 4, 2002, on the first morning that I was back in town from a brief trip, and the leading I sensed from the Lord was to worship in and anoint the gates of the city. I had no idea where the gates of the city were, so as would become a habit over the coming years, I simply asked the Lord, "Where are the gates of the city?" Within a few minutes, I had a strong impression of four locations, which happened to be three overpasses and one underpass where four freeways enter the city from the North, South, East, and West. That morning I went alone to those four locations, danced at, worshipped in and anointed with oil, the gates of the city. I didn't understand at the time why I was to dance, worship and anoint with oil, I was just being obedient to what I heard. I wonder to this day what drivers in the early morning commute thought about the sight of the old fat guy dancing across the overpasses. Little did I know either, that January 4th would become a significant date of spiritual warfare in my life for the next two years, but more about that later.

The 6a.m. prayer meeting was a Monday through Friday gathering. When I came in the room on Monday morning, I had not talked to anyone about what I had done on Friday, but three intercessors came up to me and said, "If you draw lines between the four gates you went to on Friday, where do those lines intersect?" The question was quite a surprise to me but I have learned not to be all that surprised anymore by what God reveals to intercessors and the questions He puts on minds. I replied, "I am not sure why you are asking and I don't know the answer, but here's a map so let's do it and find out." Much to all of our surprise, the lines intersected in the middle of the old Colorado Street Bridge. This bridge, is also known as the suicide bridge from the number of people who have jumped from the high arch in the middle of this bridge where it crosses over a paved road in the arroyo below. The intercessors then asked if they could go back to the four gates with me that morning and then if we could all go down to the Colorado Street Bridge to see what might be going on there in the spiritual realm.

Who's Watching the City Line?

We went out to the first overpass, which was on the North side of the city over the 210 Freeway right next to the Devil's Gate reservoir and NASA's Jet Propulsion Laboratory (JPL). Little did I know at the time that the number 210, the Devil's Gate, and JPL would all have great significance in what the Lord was about to reveal. After wandering around that gate for a while and anointing it again, one of the intercessors asked, "Where actually is the city line?" I pointed to the white marking on the other side of the roadway and told them that this was the city line. The intercessor said, "Can we go over and look at it closer?" I felt a little foolish as though any of these adult intercessors needed my permission to walk across the street to look at something, but I said, "Sure we are all adults here, let's cross the street and take a look." Much to my shock, as we were walking up to the simple white line painted on the curb of the road, I saw right next to the white line was a painted a symbol that I had learned years prior was a "demonic watcher" symbol. When I pointed this out to the intercessors, I had to explain to them, "A demonic watcher symbol is placed by someone who is placing a curse and is a demonic assignment to watch over the curse." "These symbols appear all over the world and are all very similar."[1] But here, now, was one placed next to the city line, likely representing a curse placed on the city.

In talking a few weeks later to a former practitioner of several different varieties of witchcraft, and voodoo, I would learn that the similarity around the world was because the spirit or demon associated with the person was the source of the design. The humans placing the curse may or may not be aware of drawing or painting the symbol. When others pass by this location, the demonic spirit in them or oppressing them connects with the spirit of the demon assigned to watch over the curse and comes into agreement with the curse or adds to it. Again, the human passing by may or may not be aware of the symbol left in that location, but the demonic spirit associated with them will connect with demonic assignment and come into agreement with the curse.

Do U Know?

With this particular "watcher," there was something different that I had never seen before. It was a "U" shape to the left of the watcher at a 45-degree angle above the horizontal midline of the symbol. This was to be a puzzle to me and would be the start of a download of information from the Lord. For the next two weeks, I was led by the Lord to spend nearly every waking hour absorbing information off the Internet, from libraries and out of scripture. The Lord gave me an intensive course in history, mysticism, witchcraft, Masonic, New Age, Buddhism, and mythology over that next two weeks and showed me how they all related to one another and to what He was showing me in the city of Pasadena.

As I had learned years before, we would that morning command the demon assigned to that curse to break off their assignment and go to the feet of Jesus. We then scrapped the painted symbol off the curb as best we could and anointed the location with oil representing healing of the land from the curse that had been placed.

Everybody's Watching but Nobody's Seeing

From the North Gate, we drove down to the West Gate over the 134 Freeway. Here we found paper labels strategically placed all around the gate with Buddha's and Cobras printed on them. We would learn that this was another form of watcher, and we treated them the same, by breaking off the assignment, removing the adhesive labels and anointing the locations.

At this point, we were near the Colorado Street Bridge, so walked out on the sidewalk over the bridge. I should not have been surprised by that time, but here were two watchers painted on either side of the sidewalk at the middle of the bridge. These watchers were at the location where many of those committing suicide jump off this bridge. We would also discover on the other side of the bridge on the railing, a curse painted with an arrow pointing at the U.S. 9th Circuit Court of Appeals located in a building right next to the bridge. We did more breaking off assignments, and anointing, before moving on to the South Gate.

At the South Gate, we found another watcher like the one at the North Gate and on the Colorado Street Bridge. This was becoming a pattern so we were not all that surprised when we found the East Gate surrounded by twenty-two carefully placed paper labels with the same Buddha's printed on them that we had found at the West gate. Cleaning up this gate would require coming back the next day with a stepladder to reach many of these Buddha's and remove them. On the next day, a number of other intercessors came with us to see and learn what was going on in the city and cover us with prayer as I removed these Buddha watchers from the East Gate.

A Declaration of War on the Churches

Over the next several weeks, this group of intercessors and I decided that we would go to as many of the churches in town as we could, to pray over them and bless them. There are about three hundred churches on record in Pasadena, some of which are storefronts or private homes. We were not able to get to them all or even find addresses for all of them. During the next several weeks we did pray over about ninety of them, which led to another curious discovery. At about eighty of these churches, we found watcher symbols on the property line or in front of the front door of the church. In speaking with my former witchcraft practitioner and consultant about this situation, he stated that this was equivalent to a declaration of war against the churches of Pasadena. We continued breaking off the assignments, removing the symbols, anointing and blessing the locations and notified pastors of our findings when we could locate the pastors.

As during this time I was also immersed in the research and downloads of the Lord, I would come to understand about two weeks after its discovery, the meaning of the "U," (or at least the meaning that the Lord wanted to communicate to me), on the watcher symbols we would find all over the City of Pasadena.

Endnotes

1. For more information, see the chapter on Ritualistic Curses, in *Unbroken Curses* by Rebecca Brown, M.D. and Daniel Yoder, Whitaker House, Springdale, PA, 1995.

CHAPTER 8

"U" IS FOR UNDERSTANDING

It would be about two weeks after I had started searching, before I found anything resembling the "U" which we were finding associated with all of the demonic watcher symbols throughout the city. I searched all kinds of sources including books and articles on the occult, symbol dictionaries, alphabets associated with mysticism and witchcraft and many other sources. In the meantime, the Lord was putting me through a two-week intensive graduate level course that was really opening the eyes of my understanding of the demonic underpinnings of this world. I have always been a fairly good researcher of something I was interested in, but I had never been much interested in history, mythology, occult, or non-Christian religious movements. Now the Lord was making it clear to me that if I was to be able to "do damage to the enemies camp," I was going to have to expand my study and understanding as to how the enemies' camp was set up. I was going to have to look outside of just the Bible and the books of mostly Christian authors who had little real understanding of the "ruler of this world." Since it is Jesus Himself who introduces this title for Satan into scripture, in John 12:31, 14:30 and 16:11, it seemed that He also was the best mentor to give me understanding about the enemy of our soul for the purpose of being aware of his schemes and defeating his plans. [1]

The study of this two-week period was also unlike any of the study or research I had ever done before. I did not have to search through hours of material to find one sentence that may be relevant. The Lord seemed to direct me to every relevant page on the World Wide Web, and in the libraries. At the same time it seemed that even in the car while driving, every radio program to which I listened, would be specifically about something that I was also finding in my Lord taught crash course. Then there were the people who I would meet or was introduced to, during this particular two weeks. These people also had pieces of the information that the Lord was downloading eighteen hours a day, seven days a week. I cannot say that I fully enjoyed this time (just as I never enjoyed finals week in college). I often became overwhelmed by the nature and extent to which the demonic realm had permeated every aspect of our culture and the governments in this world. I found myself at times just lying before the Lord and crying out to the Lord, "Why are you showing me all of this?" "What am I to do with this?" "Who can I talk to about it?" "How can I possibly make a difference?"

It was as if the Lord would just pat my head gently and say, "Yes, I know my son, but be patient, do not worry, for I am with you, but there is still more for you to understand before the battles that are to come." I became grateful that at least the intensive military academy training I was undergoing was only several weeks rather than the years of study this Country's military officers go through to prepare for war with flesh and blood. Unfortunately, they do not get any of the training I received to understand the spiritual forces behind and driving the flesh and blood armies of this world. I was being given special forces training to learn how to recognize the commanders in a battle, understand their strategies and be able to cut off their communications, throw their warriors into confusion and take possession of the ground that they had held under their dominion.

What Have the Masons to do With It?

I would come to understand that various Masonic groups in the 1700's, when this organization was just beginning to become publicly acknowledged, were given the mandate to restore and maintain various bodies of "enlightened" understanding or "esoteric" knowledge. It was recognized that such esoteric "religious" or "mystic" groups as the Kabalistic Priesthood, the Babylonian Religion, Egyptian Mythology, the Knights Templar and the Rosicrucian's were no longer functioning. If the knowledge and ritual practices of these groups were to be maintained, Masonic should become the custodian of these mysteries. Free choice was given to various Masonic organizations in different locations to adopt one of these esoteric groups. They were to establish their rituals and practices to maintain and bring to life that which otherwise was likely to disappear. Though there are common elements across the range of Masonic organizations in different regions, there are some practices particularly in the higher degrees, which attach to one of these earlier bodies of knowledge. I would also come to understand why Masonic is a Luciferian religion and not a society of Christian men just doing good works in the world.

I would learn of the Masonic roots of Mormonism and how many Masonic practices and rituals are still at the heart of the Mormon Church today. This, despite the many television ads and magazine articles generated to deceive the world into thinking that this organization is in fact Christian and promoting the Christ of the Bible.

Hello Queen of Heaven

I would learn that the entity that some would call the "Queen of Heaven" has its roots in Libyan religion that predates Egyptian Religion and Mythology. This entity appears in many different cultures and lands under differing names down through the centuries. There are common threads in the stories about each that links all of these differing names together.

I would learn of the Tibetan Buddhism link between The Theosophical Society, the witchcraft of Aleister Crowley, the writings of Alice Bailey, Nazi Germany and many other organizations pushing the world agenda of this day.

There U Are!

Finally, I found the meaning of the "U" and a link from there to understanding of the spiritual forces released in the City of Pasadena, California. I believe from what the Lord revealed that these forces have affected the entire world over the last sixty years.

I am going to repeat the disclaimer, which I stated in the introduction at this point. Much of what I am about to share through the following material will stretch most peoples' concept of reality. It may subject their flesh to righteous indignation or other such reactions of the flesh. As I said in the introduction;

> "This is a true story. None of the events and experiences shared has been made up for the sake of example. Everything happened just as described. What cannot be proved as factual by scientific methodology are some of the interpretations of the events and the experiences described. I can only say, Christianity is a walk of faith and faith is the key ingredient if we are to do great exploits for our God and take possession of the Kingdom. Often at the time of an event and even for a time after, faith in the results of obedience was the only thing to cling to until some evidence of the fruit of our labors would form and give substance to our faith."

I restate this because I know I have struggled at times with accepting as reality things I have been exposed to over my sixty-eight year walk as a Christian. I struggle to believe that there are actually humans out there with the mindset to live their lives believing and worshipping demons and carrying out the detestable practices that the demons lead them to do. We read daily in our newspapers of some of the horrid and bazaar things that humans have done to others. I am aware some of those in the body of Christ who hold to certain rigid doctrinal stances will likely condemn the things I am sharing here as not possibly having been revealed by God. I respect your opinion, but I know my shepherds voice.

"U" IS FOR UNDERSTANDING

Many of the Israelites that left Egypt with Moses, had no idea of where they were going or what they would encounter along the way, they simply obeyed. In fact, they did not even want to have an encounter with God but instead told Moses to do the talking for them.[2] Their lack of obedience and lack of "knowing" God lead to many falling and dying in the wilderness. Even when they were shown the Promised Land and that it was prosperous, they did not believe God that they could take possession of it and as a result that generation wandered in the wilderness for forty years until all but Joshua and Caleb had died.

As for me, I would rather fight the giants the Lord reveals than wander forty years in the wilderness and never enter the Promised Land. When the nation finally did enter, they were required to fight many battles. When they fought the battles that the Lord told them to, in exactly the way the Lord told them to, and at the time they were told, they were successful. However, there were also times that they did not carefully listen to the Lord or tried to fight a battle that the Lord did not tell them to fight and many died.

It's Not the Ones You Can See That Are the Problem

Paul tells us: "For our struggle is not against flesh and blood, but against the rulers, against the powers, against the world forces of this darkness, against the spiritual forces of wickedness in the heavenly places."[3] These are all things that we cannot see and fight against unless the Lord shows us, tells us what to do and equips for the battle. That is what this book is all about.

The "U" which I finally found in only one place, a symbol encyclopedia, is a symbol in astrology, which represents the "South Node of the Moon," or the "Birth of the Moonchild." Reading the words of that definition, "Birth of the Moonchild," jerked my senses to full alert. This was because of some facts I had been exposed to a number of months prior.

A Troublesome Trio

I had been invited to a meeting of a number of friends who were doing research on the spiritual underpinnings of the Hollywood film and television industry. Some of what was shared at that meeting was about a man who was raised and lived in Pasadena, California and who is generally acknowledged as a founder of Jet Propulsion Laboratory located in Pasadena just behind the Devil's Gate Reservoir. The Laboratory was actually established and built by the Department of the Army in 1943 and transferred to NASA in 1957, but it was built on the site of the experiments and developments of John Whiteside Parsons. Jack Parsons, as he was known to his friends, was a young rocket scientist, who developed several rocket designs that were already in use by the U.S. Military in the late 1930's. Parsons was also one of the founders of Aerojet Engineering Corporation, which was located in Azusa, California for the purpose of building the propeller aircraft take off assist rockets designed by Parsons and his group under Von Karman at Cal Tech in Pasadena.

A darker side of Jack Parsons was also coming into being during the beginning of the 1940's. Parsons and his wife had become involved with an organization called the OTO (Ordo Templi Orientis), which had opened a lodge in Pasadena in the early 1930's. I will explain this organization in more depth a bit further on. Let it suffice to say, this was a witchcraft organization founded by Aleister Crowley. Or should I say stolen from German Masonic and reworked by Aleister Crowley in London England just prior to World War I. Parsons became an active member of the OTO, and eventually became the head of the Pasadena lodge after gaining favor with Aleister Crowley and after the previous local leader ran off with Parsons' wife. In 1944, Parsons would meet a young Reserve Naval officer and aspiring science fiction writer who would become his business partner and partner in "Magick," the form of witchcraft practiced in Crowley's OTO. This new associate in business and witchcraft was none other than the future founder of Scientology, L. Ron Hubbard.

To Birth the Moonchild

After the meeting in late 2001, in which I had heard an introduction to the activities of these two men, I had done some research on my own and had run across a personal journal by Jack Parsons. In this journal, he described in great detail a two-month long witchcraft ritual, which he and Hubbard had conducted together in the early part of 1946. But the sentence in that journal explaining the purpose of the ritual, that since has been called the "Babalon Working," and the understanding to which this definition of the "U" now jerked my attention back, was the stated purpose of the ritual. The ritual was "To Birth the Moonchild." It was further explained by Parsons that the purpose of the ritual was to birth into physical manifestation the woman Babalon, the spirit described in the book of Revelation. The Moonchild is explained in other writings of astrology and witchcraft as the Goddess called Babylon, or Venus, and is the Goddess of the moon; the left eye of Horus while his right eye is the Sun God in Egyptian mythology.

It must be understood that when seeking to understand mythology and much of the esoteric writings of the occult, there are numerous reinterpretations and obscurities that are meant to elevate various leaders throughout history. Each has developed their own slight variations on the facts to prove to their followers that they are the only ones with the true knowledge. While this is the case, there still run threads within the stories that have enough similarity to them to point to some original understandings that form the basis for the interpretations that follow. In making the statement about the right and left eye of Horus, this is a belief that was collaborated by several of the sources that the Lord revealed to me through the intense study during this period. This will have direct correlations to further revelations about the City of Pasadena, which the Lord would bring to me a few days later.

This Moonchild is also the goddess entity who in this day many will call the Queen of Heaven.

The Babalon Working

Now I was even more curious. I wanted to understand the connection between Parsons and Hubbard's "Babalon Working" of 1946 and symbols being drawn throughout the City of Pasadena in the year 2002. I was curious to understand how watchers over curses that were being placed in front of the doors and on the property lines of churches in the city might be connected to this ritual in 1946.

The Babalon Working was a ritual that had been designed by Aleister Crowley himself, making use of elements of the Gnostic Mass and an ancient Rosicrucian ritual called the Rosey Cross. However, he had always considered it much too dangerous a ritual to carry out. This was partially due to his believed consequences to the individual conducting it (Crowley was already plagued by some "particularly nasty demons" he had opened the door to in the early days of his witchcraft). It was also partially due to the possible consequences to the world resulting from the physical manifestation of this particular demonic goddess. He was absolutely horrified and enraged when he learned that Parsons and Hubbard were actually conducting the ritual. This was the response of Aleister Crowley, the self-proclaimed Anti-Christ and called the "Wickedest Man in the World" by the press.

One would think even Parsons would have second thoughts when this demon actually manifested before him and spoke the words he would record in his journal. These are some brief excerpts from the beginning of the book that this entity commanded Parsons to write. It was to become the fourth chapter of a book that had been dictated to Crowley in 1903 by the manifestation of an entity that appeared to him as an "Ascended Tibetan Master."

> "It is BABALON. TIME IS. Ye fools.
> Thou hast called me, oh accursed and beloved fool.
> Now know that I, BABALON, would take flesh and come among men."
>
> "And this is the way of my incarnation. Heed!

Thou shalt offer all thou art and all thou hast at my altar, withholding nothing. And thou shalt be smitten full sore and thereafter thou shalt be outcast and accursed, a lonely wanderer in abominable places.

Ye Dare. I have asked of none other, nor have they asked. Else is vain. But thou hast willed it."

Despite the warnings of this entity and the threats to his person, Parsons none-the-less heeded the instructions of this demonic manifestation writing them down in a book called Liber 49, and proceeding with the ritual, which was completed a few days later in the beginning of March 1946. The impact on his own life would begin to manifest shortly afterward through a series of misfortunes and persecutions that took his wealth, his female companion (the sister of his previous wife) and his position as scientist from him. It would lead to his death six years later in 1952.

Parson's Casts a Spell

Shortly following the conclusion of the two-month long Babalon Working of 1946, Hubbard and Parsons' girlfriend left on a business trip to Florida. They were to buy yachts on the East coast and bring them to California where they were to be resold at a profit. When Hubbard and the girlfriend never showed up in California, Parsons' found out they had taken his money and run off together. Parsons' immediately went to Florida where he filed suit against the couple. When he learned they had taken off sailing in one of the yachts to get away from him, Parsons invoked a demon and conducted a ritual to create a storm at sea which drove the couple back to the shore where Parsons' took them to court. He recovered little through the court action, as much of his money had already been spent by Hubbard and the girl. Parsons returned to California where he was also in trouble with the Federal Government for secret military information he had shared with the newly formed nation of Israel and with Mexico. He was trying to help them develop military ordinance. His security clearances were revoked.

Whether many of the events of 1947 following this invoking of the spirit of Babalon into physical manifestation are directly related to that ritual or not is a matter of conjecture. This is greatly debated on numerous cultic web sites even today. But many would claim that Crowley's death in 1947, the founding of the nation of Israel, the sharp increase in UFO sightings, the Roswell incident, the radical shift of the Supreme Court in interpretation of the separations of church and state, and many other shifts in the age, or spiritual climate of the world in that year were directly connected to Parsons' and Hubbard's releasing into physical manifestation the spirit of Babalon. Just from the standpoint of the formation of the nation of Israel being understood by most Biblical scholars as a trigger event for the end of the age or the last days, it would seem that the release of Babalon into the world might somehow be related.

Madness and Horror in the Abyss

On October 31, 1948, Parsons is again visited by the manifestation of the spirit Babalon and this time she takes him into the underworld and leads him through rituals of the "Black Pilgrimage." Here are Parsons' words:

> "Now it came to pass even as BABALON told me, for after receiving Her Book, I fell away from Magick, and put away Her Book and all pertaining thereto. And I was stripped of my fortune (the sum of about $50,000) and my house and all I possessed."
>
> "Then for a period of two years I worked in the world, recouping my fortune somewhat. But that was also taken from me, and my reputation, and my good name in my worldly work, that was in science."

> "And on the 31st of October, 1948, BABALON called on me again, and I began the last work, that was the work of the wand. And I worked for 17 days, until BABALON called me in a dream, and instructed me on an astral working. Then I reconstructed the temple, and began the Black Pilgrimage, as She instructed."

At one point in this process, Parsons says,

> "And thereafter I returned and swore the Oath of the Abyss, having only the choice between madness, suicide, and that oath. But the Oath in no wise ameliorated that terror, and I continued in the madness and horror of the abyss for a season. But having passed the ordeal of 40 days I took the oath of a Magister of Templi, even the Oath of Antichrist before Frater 132, the Unknown God."

> "And thus Was I Antichrist loosed in the world; and to this I am pledged, that the work of Beast 666" (*Crowley's self-given title in the OTO*) "shall be fulfilled, and the way for the coming of BABALON be made open and I shall not cease or rest until these things are accomplished. And to this end I have issued this my Manifesto."

The Manifesto of the Antichrist

The Manifesto document was written in 1949 in which Parsons proclaims himself as the Antichrist. Several references are made to the motto of the OTO and many associated brotherhoods which is, "Do what thou wilt shall be the whole of the law" (*This is also called The Law of Thelema*). This is the affirmation of the concept of lawlessness that is associated with the followers of Satan and his other manifestations that we read in the explanation of the parable of the "Wheat and Tares," that

IN FAVOR OF THE SAINTS

those who practice "lawlessness," will be the first to be gathered out and cast into the furnace of fire.[4] It is because "lawlessness is increased, most people's love will grow cold."[5] "Let no one in any way deceive you, for it (the day of the Lord) will not come unless the apostasy comes first, and the man of lawlessness is revealed, the son of destruction, who opposes and exalts himself above every so-called god or object of worship, so that he takes his seat in the temple of God, displaying himself as being God.[6]

Parsons goes on to say in this document,

"And within seven years of this time, BABALON, THE SCARLET WOMAN HILARION will manifest among ye, and bring this my work to its fruition… An end to conscription, compulsion, regimentation, and the tyranny of false laws." (*Here is that lawlessness again*) "And within nine years a nation shall accept the Law of the BEAST 666 in my name, and that nation will be the first nation of the earth."

Not All Change is Good

Though I do not believe that the spirit of BABALON was manifest in one woman as I think Parsons believed would happen, we do see that within seven years of the 1946 ritual, Playboy Magazine is published. This publishing establishes an "empire" and starts a series of legal battles that open the publishing industry and the movie industry to tolerate and legalize publishing of more and more nudity, and other lessening of the standards of morality that had been in place. Not that the immorality was not going on in the background of the movie industry, government, business and elsewhere before that time. Nevertheless, starting in 1953, exactly seven years after the Babalon Working, the laws that had banned publications such as the limits that Playboy was pushing and held standards for the motion picture industry and even language on radio, began to be challenged. Within nine years after the ritual, we are building bomb shelters, and the U.S. is getting involved in Viet Nam. We see the manifestations of the immorality of the woman BABALON, who represents both love and war down through the ages, pouring out the cup of her immoralities over the peoples and nations.[84]

As a side note, in June 1952, Parsons was killed in an explosion in his garage at 1003 South Orange Grove in Pasadena (That address no longer exists). The official story is that he dropped a vile of highly explosive material but there are many other conspiracy theories suggested in the literature.

In 1951, the Chinese invade Tibet, eventually leading to the Dalai Lama fleeing Tibet in 1959 assisted by the U.S. CIA. This will become significant in later chapters of this book where we will look at Tibetan Buddhism in more depth.

In 1951, the Theosophical Society moves its international headquarters to Pasadena. Its original U.S. headquarters had been in a building that is now the administration building of the Point Loma College, formerly known as Pasadena Nazarene College, which moved from the campus in Pasadena in 1973.

1951, was also the year that L. Ron Hubbard laid the groundwork for Scientology and published *Dianetics*, named according to some after his enthusiasm for and study of the Cult of Dianna of the Ephesians.

The study of all of this later working and manifestation of BABALON in Pasadena in the late forties, I believe has its roots in Pasadena from earlier invitations of the BABALON spirit. As I was reading much of the material behind the OTO, Aleister Crowley, Jack Parsons, the Theosophical Society and the Masonic roots of Pasadena, I kept running across references to the ritual of the Rosey Cross. It was this ritual, in part, which Parsons was using during the Babalon Working. This ritual specifically has to do with the sexual union between the Sun God and the Moon God for the purpose of birthing the Moonchild. Lo and behold, the Moonchild is none other than the Queen of Heaven and whatever other name you want to call her, but is specifically centered in the names Ishtar, Babalon, and Venus. These are the primary names throughout a long history that are considered synonymous with Nuit, Inanna, Isis, Astarte, and Dianna in terms of all referring to the same spiritual entity (Some sources would disagree with the commonality of all of these names, but all of the sources agree with some of them).

Make a U Turn for Hollywood

But to get back to how all this relates to Pasadena and the "U" representing the "Birth of the Moonchild," specifically in Pasadena and in Hollywood (Hollywood being not a city, but the motion picture and television industry in general as having been birthed in the greater Los Angeles area), Babalon is continually called upon and made reference to. Hollywood has identified with Babalon since 1916, when during the filming of his silent feature length (four hours long) movie "Intolerance," D.W. Griffith enthroned Ishtar the goddess of Babylon. This enthroning was done on the largest set ever built in Hollywood and was constructed to be the gates of Babylon. The set sat at the corner of Hollywood and Sunset Boulevards for twenty years with Ishtar enthroned at the high place of the set. Griffith had not had the money to tear it down so it sat until the Government WPA tore it down in 1936. In the year 2000, the Gate of Babylon has again been constructed in Hollywood in the form of the Babylon Court shopping area, part of the Kodak Academy Awards Theater project at the corner of Hollywood Boulevard and Highland Avenue in downtown Hollywood. It is thought by some that the financial underpinnings of early Hollywood and even of Griffith's 1916 project came from wealthy families and businesses in Pasadena at the turn of the century into the 1900's. This would point to an earlier giving place to or establishing the authority of Babalon over the City of Pasadena as will be explained in the next chapter.

Endnotes

1. 2 Corinthians 2:11
2. Exodus 20:19-21
3. Ephesians 6:12
4. Matthew 13:41
5. Matthew 24:12
6. 2 Thessalonians 2:3-4
7. Revelation 17:3-Chapter 18

CHAPTER 9

THE HISTORY OF A SEAL ON KNOWLEDGE

What I am about to say in this chapter is not intended to point a finger at particular people or organizations. It is instead to illustrate how the actions of men give place to or establish either the dominion (spiritual authority structure) of Satan or of the Kingdom of God in a particular territory or city. The root establishing of a spiritual authority structure by men, leads to many other events and actions by persons living in that city. The actions of persons in later generations will come into agreement with that same spirit. This is just like I described with the demonic watcher symbol in an earlier chapter. Though I am illustrating this through the example of the City of Pasadena as the Lord revealed to me, I believe that the actions of people as led by spiritual authority structures they have allowed to dominate them, lead to the establishing of those same spiritual authority structures over the towns and cities they found and inhabit.[1]

No Coincidence

This is why I do not see Parsons as just a single anomaly in the whole world (to my knowledge this particular witchcraft ceremony, to invoke the manifestation of the spirit of Babalon into the physical world had never been done before or since, though I believe in 2003 there was some persons trying to recreate that ritual based upon web

IN FAVOR OF THE SAINTS

pages I was finding on the Internet in late 2002 and early 2003). It was not coincidence that Parsons just happened to be in Pasadena, just happened to become part of a witchcraft organization that at that time had only one U.S. lodge, which just happened to be located in the City of Pasadena in the early 1930's. I don't think that it is just coincidence that Pasadena the place of the invoking of Babalon, the goddess of war, whose shield symbol of a red star is painted on the tail of U.S. military aircraft, would also be home to fathers of modern day rocketry Von Karman and Goddard. I don't think it is a coincidence that it would be a breakthrough in formulation of rocket fuel by a relatively uneducated John Whiteside Parsons that would cause the United States Military rocket program to locate here and to take off (pun not intended) at the beginning of World War II.

It was the breakthroughs by Parsons and the research at JPL, located just behind the Devil's Gate Reservoir, which also would lead to the rockets that soon would be tipped with the nuclear weapons. The development of those nuclear weapons, were in part, as a result of a 1939 letter by Albert Einstein who had been a visiting professor in the 1930's at Cal Tech located in Pasadena. These Nuclear tipped ICBM rockets would strike terror into the hearts of many of us living in the world of the late 1950's.

I do not now see all of these and many more things associated with Pasadena as just coincidence in light of the root establishment of this spirit of Babalon in the very founding of the city. This becomes a very important understanding not only for Pasadena, but also, for any city where one is attempting to understand why some things go on in that city. It is important to understand the over arching spiritual dominion or authority over that city. It helps to know how did it gain authority and what can be done to change the spiritual dominion. It is my belief through this experience and others, that ultimately we must be heavily reliant upon the Lord to point to the history, interpret the history, the events and the outward evidences. We must also then allow Him to lead us through the warfare to change the spiritual dominion. Back to that principal that I introduced in the very beginning of the book; "we must hear the Lord, and obey Him exactly."

A Masonic Seal

I do not know that the founders of the City of Pasadena fully understood what they were establishing in the spiritual realm in the same way that I am about to share with you. I do know that they were part of an organization and organizations, which were heavily immersed in ritual related to the spirit and religion of Babalon[2]. I do not know whether witchcraft organizations in Pasadena and other organizations that have located there since, understand in the natural why they are there. However, I am relatively certain it is because of this spirit that was established and given dominion in the city at the founding. What I am about to share is the unraveling of information about that founding that the Lord revealed during a particular night in January of 2002. This revelation would give understanding to why many of these other events occurred in this city. It would also help to explain how this city brought the spirit of Babylon into the Hollywood industry and why now in the year 2002 witchcraft demonic watcher symbols throughout the city had attached to them the symbol of the "Birth of the Moonchild."

Historically the city of Pasadena was founded as the Orange Grove Growers Association in 1875 (the same year as the founding of the Theosophical Society by Helen Blavatsky). It received its name "Pasadena" somewhat mysteriously as a postal location, before the name was actually voted on and adopted by the residents. The name was made up of a number of local Native American words meaning something like "the Crown of the Valley." This may be one reason put forth at least publicly, for the adopting of a city seal in 1886 that has a prominent crown on it. The crown, by the way, is patterned after the coronation crown of the Royal Family of England, which is also tied very closely with other Masonic secrets, but that is the subject matter for books written by others.

The founders of the city came from an area of Southern Indiana, which had strong roots of Masonic and witchcraft. Through research, it has been determined that most if not all of the families that founded the city had strong roots in Masonry. It is likely for this reason that the first "secret society" in the city, which history tells us everyone in the city at that time in 1879, had been made charter members, was based

IN FAVOR OF THE SAINTS

in Masonry. Several years later, the first Masonic Lodge was established, and when a committee was formed in 1885 to apply to the County of Los Angeles for incorporation of the city, it was the Grand Mason of the lodge who headed that committee. The city was incorporated in June of 1886 with eleven trustees and officers, all of whom were either charter members of one of the several Masonic organizations that were in the city, or at least were associated with one of these organizations. The city seal was adopted as the fourth ordinance enacted at the very first meeting of the trustees in June 1886. That means that the official seal had to have already been thought through, and constructed prior to that first meeting. The seal as illustrated below is a crown, with a Maltese type cross on top, a key passing through the crown pointed downward, a chain around the crown, the name of the city, two stars, and the date around the chain and then a twisted rope around the outside of the seal.

The Cross and the Rose

As I was looking at the history of the founding and as the Lord was directing me in my search to find a connection to the Masonic roots of the city and the association with the "Birth of the Moonchild" I had looked briefly at the city seal. But at this particular point and on this particular evening in 2002, I was more focused on the city flower, the crimson red rose, and its relationship to a rose described in the ritual of the Rosey Cross and the link to this being the flower of Babalon. This ritual was described in Parson's journal as part of his experience during the ritual of 1946 carried out by him and Hubbard.

I had my senses stirred by the description in this ritual of the woman Babalon dancing amid 8 green flames and settling into a blood red rose of 7 times 7 petals, a rose of 49 petals representing the number of Babalon. Over this rose is the cross which represents the Sun God, and below the cross the disk of the sun and a hexagram.

Knowing that the official flower of Pasadena is the Rose and it is of a dark red color, and that Pasadena is the home of the Rose Parade on January 1 of every year, I began to wonder if there was any connection between the rose of the ritual, and Babalon being called forth in this city. I did more than wonder as I also heard a brief segment on National Public Radio (NPR), Station KPCC, located at Pasadena City College, talking about how the rose was the symbol of secrecy. It was used in Roman and Greek periods as a sign that conversations and actions occurring in a party or dinner where a rose was present on the table or hung from the ceiling, were considered confidential, or secret, and were not to be spoken of outside of that location. This led to the rose design in the metal work of ceilings in some restaurants. Conversations "under the rose" were to remain in confidence. I checked this out in the encyclopedia and found what I heard to be true. The definition of "sub rosa" or under the rose was this veil of secrecy.

I also learned, that the blood red rose or crimson rose is the flower of Venus and of Babalon.

My youngest son, who was at the time a student at the Pasadena Art Center College of Design, walked into my home office that evening. I knew that he had been working on a project with the city of Pasadena during the previous fall that involved the cities' identity logos and the design of image banners for various parts of the city. For that reason, I asked him if he had run across anything in the city image material that talked about a rose of 49 petals or 7x7 petals. He said that he did not recall anything similar to a rose of 49 petals, but he would go down to his room and look through his material on the project.

Have Fun Dad

My son is very sharp regarding images, logos and symbols, and one of his key interests in graphic design is coming up with logos, colors and symbols that represent the core of a particular company or corporation's image. A few minutes later, he returned and said, "I didn't find anything about the rose, but here is something you might be interested in." "I see in it symbols of many of the things which you have been studying and looking at in the material in front of you dad." With that, he handed me a copy of the original City of Pasadena Seal that was adopted as the fourth ordinance of the City in June 1886. He pointed out a few things that he was seeing and sure enough, I could see the correlation of the 7x7, the cross and the sun disk described in the ritual of the Rosey Cross. My son said, "Have fun dad," and left the room.

I was having anything but fun at that point, in fact I became very overwhelmed by what I was finding. I could see that there were elements present in the Crown that were very similar to a number of things that I had run across in relationship to the Gnostic Mass, the Rosicrucian rituals, and the practice of Magick. I soon found myself in another of those moments of crying out to the Lord, I am overwhelmed! I don't know what to do with this information. I don't know who I can talk to about it. I don't even know what it is all about, it is a mystery to me. Suddenly I do not know why, I thought of the words in Daniel, "…there is a God in heaven who reveals mysteries."[3] I begin crying out, "this is a mystery to me and I need the God in heaven who reveals mysteries to help me understand this mystery."

It was late in the evening, about 11:30 p.m., I was tired, and so I went to bed.

Endnotes

1. See for example the books by George Otis Jr., *Twilight Labyrinth and Informed Intercession*
2. The alternate spelling of Babylon as Babalon is used primarily as reference to the goddess rather than the city in witchcraft circles.
3. Daniel 2:28

CHAPTER 10

THE REVELATION OF THE SEAL

That night, at 2:30 in the morning the Lord awoke me with this phrase repeating over and over, "The key is in the crown." I knew in my head that literally, the key passes through the crown in the seal, but what I understood the Lord to be saying to me was, the key to understanding this mystery is in the crown. I got out of bed and went to my desk. I repeatedly gasped in surprise during the next four hours as the Lord showed me every detail of every element in the city seal related to various aspects of these rituals and "secret understandings" described in some of Crowley's material.

The even more amazing part of the revelation of that early morning was the four times the Lord stopped me and gave me a scripture to look up and study that in every case related directly to the part of the seal that I was examining at that moment. I am not going to set out every detail of the four-hour download. It is much too tedious, and off the point that I believe should be understood here, but I have included the much more in depth description in APENDIX B. The point here is, there is a God in heaven who understands mysteries and is able to explain them to you. Ask Him.

Here is a summary of what the Lord revealed during the four hours of that early morning.

The two larger openings in the crown represent the eyes of Horus, which were, the right being the sun god, and the left the moon goddess. (I am describing right and left as though you are looking out of the eyes from the inside of the crown or the left and right position of your own eyes.) This left eye again represents the moon goddess who is identified with Isis, Inanna, Ishtar, and Babalon.

The Key represents the authority to lock and unlock. In relationship to the left eye of Horus, it is the key of authority to unlock the underworld given to the Moon Goddess. Thus, we see the key in the eye of the Moon goddess, the left eye or opening of the crown. The cloverleaf design of the top of the Key is an ancient symbol of authority. On a newer version of the city seal, the bottom of the key is a letter "E" which represents the East, which is of great significance with the higher levels of Masonic and with Tibetan Buddhism.

Groupings of five items appear a number of times in the crown and represent the five elementals of all life. Various secret societies make reference to the five senses, the five aspects of the mind, the five basic genomes of man, the five elements of the spiritual realm and many other elemental five's. Five is a significant number in many of these rituals as it also relates to earth, wind, fire, water and spirit. This same understanding also pops up in Tibetan Buddhism.

Groupings that have a numerical value of twelve appear which represents the twelve astrological signs and also relates to the Tarot.

The Sun's Cross Not the Son's Cross

The cross on top of the crown is not just any cross but a cross of five elements. This is as described in the ritual of the Rosey Cross, where this cross again represents not only the Sun God, but also the four elements of earth, wind, fire, water and the fifth of the spirit.

The particular design of the cross is very similar to a specific pentacle that is very much different from every other pentacle or pentagram. (I will describe the concept of pentacles in more depth a few pages from now as I tell how the Lord revealed that information)

Rituals involving these pentacles are used to call up or invoke various angelic (demonic) beings to receive instruction from them. With all of the other pentacles, Bael is called upon in the ritual. This pentacle of the cross instead is related to the Sun and is used to evoke an entity, which appears for the purpose of telling you how to break your mental bonds and be free; free of the mental bonds of guilt associated with sin, so that "There is no law beyond Do What Thou Wilt." This is called the Law of Thelema, or again the concept of lawlessness.

Below the cross is a circle that is spoken of as the disk of the Sun in the ritual of the Rosey Cross.

The two parts separating below the cross and disk symbolize entry into the sexual organ of the woman. I do not have specific reference for this other that the highly sexual nature of the rituals involved and the whole recurring concept of the birth of the moonchild, which is the physical manifestation in the material world of the spirit of Babalon. This is exactly what Jack Parsons set out to accomplish. In Astrology, the Moonchild is Venus, or Babalon.

Overall, the top of the crown represents the union of the Sun and Moon sexually to birth Babalon to which authority is given by the key to open the underworld or the Abyss. This relates to the ancient legend of Astarte, one of the wives of Seth who became trapped in the underworld. Inanna, Ishtar, and Babalon are later incarnations of this same story.

The first circle is like a chain and consists of 64 elements or links. I am not going to go any further into this here, other than to say that 64 is a significant number in this design.

Between the inner chain circle and the outer rope circle are two five-point stars representing the morning and night aspects of Babalon sometimes differentiated as Venus being the morning star and Babalon being the evening star. Some sources also refer to the two aspects of Babalon as the Goddess of both Love and War.

The outer circle is like a rope and as such is a circle that is meant to bind in. This circle as a rope has 96 twists. The numerology of this is pretty obscure but has to do with the number of the beast in Crowley's system of witchcraft.

I have not gone into this detail (and much more in APENDIX B) to impress you with my knowledge of the occult and secrets of witchcraft and Masonry, because what I have come to understand only scratches the surface. I have only put this information here to illustrate what the Lord was revealing to me about the "esoteric" and hidden knowledge that these organizations have incorporated into their initiations, rituals and symbols. Then the Lord used the understanding of these mindsets to help me discover how the enemy has managed to hide himself in the plain sight of most of the people of this world.

A Key Verse Revelation 20

At this particular point of the morning hours, I was sitting and pondering the Key in the crown and the chain circle surrounding the crown when the Lord gave me the first scriptural explanation. I heard in my mind simply, "Revelation 20." It did not occur to me what that scripture was about, so I picked up my Bible and looked it up. My jaw dropped as I read,

> "And I saw an angel coming down from heaven, having the key of the abyss and a great chain in his hand. And he laid hold of the dragon, the serpent of old, who is the devil and Satan, and bound him for a thousand years, and threw him into the abyss, and shut it and sealed it over him, so that he should not deceive the nations any longer, until the thousand years were completed; after these things he must be released for a short time."[1]

Here we had the chain, the key and the fact that in the city seal the key is pointed downward toward the abyss with authority over the key given to Babalon. It was at this point that I also realized the chain was a circle around the crown and that in witchcraft, circles are drawn to keep something in or to keep something out. In this seal there are two circles, with the outer one of rope representing binding and the beast. I came to the understanding that represented here was the chain and key, as foretold in Revelation 20, to be used to bind the dragon in the abyss for a thousand years. In this seal/symbol, we had the beast forming a protective circle around the outside of those items and instead giving to Babalon authority to access the abyss.

The Dalai Lama Has the Key

This would make more sense to me about a year later when dealing with issues of sand mandalas built by Tibetan Buddhists. I would realize that the Dalai Lama was going around the world being given the keys to many cities as he traveled. He was symbolically given political and physical authority over that city. Then in conjunction with the symbolic authority of the key, a mandala built in that city, was used to open the abyss in the city and invoke forth the "deities and demons" to inhabit the symbolic palace that the mandala represents. This combined act gives spiritual authority over the city to the demonic realm. I will explain this further in later chapters.

This would become very important information in the city of Pasadena where the key and symbolic authority had already been given to the Dalai Lama, and for future encounters in other cities across this Nation. It also would become the basis for a prophetic act done in the City of Pasadena about a year later. I will describe the "Change the Lock" prophetic act in a later chapter.

Numerology and Witchcraft

Next, because of the importance of numerology in Crowley witchcraft and in Masonic, I was counting up all of the active elements of the crown.

The total of the active elements comes to $96+64+1+49=210$. I did not try to arrive at this number. I was simply adding the numbers that the Lord was pointing out. But, when I saw the total as being 210, the question crossed my mind if this had anything to do with the numbering of the 210 Freeway. The construction for this freeway started in Pasadena and stretched in two directions out from the center of the city. The freeway is both North and South and East and West in the City with the ninety-degree bend at a location very near to the previous location of the most prominent Masonic Lodge in Pasadena's history. The number 210 is also the "Magick" number of the name, John Whiteside Parsons according to one OTO source. This piece of information I found on a sheet of paper lying on my desk. That night this sheet of paper was on top of the four-inch high stack of things the Lord had me download off the Internet during the previous two weeks.

The Numbers in 7

At this point, the Lord gave me the scriptural reference of Numbers Chapter 7. I read this chapter several times and nothing clicked until I started taking note of the numerical values mentioned in this chapter and started penciling them into the margin of my Bible. This passage describes the offerings given at the consecration of the Tabernacle in the wilderness. Offerings were given by a priest of one of the tribes on each of twelve days. The offering given was identical each of the twelve days, only the priest and the tribe represented were different each day.

Here are the offerings: a silver plate made from 130 shekels of silver, a bowl made from 70 shekels of silver and a gold pan made from 10 shekels of Gold.[2] As I wrote these numbers in the margin of my Bible, I noted that this adds up to 210 shekels of precious metals! Isn't that a coincidence? If it has no significance, why did the Lord show this to me specifically in relationship to the seal of the city and the number of 210 that keeps showing up in relationship to the City of Pasadena? The offerings in the silver were to be of flour and oil and were mixed for a grain offering. The offering in the gold pan was an incense offering. I had the impression the Lord was showing me that this has something to do with healing, nurture and prosperity represented by the grain offering, then worship and prayer as represented by the incense offering. I would later learn that during the consecration of a Masonic lodge grain and oil is poured into the corner stone for this exact reason of representing healing, nurture and prosperity. Why the silver plate and silver bowl and a gold pan, why 210 shekels of precious metals, I don't know yet, but I believe there is significance here that relates to Pasadena. Perhaps you, as you are reading this will have received more information from the Lord.

The next offering was 1 bull, 1 ram and 1 male lamb 1 year old, for a burnt offering and 1 male goat as a sin offering. These numbers as I wrote in the margin of my Bible are 111 and 1.

The Cabalah and Hidden Names

Why 3 animals as a burnt offering and 1 as a sin offering? I believe this has something to do with holding back the demonic celestial beings from entering into the affairs of man. I say this because of the Cabalah. Here is the reasoning that I believe was revealed to me by the Lord on that night. The Cabalah was a rose like symbol onto which were written the 22 letters of the Hebrew alphabet. This Cabalah was then used as an encrypting tool to create stick symbols that spelled out the names of the angels for the Kabalistic Priesthood.

This group of Jewish priests claimed that when Moses came down off Mt. Sinai, he also was given the names of the principal angels and demons, but was instructed that these names were not to be called upon. The Kabalistic Priesthood, at some point of history, violated that injunction from God and began calling on these names. However, this had to be done in secret, because the majority of the priesthood held that this should not be done.

The Kabalistic priests created and began using the Cabalah to encrypt these names by drawing lines between the letters of the Hebrew alphabet to spell out these names. Then just the lines were extracted from the Cabalah to form the stick symbol that now represented the name of that angel. This also became the root of some of the numerology, as numerical value was assigned to each of the letters of the alphabet and thus a numerical value of a name. This practice is still alive today in Crowley Witchcraft or Magick and other forms of occult practice. You will see these angelic stick symbol names inscribed upon various implements used in witchcraft rituals such as the chalice, and the air sword.

In the past century, Aleister Crowley developed an English language equivalent to the Hebrew Cabalah, such that any word spelled out in English would have the same numerical value as that same word in Hebrew. This English Cabalah, Crowley called the 111 Cabalah. This number 111 now penciled into the margin of my Bible started me thinking; "Since the angels are described in scripture and represented by idols found in Buddhism and Hinduism, as having three faces of animals or birds and one face of a human, this particular burnt offering in the book of numbers has something to do with maintaining the separation between man and the angels, and the prohibition against calling upon the angels' names."

The goat in the occult is the representation of Satan. The goat in representing Satan also represents the true original sin, which was of Satan in his rebellion and dishonoring of God, before the sin of the woman and the man. Since this is the source of the sin, so it also is the offering sacrifice to counter the effects of sin.

Weird Numbers

If you want to get weird with numbers, this also may relate to Pasadena. 111 as the number one hundred eleven (the burnt offerings) has the number one subtracted (or sin offering) and we get 110, the current number of the first freeway built in the United States, in Pasadena. So, we have both the numbers 110 and 210 contained in Numbers Chapter 7 offerings to consecrate the Tabernacle in the wilderness. Again, I believe all of this has to do with life as it was intended by the observance of the Lord's commands for nurture and healing and worship and prayer. Also, burnt offerings that may have something to do with holding back some spiritual force affected by celestial beings and the recognition that sin would need to be dealt with.

The next offering in Numbers chapter 7 is a peace offering of 2 oxen, 5 rams, 5 male goats and 5 male lambs. This number I wrote in the margin was 2555. I had the impression at this point to divide 2555 by 7, it is 365. Again, my impression at the time was that this number could represent 7 years, the number of years of lack of peace or of tribulation in the books of Daniel and Revelation. But there is another number here by just adding 2+5+5+5=17 as is often done in numerology.

A Revelation of 17

As I looked at the number 17, the Lord gave me Revelation 17. The center of this chapter, verses 9 through 13, deals with the beast of 7 heads and 10 horns (17 elements). These are said to represent kings and kingdoms with which the woman Babalon has committed immorality. It seems entirely possible to me and the strong impression I had that night, was that the 17 peace offerings in Numbers 7 relate to offerings intended to maintain peace in relationship between 17 future kingdoms of the world, and God. Again, I think God was trying to tell the Israelites something about their responsibilities and authority through the offerings and the effects that maintaining them would have on the future. Eventually the offerings would be done away with and we see that instead of a relationship of peace (shalom = an authority structure that is without chaos) being maintained between these kingdoms and God, all of these kingdoms "commit acts of immorality" with the great harlot.

Clearing the Waters in Revelation 22

The final passage that the Lord gave in that morning of revelation was in the 22nd Chapter of the Book of Revelation.

> "And he showed me a river of the water of life, clear as crystal, coming from the throne of God and of the Lamb, in the middle of its street. And on either side of the river was the tree of life, bearing twelve kinds of fruit, yielding its fruit every month; and the leaves of the tree were for the healing of the nations. And there shall no longer be any curse; and the throne of God and

of the Lamb shall be in it, and His bondservants shall serve Him; and they shall see His face, and His name shall be on their foreheads. And there shall no longer be any night; and they shall not have need of the light of a lamp nor the light of the sun, because the Lord God shall illumine them; and they shall reign forever and ever.

And he said to me, "These words are faithful and true"; and the Lord, the God of the spirits of the prophets, sent His angel to show to His bond-servants the things which must shortly take place. "And behold, I am coming quickly. Blessed is he who heeds the words of the prophecy of this book."

And I, John, am the one who heard and saw these things. And when I heard and saw, I fell down to worship at the feet of the angel who showed me these things. And he said to me, "Do not do that; I am a fellow servant of yours and of your brethren the prophets and of those who heed the words of this book; worship God."

And he said to me, "Do not seal up the words of the prophecy of this book, for the time is near. "Let the one who does wrong, still do wrong; and let the one who is filthy, still be filthy; and let the one who is righteous, still practice righteousness; and let the one who is holy, still keep himself holy." "Behold, I am coming quickly, and My reward is with Me, to render to every man according to what he has done. "I am the Alpha and the Omega, the first and the last, the beginning and the end." Blessed are those who wash their robes, that they may have the right to the tree of life, and may enter by the gates into the city. Outside are the dogs and the sorcerers and the immoral persons and the murderers and the idolaters, and everyone who loves and practices lying.

"I, Jesus, have sent my angel to testify to you these things for the churches. I am the root and the offspring of David, the bright morning star."

And the Spirit and the bride say, "Come." And let the one who hears say, "Come." And let the one who is thirsty come; let the one who wishes take the water of life without cost".

This chapter is interesting as it relates to Pasadena. It is this bit of information that I had not connected until I was sitting here reading the words of the chapter again. The beginning of Chapter 22 speaks of a river of water of life clear as crystal and of the tree next to it with 12 kinds of fruit.

HAHAMONGA: Changing the Name of the Devil's Gate

I spoke earlier of the Devil's gate reservoir as the location where Jack Parsons had done a number of his rocketry experiments, the location behind which Jet Propulsion Laboratory would be built and the location near to which I found the demonic watcher symbol with the "U" on it next to the city line. In the late 1990's, a prophet of God, Lou Engle, from Harvest Rock Church in Pasadena, would be led by God to take a small team to this reservoir, do a prophetic act there and declare that the name of the reservoir would be changed in the near future. In 1999, in a movement that had been started by the chief of the Gabrielino Shoshone Nation, the original and first inhabitants of the area, the name of the reservoir was changed to Hahamonga meaning "Fruitful Valley, Flowing Waters" and a plan was put in place to restore this watershed area from a Super Fund toxic cleanup site back to a natural place of beauty for the recreation of the people of Pasadena and Los Angeles. The Gabrielino people had originally been called Tongva before they were rounded up and forced to become workers at the founding of the San Gabriel Mission in 1771 a few miles south of the future location of Pasadena.

A few years after the renaming of the reservoir and the watershed in 1999, The Pasadena Call, a gathering of twenty-five thousand youth was held at the Rose Bowl located about a half-mile downstream of the reservoir. In the late afternoon of this February 2003 event that had been oppressively hot and dry all day, Lou Engle and Elizabeth Jensen, a native Tongva prophetess, stood up and in a prophetic chant led the crowd in proclaiming HAHAMONGA over the Arroyo Seco (dry riverbed) flowing out of the former Devil's Gate Reservoir leading to the Los Angeles River.

In that prophetic proclamation, they were speaking life over this area. They were speaking restoration of the spirit of God to the Arroyo. In days long gone, the Arroyo had bristled with life and the ground had been a productive source of fruits and vegetables for the Tongva people. In the early 1900's, revival meetings were held in tents in the Arroyo. This was shortly after the outpouring of the Holy Spirit at the Azusa Street meetings in 1906. The Azusa Street meetings were very near the location where this Arroyo joins the Los Angeles River. As the crowd of 25,000 in the Rose Bowl on that winter afternoon in 2003 shouted HAHAMONGA, HAHAMONGA, HAHAMONGA, a cool and gentle breeze drifted into the Rose Bowl and broke, like a cool drink of refreshing water, the oppression that had rested there through much of the day. This was a wonderful climax to the years of work of a number of spiritual warriors and prophets over Pasadena.

A Demon Infestation at the American Film Market

As these two prophets stood and proclaimed change over this area, just a few miles away the prophetic warnings of another prophet would be ignored, as the demonic presence in the LA basin would come to rest over the American Film Market (AFM) in Santa Monica. This annual event is where the films that will be produced over the coming three years and shown throughout the world are bought and sold by studios and distributors from around the world in transactions in excess of $500 million. Through the media arm of Hollywood, Babalon the great harlot, who sits on many waters, was in the process of committing her acts of immorality with the kings of the earth, and making those who dwell on the earth drunk with the wine of her immorality.[3]

The shifting of demonic principalities from one region to another as the result of the Saints actually taking possession and occupying one territory, has led to the development of what I, and others, are now calling "Occupational Theology." We have learned through a number of experiences in the past fifteen years, that it is not sufficient or even necessary, to hold mass and costly rallies in order to shift the dominion over a territory. We have seen just a hand full of completely obedient saints cause dramatic changes in the spiritual canopy over a city or region. Nevertheless, if the saints do not continue to occupy the region and enforce the authority of the Kingdom over the demonic forces that seek to regain their control, the city or region will quickly slip back into a condition even worse than existed before. It only takes a few to sweep the house clean but if it is not filled with and continued to be occupied by those who will, in the Spirit, function as priests of God over the people of that area, "the demons will come back seven fold and the later state will be worse than the former."[4]

This was the case with the American Film Market (AFM) of 2003. Great strides had been made in the previous year by a number of prayer walking warriors, to bring a family friendly agenda to the AFM in stark contrast to all of the previous years. That headway would be lost by the lack of follow through and only three individuals were left to stand against the horrendous onslaught of demonic assault on the AFM in 2003. Family agenda was buried as the demons focused the millions of dollars of sales on the few demonically inspired films presented rather than the dozens of family friendly entries. To cement the demonic hold on the AFM for the future, the dates of future AFM's, were changed from its traditional February timing, to be now be held over the Halloween Holiday in subsequent years. The enemy aligned his forces into the time of the year when the most demonic activity has free reign over the spiritual atmosphere and over the AFM.

A God Who Reveals Mysteries

Now back to that night in January 2002, what a night, and what a God who reveals mysteries. However, the revelation of the seal was not yet done. A few days later I talked to a city official about the seal only from a historical point of view. I did not reveal to that person any of what had been revealed to me, as the Lord had said it was not time yet to do so. There were things to do in the city and these would be hindered if this were revealed to the wrong people before the proper time. However, I did ask the official if there were plans to alter the seal because I had heard that this was being considered. He responded that there were no plans at present to alter the seal even though there had been some complaints that felt there were parts of the seal that were not appropriate on a symbol representing a government body. Though the official did not say so, I believe he was referring to the cross on top of the crown as representing the Son of God Christ, not the Sun God I knew it to represent.

Since I did not have any written source that specifically illustrated this cross as representing the Sun God, I asked the Lord this question, "Can you show me something in black and white drawing or text that specifically proves that this particular style of cross represents the Sun God and is not a Christian symbol?

Going Shopping God's Way

A few days later I was walking down a street in Pasadena when I heard the Lord say, "go into this book store that you are next to, I will show you a book, take it from the shelf and open it to page 405." "You may then buy the book because you will not be attracted to it, but I have other things to show you, which you will also find in this book."

I went into the store, wandered around for a while looking at a number of shelves, but finally a particular book caught my eye and I pulled it down and opened to page 405.

The book I took down from the shelf that day was a handbook for

THE REVELATION OF THE SEAL

beginning practitioners of the Aleister Crowley form of witchcraft called Magick. This page was a section in that book describing five different pentacles, which are used to call upon different demonic entities in order to receive messages from them. Most people are familiar with the term Pentagram as a five-pointed star associated with witchcraft and astrology. However, few understand that the pentagram is only one type of pentacle, which is used for similar purposes. Of the five pentacles in Crowley Witchcraft and in other forms of Luciferian religion, all of those except the one of this cross are used to call upon Bael and then an entity will appear which will give some instruction or message. This cross pentacle, of which we are told, "This one as different, than all the rest," calls upon the Sun God and the entity, which appears will "tell you how to break your (mental) bonds and be free." This is further explained in other documents as freeing your mind from the association of guilt related to sin so that you are free of the bondage of the law and become a law unto yourself, "Whatever thou wilt shall be the whole of the law." This is the Law of Thelema or the principal of lawlessness as discussed previously.

In Summary

To summarize this long and perhaps confusing chapter, what I learned in one night by direct revelation of the Lord in answer to specific prayer for Him to reveal a mystery to me, was this; The symbol and the seal of the city which was put into place by the Masonic founders of the city in 1886, is a description of the authority given to Babalon in this city and describes a future act of two men practicing a form of witchcraft. The rituals carried out in 1946, had been in some form at the heart of higher degrees of German Masonic at some time before or around the turn of the century into the 1900's. This seal represents the sexual union between the Sun God and the Moon God for the purpose of birthing the Moonchild, Babalon and giving authority to Babalon over the key to the abyss. Meanwhile the beast is forming a circle of protection or binding around this whole process.

This has been a rather lengthy illustration of the types of revelation that the Lord might give to gain understanding of the root issues in a city. If I have not completely lost you by this point, and you are not convinced that I have gone stark raving mad through this process, hang in there for the next chapter and see where this understanding will lead in battling for a change in the spiritual dominion over a city.

Endnotes

1. Revelation 20:1-3
2. Numbers 7:13-14ff
3. Revelation 18:3
4. Matthew 12:44

Chapter 11

So Now What Do I Do Lord?

From the reading of the last three chapters, you might infer that I endorse or that I am telling you the practice of delving into all sorts of non-Christian and occult materials is necessary. I wish to strongly state that I do not endorse or recommend in any way, such a practice. There are some people involved in spiritual warfare and spiritual mapping though, who by the Lord will be led to do so. That is the whole point of this book with respect to Spiritual Warfare. This warfare, or rather the understandings of how to conduct oneself in this warfare, must come from the Lord. You must hear Him clearly, understand what you hear (which may require asking specific questions of the Lord), then you must do only what the Lord directs, in exactly the way and time in which He directs. You must obey Him exactly. I feel that I cannot over emphasize this aspect of spiritual warfare, because we cannot expect to exert the authority given to Christ if we are not in absolute submission to that authority.

Note, I said absolute submission to Christ. This at times may place us in conflict with our submission to other human authorities, which as a general principal of scripture we are to respect and be in submission to. If those human authorities are themselves in absolute submission to Christ alone, and not to human doctrines and philosophies, this should not pose a problem. However, human authority is often ruled by human judgment, pride or fear, which may allow the flesh in others to come against your absolute obedience in the Lords direction to you.

It is at these times that you must absolutely know the Shepherd's voice and be certain you can distinguish it from the voice of someone who is not the Shepherd.[1] It is not our power or might, understanding, or wisdom, by which we are able to dislodge the dominion of Satan from over individuals, our cities, states, and our nation, it is "by my spirit, says the Lord."[2]

A Caution About Researching the Occult

What I have shared with you in the last three chapters is simply a small portion of the learning with which the Lord had to prepare my mind so that I would be able to see the root issues and understand the things He would lead me and others to do in the next several years following this revelation. I made no attempt to gather information from the sources which the Lord revealed other than that which He directly led me to and then only for the purpose of understanding the historical actions of others and never for my carrying out any portion of those abominable practices. Even the book on Crowley witchcraft, which the Lord had me purchase along with other resources, is in a locked cabinet that has been sealed in the spirit. I have had no curiosity to examine any of its contents beyond exactly those pages that the Lord has directed me to for the specific purpose of understanding things I have found in other places that the Lord has led me to look.

I find this also an important principal that you not find attraction to the things of the occult other than specifically what the Lord uncovers for the purpose of understanding. I have had two requests from members of the spiritual mapping group I was a part of to look over the book on Crowley Witchcraft. I have asked, in both cases, that the individuals do so in my office, which was first sealed with prayer to prevent any influence from the demonic realm. Both of these individuals after a few minutes of thumbing through the book or reading a portion, have handed the book back with the explanation that they felt restrained by the Lord not to read any further. They found that there was a growing curiosity in them to understand how to exercise the powers taught in this material.

I personally have not done further research into numerology, or dream interpretation even though I know of persons in the Christian community, who I highly respect, who do teach or use these practices. There is a large body of literature to aid you in developing these understandings in your life, but the Lord has not led me there. I find that if there is a dream that the Lord wants me to understand, he will give me the interpretation. I have never had to rely upon any book or list of symbolic meanings to arrive at that interpretation, except for the few times in which I was asked for an interpretation and the Lord had showed me nothing. I have since realized that if the Lord has showed me nothing, I am not the one to interpret that dream. There are plenty of instances where the Lord has immediately given me an interpretation even before I was asked for one. I now clearly tell people, when asked about interpreting a dream, that I am not in the ministry of dream interpretation so I do not know if I can be of any help to them unless the Lord chooses to show me something, but I will ask Him.

The same goes for numbers. Other than some generally accepted understanding that five represents grace, and the number three, the trinity. I find myself at a loss to explain the meaning of a number when someone asks unless the Lord had specifically revealed something to me for that particular time and place. I have read a few Christian books that go deeper than that, but I cannot say that I even remember what I read as it is not something the Lord has enabled or indicated I should retain. I state this also in regard to all of the numbers of the previous chapter. I have no idea of the meaning of all of those numbers, beyond what the Lord revealed through the intense download of those two weeks prior to the revelation of the seal and the resultant understanding that these numbers were and are important to practitioners of these occult workings. These were specific revelations that the Lord used to get me from one place in my understanding to another place in my understanding.

My only other curiosity with numbers is from years of experiencing the Lord leading me through the study of a topic in the Bible and quite often finding that the thread He is leading me on will involve the same chapter and verse numbers in multiple books of the Bible.

Many times when the Lord has awaken me in the night, He calls my attention to the hour and minutes on the clock as the chapter and verses that I am to look at to see what He is waking me to communicate. This form of communication from the Lord might be categorized by some as superstition, unscientific, or otherwise misunderstood; but apparently, this is one way that the Lord has found works to get my attention in the middle of the night. Other friends and ministry leaders have told me of far stranger ways that the Lord speaks to them (Far stranger, to me anyway!). The Lord is the Lord. He can choose to get our attention in any way He wishes. The question is, what will it take, to get your attention and then will you be obedient like Samuel to run to Him and say, "Speak, for Thy servant is listening?"

A Clear Warning

Because I have shared some of the things in the last three chapters with numerous people, I have automatically, been thrust into the role of an expert in this field by some. I am not. I know very little beyond what the Lord had revealed for this particular instance. Though some of the knowledge and understanding is and has been applicable to things, which the Lord would reveal in other situations, and in other cities, it must be the Lord who reveals the applicability to any situation other than the specific one for which it was revealed to me. There are people to whom the Lord has shown a lot more about Masonry, numerology or mythology than He has shown to me. What I have shared here was only what was necessary for me, and a few others to understand some of the root issues in this particular city. I have shared the information, as an example of the depth of the Lord's revelation that may be needed to bring us to a point that we are able to stand in warfare against a particular enemy, in a particular battle. In later chapters, I will also share an understanding of Tibetan Buddhism that the Lord has had to prepare me with to be able to stand in some of the current battles in that war.

Is this warning and disclaimer clear enough?

The God in Heaven who reveals mysteries had just revealed a mystery and all of the knowledge to be able to understand that mystery. So now, what do I do Lord? This is a next general principal of spiritual mapping and spiritual warfare that I have found true around the world.

There is More than Meets the Eye

It is not enough to merely have knowledge of what and where the points of evil are in a location or city, or even to understand what the root issues are that have placed and have held the dominion of Satan over that location. We must then understand if that dominion is still in place in that location, still attached to the same roots, and are there current manifestations of those roots that need to be dealt with. We must understand that many of the points of evil publicly identifiable are not necessarily the root which must be pulled up to remove the demonic attachment, but are simply the fruit and branches feeding off of the root, or the symptoms of the underlying problem.

A few years ago a group of intercessors decided that they were going to deal with the problem of video pornography of which a particular area of greater Los Angeles is the number one producer in the world. They decided to pray in front of a few retail outlets of pornography in one location of the San Fernando Valley. The problem was that it was not these locations that were producing the pornography. They were simply the visible fruit and symptoms of the underlying root system. The locations that are producers, number in the hundreds and are spread across four or five different cities or communities in the San Fernando Valley on the North side of Los Angeles. Even these were not the root structure of this problem, simply the branches.

They did not consider that the ability of these pornography factories to function lie in financial, political and spiritual backing that has its focus in another very respectable part of Los Angeles, miles away. Though this had been revealed to an individual and was communicated to the intercessors, they tried instead to cut off a few pieces of the fruit, which quickly grew back, rather than using their spiritual authority to pull up the root. They did nothing, which actually changed the dominion over the area. They simply picked a fight with a few of the demons in the area and as a result took a few blows to themselves. The prayer over the pornography stores was not a wrong thing, but did not have the expected result, because the dominion over the area had not been removed, they had not pulled up the root, which the Lord had revealed. This issue still exists today, because no one has yet followed the Lords instructions given through a prophet, on how to deal with that root. A few of those intercessors are now at least looking in the direction of the root and the area of the city where it is buried.

One is not always the Prime Number

This brings me to another point. Some things the Lord will reveal to us, He will equip us to do by ourselves. Nevertheless, other things take the unity of a number of people in order to have a sufficient anointing to be able to bind and remove. Remember the lesson from Argentina about Psalm 133? (Unity brings anointing) So again, you must hear from the Lord what to do.

I have made it a practice to ask everyone that participates in a prophetic act or a prayer walk to ask the Lord specifically if they are to participate in this particular act. If they hear nothing or a negative from the Lord, I ask them not to participate. It is for his or her own protection, because everyone involved must be in agreement and in unity. It is this unity of all hearing the same thing from the Lord, all being of one spirit that really has power and anointing on it for defeating the enemy. (See also putting on the Belt of Truth in Chapter 5)

A Plan for Pasadena

Now, since you are sitting there wondering, "When is he going to tell me what the Lord said to do about Pasadena?" Let's get into it.

SO NOW WHAT DO I DO LORD?

What was to be done involved a whole series of events and prophetic acts over a three-year period, but there are still issues that are ongoing. Some of these things to be done were revealed to me, but other things were revealed to other members of a spiritual mapping group, which I did not even meet until several weeks after the revelation of the seal on that one night.

What the Lord showed me to do on that night of the revelation of the seal was an identificational prayer of forgiveness and reconciliation over the people, the places and the events that had given place to this dominion of Babalon over the city. The Lord gave me the words to the following prayer and told me it should be spoken over the various locations where these events in the city's history took place. He also told me that eventually it would be necessary for a city official to pray this prayer in identificational repentance, even as I was doing in the meantime. But the Lord said it would be years before the city officials would understand and be ready to do this.

Prayer of Identificational Repentance for the Root Iniquity in Pasadena

Lord Jesus and to our Father the Lord God Almighty, I repent on behalf of the men and women who acted to evoke this great evil and who have continued to give authority to Babalon in this city. I repent on behalf of the men and women who have and continue up to this time to evoke the sun god to break their mental bonds and be free to sin without guilt. I repent on behalf of the men and women who have and continue to seek out Babalon in order to shake off and free themselves of limitations and the covering, protection and signpost of the commandments you have given Lord God Almighty. Lord I repent on behalf of the further work of Jack Parsons, L. Ron Hubbard and Marjorie Cameron as they foolishly acted to loose Babalon into the material realm.

To the Most High God, to the Lord God almighty, and in the name of our Lord Jesus the Christ, who is our advocate, we petition you almighty Father that the celestial and angelic beings which have empowered the opening of this city to the rule and authority of Babalon be rebuked. Further since you gave all authority on earth and in heaven to our Lord and Savior, the Lamb that was slain before the foundation of the world, and you have given us authority such that whatever we bind on earth shall be bound in heaven and whatever we loose in earth shall be loosed in heaven[3], we therefore, this day bind up the beings given authority and invited into this city by the founders and trustees of this city, and we loose from those beings the keys to Hades and death, and ask that they be returned to the rightful authority. We bind the workings of all those in this city who have sought to use the "stele of Osiris[4]" to further bring the powers of the underworld into this city and create a wall of protection for themselves. We loose them from the bondages of the fear of death[5] that they have brought upon themselves and others in the city. Lord we bind the working of any other person or group that has called upon, evoked or sought to use the power of beings banished from Heaven[6] and we instead loose Your Kingdom almighty God and Your Holy Spirit to enter their lives, demolish the strongholds and blindness and turn their eyes and hearts to you.[7]

We ask that your warring angels and messenger angels be sent to the men and women in authority in this city as they make decisions about the seal and identity of this city in the coming months. We pray that the eyes of their understanding[8] would be opened to remove this ritual and invitation of Babalon to reign over this territory. We pray that your Holy Spirit would lead them to place this city solely under the authority of Jesus Christ and the reign of the Kingdom of God.[9]

Lord, we plead the blood shed on the cross over the members of the many cults and ancient religions in this city and throughout the world.[10] We ask Lord, that the blindness be removed from their hearts and that Lord, the strongholds, philosophies and filters over their minds, which have lifted other gods above you, would be demolished, that they would repent of their wicked ways and be restored, healed and saved by the already accomplished working of your blood.

We bow before you Lord Jesus only and ask that you would further reveal the mysteries that have been hidden under the rose so that all men, women and children in this city might come to the knowledge of salvation, repent, be healed of the iniquities of the fathers of this city and be delivered of the resulting physical, mental and spiritual sickness in this land.

We thank you Lord that we know this work is already accomplished in you.

God Reveals Locations

Over the next month after the revelation of the seal, the Lord took me to a number of places around the city, which I was able to locate through documents, photos and maps. Some locations the Lord had to point out because buildings had long since been torn down. I prayed this prayer and as He also showed me, I anointed each location with oil for healing.

In the middle of this time, I met for the first time, the leader of a spiritual mapping and warfare team that had been working in Pasadena for a number of years. I had not previously connected with this team because I was just in different circles of people and besides the Lord rather suddenly dropped me back into this aspect of ministry just a month earlier.

When I showed this leader the material in the last several chapters, he was amazed and asked how many years I had been researching and working on this. When I told him that this had all come from the Lord in the previous two weeks, that really floored him, but we struck a quick friendship. A short time afterward a number of my new fellow warriors set out to re-follow my steps. The Lord would give various ones additional prophetic acts to do at the locations to which the Lord led us.

There is one interesting point regarding discernment and hearing from the Lord out of this example. As I was going to the various locations, I was not certain of the location where the trustees of the newly incorporated city had met and adopted the seal by ordinance at their first meeting. I knew approximately where this was from historical descriptions of the buildings downtown in 1886. Those buildings had been torn down and rebuilt slightly different three times. As I was walking down the street in the approximate location and asking the Lord where it was, I suddenly got a chill and the hair on my back stood up. I stopped and turned toward the building next to me to see in its art deco design, two goat heads on either corner of the building. As I looked at the location, and compared it to the pictures I had of the buildings in place in 1886, I realized that this building with the goat heads on it was right on the site where the office in which that first meeting had taken place was likely located. Several weeks later when I came back with the group, as we entered that block, I told the others that I believed that the Lord had revealed to me the location of that meeting, but I was not going to tell them where I believed it was. I asked them to ask the Lord about this and then to discern from the Lord where that location was. Everyone in the group discerned the same location as they felt something in their spirit when they walked by that location. We were in agreement. The courtyard of this building, which had been locked when I had previously been there, was this time unlocked and we were able to enter into the courtyard to carry out our prophetic act. This was a good indication that the further work was to be done by this group rather than by myself on the first pass.

SO NOW WHAT DO I DO LORD?

After this initial identificational repentance and healing work, the Lord would point out various issues that we would deal with over the next two years. This would lead also in 2003 to dealing with some specific issues regarding the key of authority of the city and the relationship of this key to the Dalai Lama. I will come back to this in a later chapter to keep things in somewhat chronological order and to lay the groundwork to understand how this relates to Tibetan Buddhism.

In the next chapter, we will begin to enlarge the place of our tent and lengthen our cords[11] as I describe the next series of things that the Lord would reveal.

Endnotes

1. John 10:4-5
2. Zech 4:6
3. Matthew 16:18, 18:19
4. also **ste·la** (stē'lə) *pl.* **steles** also **ste·lae** (-lē) An upright stone or slab with an inscribed or sculptured surface, used as a monument or as a commemorative tablet in the face of a building.
5. Hebrews 2:15
6. Revelation 12:8-9
7. 2 Corinthians 2:3-5
8. Acts 26:18
9. Hebrews 2:8
10. Numbers 16:46-47
11. Isaiah 54:2-3

CHAPTER 12

ENLARGE THE PLACE OF YOUR TENT

I had learned a very interesting lesson from the Lord about the sphere of our influence or authority back during my years as an officer in the Fire Department. As I progressed through the ranks in the Fire Department from Fire Fighter, to Fire Fighter Specialist/Apparatus Engineer, to Captain, and finally to Battalion Chief in a large organization covering a large territory, I had more people and territory under my tutelage and supervision. The interesting thing about that is that I began to observe early on, that I also had spiritual authority in the same sphere and territory as my secular County designated authority. Though I can now go back and see that this was the case from the time I was a Fire Fighter/Paramedic usually just dealing with one other person at a time, and as an Apparatus Engineer with a crew of one or two that I would supervise, it was not until several years into my position as a captain that I begin to consciously understand this principal.

When I became a Captain in 1982, my sphere first spread to a station where I supervised about 50 people including explorer scouts, Call Fire Fighters (similar to volunteers) and all three shifts (as there were no other regularly assigned Captains at that time in that station). In addition, I was responsible for the fire prevention, fire suppression, rescue services and emergency medical response (Paramedics) for a city of about fifty thousand people and many square miles. Later in the 80's I would be assigned as a full time Chaplain for the Department, which was not primarily a ministry position, but also involved general welfare issues. It involved insuring medical treatment for injured firefighters, feeding crews on major incidents, providing fluids, goggles, sunscreen, spare gloves and other things to units on the fire line, overseeing Workman Compensation Claims and assisting Department members with retirement planning and processing. On the spiritual side I made hospital calls, death notifications, conducted funerals, dealt with drug and alcohol problems, and whatever else twenty-two hundred department members, their families, and several hundred retirees and their families needed. These approximately forty-five hundred people were spread all over three states and I was at their beck and call twenty-four hours a day. Many of you pastors out there know exactly what I am talking about and this is exactly the type of busyness that keeps you from exercising greater authority over the territory into which you have been placed as a gatekeeper. How would you like to pastor that church made up 95% of people who were not Christians, lived spread out over thousands of square miles and had no other church affiliation to which they could be referred? Anyway, the point is not how impossible the job was, but that this was expanding my sphere of both secular and spiritual authority. This led to my next job assignment that involved forming a unit in the Fire Department to enforce State and Federal Laws over all handlers of acutely toxic chemicals and materials in Los Angeles County. This job also required me to work with State Legislators to modify the State Laws, and to work with other Fire and Health Departments all over the State of California to develop guidelines for the enforcement of these laws.

Changing the Dominion Over a Fire Station

The first real example of a sphere of influence over a whole station came in the mid 1980's, when I was assigned to a station that was filled with pornography. That spirit was over the whole station and affected everyone assigned to that station. At the time, I was chairman of the missions program of my church, which was under spiritual attack as I related in an earlier Chapter. I had quite a lot of home work to do for that program so would bring some of that work with me to the station to work on in the evenings when we were free to watch TV, make calls to home, read or whatever else. I would go down to the station office, which was located at the other end of the station from the recreation room, where the television was continually playing pornography. Even with the office door shut, I could still hear the sounds of the trash being viewed by other station members. Within a few days of being in that environment, I would find myself getting angry with and not wanting to talk to church friends and family who would call on what we called the "house phone." That phone, for private use by station members, was located in a small hot somewhat soundproof booth in the Recreation room. But what made the booth sound proof and hot was a door with a large double pane window directly facing the lurid action on the TV screen ten feet away. Another problem was that I would bring the mission materials to work and realize the next morning, as I would be leaving for home, I had left the materials in the car and totally forgotten they were there to work on.

About four or five 24-hour shifts of this immoral assault was about all I could take before I knew I had to do something to change the spiritual atmosphere, or the spiritual dominion over this work location and home away from home. While at home on my next day off, I prayed and asked the Lord what I could do in the spiritual realm and the physical realm to affect change in this situation. The Lord challenged me to prayer walk the perimeter of the station every morning and to pray during my daily prayer time for every individual assigned to the station. I did this for two weeks during which the situation began to change. At that time, there was no Department policy that could be enforced to bring this 24-hour a day barrage of pornography under reasonable control. So at the same time as I was doing the prayer walk of the station and praying for the individuals, I also took action in asking the Lord to show me what I could do in my authority as a Captain to put in place some sort of policy. I talked with my Battalion Chief, a Christian, about the situation and he told me that this issue had been a topic of discussion at a recent International Fire Chiefs convention. Our department still had not dealt with this policy issue, but he said that he would stand with me in whatever the Lord would show me to do. I also learned that the Battalion Chief on one of the other shifts of the three-shift cycle was actually duplicating and providing some of this material to the station and would sit with that shift and watch it. He had a side business in distribution and sales of this stuff. Well, after praying about it, I researched all of the departmental policies and County law regarding public facilities. What I discovered is that the fire stations are public facilities and therefore the public can enter at any time during normal business hours. Based upon this and general statements in County policy regarding conduct of business with the public, I was able to draft a memo requesting that viewing of video pornography be limited to between the hours of 10p.m. and 6a.m., times when the public were not likely to be entering the station. This time frame was also meant to protect family members, who quite often would stop by the station and enter by the back door directly into the recreation room. I added to the memo, that if station personnel did not voluntarily comply with this request, I would take the issue to higher levels of authority in the Department.

I got an immediate negative reaction to the memo from the other captains in the station. As I was leaving the station the next morning, one individual with a severe addiction to this visual trash was sitting in the recreation room at 7a.m. watching a pornographic video. I told this man who was not on my shift, but subordinate rank, that my memo had been a request but that I would take disciplinary action toward him if this continued. That man's Captain immediately called me up into the front office and started balling me out as to who did I think I was to try and tell his men what to do or not to do, and don't you ever do that again. He also made a few comments about pushing my moral standards on others, which I pointed out to him I was not, because if it were solely up to me the material would not be in the station at all. I was simply trying to bring reasonable limits that would promote, not tarnish the image of the station and of the Department as a whole. I left that morning with my stomach churning at this severe break in relationship with a co-worker, who also professed to be a Christian.

Faith in the Results of Obedience

I need not have worried, because I had done exactly what the Lord had showed me to do and I should have had faith in the results of that obedience. When I returned to work my shift the next morning, the TV was not on, and the memo I had written had been moved to a prominent place directly over the TV. The same Captain with whom I had the run in the previous morning, asked me to come up to the office with him. When we were in the office, he apologized for his words and attitude the previous morning and then told me what had happened during their shift.

Their Battalion Chief, who was the one bringing much of the porno and watching it with them, had come by the station that day while I was off duty. Immediately the station personnel took him over to the bulletin board, showed him my memo, and asked him what they should do about it. The Chief who had been duplicating and selling video pornography said to them, "I think that this Captain is a pretty wise man and I think you should do what he is suggesting."

Shortly after that, the one man who had been at the center of the problem in the station transferred out of the area. He was going through a divorce and moved to a different area of the County. Several years later, his life had significantly changed for the better in a station where there was no pornography permitted. I would learn that he married a Christian woman and had himself become a Christian.

I put this story in this book, because it illustrates the power we have in the secular realm by using our authority in the spiritual realm even in the workplace. I was not aware enough at that time of the issues in the city where that station was located, or even of the authority I had in the spiritual realm that I could have used beyond the station walls. I would not learn that until about eight years later when I had been promoted to Battalion Chief and stationed in the City of Carson, California.

Carson was home to several major refineries and large toxic chemical processing plants. I was assigned there because of my experience the previous four years when I had been running the unit in the department that regulated the storage and release risk prevention programs that dealt with many of these facilities. They all presented significant fire, explosion and toxic hazards in the area.

Praying Shalom Over a City

It was not uncommon for explosions to occur on a weekly basis in some of these facilities and the stations of this Battalion were used to dealing with several major fire or explosion incidents a month. There was also a little higher than average house fire rate in that city. The stations kept pretty busy.

By this point of my spiritual understanding in 1992, it was my regular practice to pray over the city where I was working. I prayed for its general protection and for safety of the citizens as well as the department personnel. It was not until I had been overseeing that battalion for about a year that personnel in several of my seven stations begin complaining to me that we never had any fires or explosions on our shift and "the other shifts were having all the fun." Well, I don't exactly find fires and explosions fun, because I thought it was our responsibility to prevent such things from happening. Those comments caught my attention and I went back and checked logbooks. Sure enough on our shift, we had never had a major fire or explosion in the year I had been there. We did have to go right to work first thing in the morning a number of times to clean up what had happened on the previous shift, but none of these incidents had started on our shift. I just pondered these things at that time as there was much other work to handle and I just kept up with the prayer over the city quietly.

In 1994, I transferred to another Battalion where now I had seven stations in seven cities under my responsibility. The trend pretty much continued. We had fires and other incidents, but again at a much lower rate than the other shifts. One night a volunteer photographer for the department came into the station to chat with the guys. As he was leaving, he joked, saying he was going home to turn off his scanner, because nothing ever happened on our shift worth getting out of bed to take pictures of. Again, I looked over the logbooks, and he was right, we averaged about one third less than the total incidents of each of the other two individual shifts. More pondering!

Sing Over Your Cities

One day I am driving along the freeway on my twenty minute commute to work and a strange thing happens. I hear the Lord say, "Sing over your cities." I wondered what I should sing. How does one sing over a city? I could not remember having seen that anywhere in the Bible. Then I started thinking about what my responsibility and authority was over these seven cities. I was responsible along with the men of my stations for rescue from traffic accidents and building collapses and other rescues requiring special skills, for healing and emergency medical treatment through the paramedic program and for deliverance from the harm of fire. What do you know! We were providing salvation to the cities, for these are all meanings of the word "salvation." So, I started making up songs of rescue, healing and deliverance over the cities, which I sang all the way to the station. The seven stations for which I had responsibility each averaged between fifteen and twenty-five alarms in a twenty-four hour shift. However, on this shift, this day that I sang over the cities, the busiest of my stations had only five alarms and they were all false alarms. I continued to ponder these things!

About two weeks later, I was driving to another battalion to work for a chief that was on vacation. This was a battalion similar to mine in size and make up, but in a different part of the County. As I was driving along, again I hear the Lord say, "Now sing over these cities." Okay, at least this time I knew what to sing about, so I started singing salvation songs of healing, rescue and deliverance over this group of cities. This battalion was actually a little busier than mine was with most of the stations pushing more toward the twenty-five responses per shift than the fifteen end of the record. Except on this day, these cities were sung over! This time, there were only five responses in the entire battalion on that day.

Now I understood what the Lord was trying to show me. We

can call upon our spiritual authority to affect our secular physical responsibility. Also that our spiritual authority extends to the limits and beyond of our secular authority. This concept has been developed in the market place, the business world, to some degree by Rich Marshall in his book *God@Work*[1], and by Ed Silvoso in his book, *Anointed For Business*[2], but at that point I had not heard anything like this applying to government workers other that some prayer movements that were praying for those in authority as Mayors, Fire Chiefs and Police Chiefs. I had not heard any one talk about government workers praying over the cities and the areas of their responsibility because of the spiritual authority attached to their secular area of authority.

You Too Can Have Spiritual Authority

Let me state here that having a job that involves secular authority (sphere of influence) over an area of a city or territory, is not the only way in which you might gain spiritual authority. I am using an example of what I discovered as it applied to me. I know housewives who do not work outside the house, who are not considered church leaders, or leaders of any organization and who have no appointed secular or religious authority. Yet, they appear to have great spiritual authority over a region simply because of their obedience in listening to the Lord and carrying out the acts and worship of which He instructs them.

This would now shape my understanding and release me in a lot more freedom in 2002 not to be surprised when the Lord would begin showing me spiritual warfare issues on a countywide level and bringing people and strategies to deal with them. I had already been in secular areas of authority over the County and even over the state to a lesser degree, so now He began calling on me to exercise spiritual authority in the whole county and to a lesser degree in the whole state.

A Festival of Sacred Music?

I was made aware in the spring of 2002 of an event scheduled for late September through the end of October, in the County. The event was a worldwide festival of sacred music, scheduled for every three years after having been instituted by the Dalai Lama in 1999. This was being held in cities all over the world, but in the County of Los Angeles, it involved fifty-six separate events at different venues around the County. In reading over the announcement of this event, I quickly realized that the sacred music was not limited to the church hymns I was familiar with, but also included such offerings as yoga dance, whirling dervishes from Turkey, and worship of the goddess of the sea. I did not know much about the Dalai Lama and Tibetan Buddhism at the time, but again the Lord begin to quickly dump education and revelation upon me as I realized that this festival, particularly as being implemented was putting into the atmosphere over Los Angeles County songs of worship to the god's of this world. Since, I remembered how powerful that principal had been in singing over the cities I had secular authority over. I could only imagine what the effects would be of these fifty-six instances of putting demonic worship into the atmosphere over the ninety-six cities of Los Angeles County. For months, I tried to talk to pastors and various prayer groups about what the effect of this might be and shouldn't the churches do something to counter this spiritual assault of the heavenlies? I found a couple of small prayer meetings that were somewhat understanding and at least prayed over the issue in their prayer meetings.

All Those in Favor of Tibetan Buddhist Prayer in the Schools?

Another issue about this festival, which caught my attention, was the issue of prayer in schools. We all know that since 1963, school officials nationwide have been restrained from requiring students to pray or to lead in a prayer in their role as a school official. (The supposed wall of separation between church and state) Well, in 2002, teachers in the many of Los Angeles County's school system's, were requiring their students to construct "Tibetan Prayer Flags" that were taken to the various fifty-six venues throughout the Festival of Sacred Music and flown over and around the performances of the "Sacred Music" and witchcraft rituals.

Oh, you see, forcing a student to be involved in prayer, is only banned if that prayer happens to be related to the God of the Bible and the practice of Christianity on which this country was founded. I guess the Justices back in 1963, felt it was perfectly ok to force students to pray to demons, because that has nothing to do with religion or church even though demons, and the fallen "god of this world" is mentioned in the Bible. It was obvious that the "Sacred Music" has nothing to do with religion, because a State run university, UCLA, was sponsoring and coordinating this massive Festival. There you go folks, your tax dollars at work offering a smorgasbord of religious beliefs other than Christianity for your sampling.

I am to do What with 13 Poles and a Canopy?

In one of the early-morning prayer meetings at my church, as this festival was beginning in September, I was sitting on the floor of the prayer room listening to and agreeing with the prayers of another person in the meeting. Suddenly, I heard the familiar voice of the Lord in my head. He was simply naming off locations with which I was familiar. "The Malibu Lagoon, Santa Monica/Venice, Wayfarers Chapel Portuguese Bend." As this continued, I quickly grabbed a pencil and paper and begin writing these places down. "The Tongva Indian village of Pavugna in Long Beach, East of Whittier, over Pomona at the East end, Lake Los Angeles, Ave A and Highway 14, Frazier Park at Interstate 5, Balboa Avenue West of Interstate 5, Santa Suzana Pass/Rocky Peak, The West Lake, and Mount Wilson." There were thirteen locations in all, and as I looked at the list, the Lord then said, "You are to lift a canopy of prayer with its center pole at Mount Wilson and worship from all of these locations simultaneously." I quickly shared what the Lord had just delivered with the others in the prayer meeting. I wondered how I would pull together this prayer and worship over the whole County, as it would require at least thirteen people scattered over hundreds of square miles. Most of these points formed a perimeter of the County, an area bigger than some of our smaller states. Mount Wilson was somewhat in the center and the location of most of the TV and Radio station antennas for the Los Angeles area.

I had done prophetic acts before, but generally by myself or with just a few people all at the same location. I was not sure if I even knew thirteen people who would consider participating in such an undertaking as this. It would also require long drives for most of those participating.

The second question that came immediately to mind was timing and purpose of this act. I immediately assumed that since I received this word during the Festival of Sacred Music, this act had something to do with that event. The Lord gave no direct indication that this was the case; in fact, He gave no direct indication at that time of anything having to do with timing or purpose. Later that day, I wrote up what I had heard and began sharing it with everyone I ran into. The general comment in response was something like, "That sounds interesting." No one seemed to think that this was of any great importance or urgency and I had not even found one person who indicated a desire to participate during a several week period. Just as I was beginning to ask God if I had hear Him wrong about this Canopy or if I was not being aggressive enough to pull people together to make this happen, a brush fire started in the San Gabriel Canyon. This Canyon is in the mountains that line the North edge of the San Gabriel Valley, a large populated valley to the East of Downtown Los Angeles. Pasadena City whose name means something like "Crown of the Valley," lies at the North West corner of this valley, against the foot of the mountains, with Mount Wilson towering five thousand feet directly above Pasadena.

A Fire and Faith

This fire according to the local newspapers and the Los Angeles Times was started from candles being used in a witchcraft ceremony up in the brush along the canyon road. The articles stated that according to rangers, it was not uncommon to find these witchcraft rituals being conducted up in the Canyon. The fire from this one was quickly out of control and was burning Westward toward Pasadena where a similar fire a number of years before had suddenly swooped down on the East end of Pasadena early one morning destroying a large number of homes.

We had a weather condition in Los Angeles called an inversion layer. This is a layer of warm air above the ground and a denser, cooler layer along the ground, which is trapped by the warm air above and does not tend to penetrate the warmer air above. The Los Angeles area is notorious for this condition that also holds the smog pinned to the ground in the basin of mountains that surround Los Angeles. This is not the normal condition of the atmosphere in most other areas, as normally the air is warmest near the ground and proceeds to get cooler at a rate of about 3.6 degrees Fahrenheit per thousand feet elevation. However, on this morning in September, we had an inversion layer, which was holding all of the smoke of this brush fire to within about fifteen hundred feet of the ground surface, and it was miserable.

The event taking place that morning, which also helped to make this morning stand out to me, was the beginning of The Call School at Harvest Rock Church in Pasadena. I had been asked to film a video of the opening of this nine-month discipleship school made up of young people from around the world who had attended various "The Call" prayer and fasting events. They were young people who were committed to a radical walk with Christ. Dr. C. Peter Wagner who was helping to sponsor, and accredit this under the Wagner Leadership Institute was there at Mott Auditorium on the former campus of the Pasadena Nazarene College and now U.S. Center for World Mission. The notable effect of the inversion layer at that location was the auditorium was filled with a smoke haze that morning and it was very irritating to a number of people throughout the morning.

At noon, I left to go back to my office, which was about fifteen miles East in the City of Arcadia. As I was driving the two miles from the Auditorium down to the 210 freeway, which runs East-West along the North side of the valley, I begin thinking about the brush fire. I was a retired twenty-four year veteran of the Department, which had principal responsibility for the area where the fire was now burning.

Suddenly the realization popped into my head that this fire had started in the area that had been under my responsibility as a Battalion Chief. Something that I probably would best describe as, a gut rush of faith, begin to well up in me. I began to prophecy over the fire for the "wind to reverse 180 degrees and blow the fire back upon itself, for the inversion layer to be broken and the smoke to lift, and Lord I am even asking for it to start to rain." That all sort of burst forth out of my mouth and felt like a good burp that cleared a pressure inside and now I could get back to the business at hand. In the ten minutes it took to drive to Arcadia, all that I had prophesied occurred and as I was coming off the freeway ramp in the City of Arcadia, it was raining large drops on my windshield. Well, I had apparently not been specific enough in my prophetic proclamation, because though the smoke lifted and the wind turned 180 degrees, it also picked up speed and blew the fire right past its starting point, on toward the East, burning a number cabins in a Forest Service area North of the town of San Dimas. The rain only lasted for a couple of minutes and had no effect on the fire.

What's the Point?

Over the next several weeks, the fire continued to burn toward the East but at a slower rate. One of the side results of the fire was that the Forest Service shut down "indefinitely," all roads accessing the National Forest areas of Southern California including access to several of the thirteen points of the Canopy that I still knew was a command from the Lord. I was immediately back asking the Lord's forgiveness for not having pursued this aggressively enough to complete this prophetic act before we now did not have access to these several areas. The Lord answered, "Don't worry about that, the time is not yet, and you need to understand why these points."

I waited fully expecting that now the Lord was going to tell me why these particular points. He did not, but as I would begin researching again over the next several weeks, He would reveal sources to me that explained that each of these represented a false religion, a false worship, a false god, or root iniquities of County and Federal Government that happened in Los Angeles County. He would also reveal that each of these thirteen points was a gateway or along a ley line that was connected to a city North of Los Angeles County. I will talk more about these ley lines in the next chapter as I tell more about the canopy and its effect.

Now that I knew the canopy was not part of dealing with the Festival of Sacred Music, I began to look more closely at some of those events. I did convince several warriors throughout the Los Angeles area to pray over several of the events and to actually prayer walk the venues of some. Our main focus was toward the last event of the festival, which was also one of the free, open to the public events. It was on the Santa Monica Beach right between the water and two "art objects" which the Lord had revealed to a number of people to be Asherah poles, (more on that later). This event was called, "Honoring the Sea." I and several other friends were able to recruit several intercessors to attend this event just before the end of October. But first, back to the brush fire that was still burning after almost four weeks.

Through the end of September and the first half of October, this fire continued to move slowly across the mountain range until it was right up against the little village on Mount Baldy. Day after day, the news would report that the village was threatened but not yet burning. All through the first weeks of October, every time I would hear the news, I would recall the prophetic words I had spoken which had such a dramatic effect on the fire. I knew that those words came from faith and the knowledge of my authority in the Lord over the territory where the fire started. Now I kept praying, "isn't there someone out there who has authority over the region where the fire was now and understood their authority to prophesy over this fire?"

Enough!

Apparently not! The fire continued to burn in inaccessible mountain areas and now for several days threatening this village that had never suffered fire damage before. Finally, one afternoon, I believe October 25, I was listening to a news report regarding the fire that was now saying that it appeared that this fire, still threatening Baldy Village, was likely to burn unchecked for another month or more. That same gut reaction of faith welled up once more and I exclaimed aloud, "Oh no, it won't." With that, I began calling upon the Lord to bring rain that very night which would extinguish the flames and put an end to this fire within 24 hours. (I guess I learned in my spirit from the previous request to specify that the rain should this time put the fire out) That is exactly what happened. I was not aware of a forecast of rain; there were no clouds in the sky. However, later that night it started raining primarily over the area of the fire and the fire was put out within 24 hours. In fact, it did not rain very much over any other part of Southern California.

Pagan Worship in the Beach

The last lingering rain clouds were still in the sky over Los Angeles as a group of ten intercessors and prophets walked past the Asherah poles out onto the beach at Santa Monica at 5p.m. on October 28, 2002. We joined the TV cameras and about fifteen hundred onlookers, mostly dressed in white (per the event notice), who had been urged to bring their drums and come to participate in the worship of the goddess of the sea, Yemanja. The music started with a fierce looking group of New Caledonia (in the South Pacific) Island warriors in grass skirts and with spears, tattoos and faces made up with black and white paint. They did a ritual dance and chant that was rather hair raising to set the tone for the evening. Next to get things into the Brazilian mode for the ritual of this Brazilian manifestation of the goddess that is worshipped all over the world, there was a Brazilian drum band and costumed female dancers with white feather angel wings and masks on and showing a lot of bare skin.

Finally, the procession of Yemanja entered the beach preceded by a man carrying an Idol of the mermaid like goddess over his head followed by the rest of the procession. In the center of the procession was a young woman who appeared to be in a trance and was dressed in a mermaid like costume with metallic gold and iridescent make up on her face. She was attended by two other young women also dressed in mermaid costumes. The rest of the procession was musicians, dancers and priestess's to preside over this pagan rite. The ritual began with dances, then mock warfare and finally it was time for the Goddess to dance. As she arose, still trance like, she danced out into the evening surf as the participants and onlookers threw fruit, vegetables and flowers into the waves as an offering.

Mind you, this was not occurring in Africa or some other dark third world country, but was on Santa Monica City Beach, Public Government owned property right next to the heart of much of the Motion Picture and Television industry that beams itself into every corner of the world. This was not a made up movie being portrayed as reality. It was a spiritual reality impressing itself upon the writers and producers that spread the immorality and demonic agendas of the great harlot all over the world.

As all of this was going on, I became aware that the intercessors that came with us were all in tears at this affront to true Lord God Almighty of the earth and sea. I was also aware that there were ominous changes taking place in the sky above. A long strait black roll of a cloud was forming overhead and extended from our location to the North and the South as far as the eye could see. On the South, it passed over the Palos Verde Peninsula toward the Los Angeles and Long Beach Harbors. What concerned me most at the time was that the cloud looked angry and ready to burst forth in lightning.

I stepped closer to the surf line to get one last video shot before suggesting to the intercessors that we get out of there as this crowd might be struck by lightning from the cloud above. A sudden wave surged in and I felt the cold water overwhelm my shoes and my long pant legs all the way up to my calf on both legs. Ugh, I guess I was going to have wet pants, socks and shoes for the drive home. I gathered the intercessors and we started up the beach when I suddenly realized that neither, my pants, shoes or socks were wet. I asked a couple of the intercessors who had seen the wave wash over my feet to feel my socks and pants. They confirmed that they were completely dry and the sand was not even sticking to my shoes. The Lord would tell me later that this was because He did not want me wet with the water that had been dedicated to this goddess.

West Coast Ports Shut Down

As for the cloud, lightning did not come down on the pagan worshippers, but I would learn the next morning that all of the seaports on the West Coast had been shut down by management because of a work slowdown by workers and threatened strike. The ports all remained closed for two solid weeks at a loss to the American economy estimated at nearly $30 Billion dollars. The ships that piled up in the channels waiting to enter the ports when they finally did reopen created a backlog that took months to clear. Did this have anything to do with the demonic worship out on the beach that evening? Did the very unusual cloud that formed over the ritual and the harbor ports have anything to do with this shutdown of the ports up and down the entire West Coast of the U.S. that night? I do not doubt they did, as at this point in my life, I have seen other direct correlations between pagan rituals, weather, physical destruction and economic loss.

Perhaps this shutdown of the ports and the associated economic loss could have been prevented if others and I would have had more understanding of the necessity to take preemptive spiritual action prior to the Festival of Sacred Music. Maybe we could have shifted the spiritual dominion created by this festival. Maybe if some of the prayer groupings and pastor fellowships in Los Angeles, who claim to be watchmen on the wall and gatekeepers, understood spiritual dominion and the authority they have in the spiritual realm over their city, they could have made a difference. If they understood that their authority is not just over their church building, but they can also have impact on the city by taking prayer and worship out into the streets. If they would just set their foot to the land outside of the comfort and protection of those walls with their hearts completely given over to the Lord, and not to the busyness of maintaining their individual institutions, they would perhaps understand a God of whom it is said, "the eyes of the LORD move to and fro throughout the earth that He may strongly support those whose heart is completely His."[3]

I cannot say that I fully understood at the time either, but with six months warning and talking to everyone I met about this Festival of releasing demonic worship into the atmosphere, I would have expected to have found some other leadership who would have the wisdom and spiritual understanding to block this demonic manifestation.

It seems it is about time that we start learning to take possession of the Kingdom we have been made to be, and rule over it, so that the Ancient of Days will rule in favor of the saints, and we might see an end to the stealing, killing and destroying under the dominion of Satan.[4]

Let's now move ahead to understand what the Lord did show to bring protection from future events as we learned to create a canopy of protection formed through prayer and worship over the County of Los Angeles.

Endnotes

1. Marshall, Rich, God@Work, Shippensburg, PA: Destiny Image, 2000
2. Silvoso, Ed, Annointed for Business, Ventura, CA: Gospel Light, 2002
3. 2 Chronicles 16:9
4. John 10:10

CHAPTER 13

SPIRITUAL MAPPING THIRTEEN POINTS OF UNDERSTANDING

During the month of October 2002, I was trying to get groups throughout Los Angeles to recognize and take spiritual responsibility in the territory during this demonic festival of "Sacred Music." I was also, for my own part, taking responsibility to obey the Lord to understand the meaning of the thirteen points that He had revealed to me in that prayer meeting in September. The fire was burning in the San Gabriel Mountains, and the roads were closed to all of the National Forest areas around Southern California with the Forest Service stating that this closure may continue for a year. I had no idea when we might be able to carry out this prophetic act over the County, but the Lord did not seem worried about it and therefore I was going to be obedient to what I could do until further direction from the Lord.

I first made a large copy of a map of Los Angeles County and precisely as I could, marked the location of each of these thirteen points on the map. At first, I also tried to mark the location of the fifty-six events of the Festival of Sacred Music to see if there was any correlation. Finding nothing obvious, I then begin drawing lines connecting the thirteen points with each other. That is when something very interesting began to appear. There did seem to be some pattern emerging as several of the points fell on the same lines and the center East-West line was in line with a Base Line used to lay out the surveying points and original mapping for the States of California, Arizona and New Mexico.

IN FAVOR OF THE SAINTS

Running along this base line is a portion of the old Route 66, known to many as a ley line (See APENDIX A, for a definition of ley lines) that connects the Santa Monica Pier at the Pacific Ocean with the City of Chicago. Seeing that correlation raised my curiosity and as a fluke I purchased a State of California map, drew lines from each of the thirteen points through the Northern point of Frazier Park, and extended these lines across the state map.

Frazier Park

Much to my amazement, every one of those thirteen points would connect through the point of Frazier Park to a city or several cities in another part of the state. This seemed significant, as Frazier Park is like a funnel or faucet through which passes much of the flow of commerce, food products, communication, electricity, oil and gas pipelines, and water, between the Southern end of the State and the North. I would learn that as it is a gateway in the natural, physical world, it also is a spiritual gateway between the North and the South and at least the thirteen points in Los Angeles County have a spiritual link between them and cities in other parts of the State. That would be rather plainly illustrated to us through a divine appointment that the Lord arranged on the day we actually erected the Canopy of Prayer and Worship.

Malibu Lagoon

I also then began researching the points that the Lord had revealed to understand the significance of each. I was already pretty familiar with the Malibu Lagoon, having spent a fair amount of time there, as a young boy growing up not far from that location. I understood that a Native American Village had once been located there but that now this site was just below the view of a Catholic monastery and retreat center. This center was named after the leader of the Spanish Monks who ventured into California in the 1700s to form a chain of missions that enslaved the Natives to work and build the missions in the name of civilizing them and making them into Christians. Most of these natives, who had dwelt on these lands for perhaps thousands of years prior, would be destroyed within fifty years through murder, abuse and the diseases that came with the European settlers that followed the establishment of the missions.

The Malibu Lagoon is also the setting of many Hollywood movies, and the temple of the worshippers of sand, surf and sun that practice their religion there in Malibu. Right next to the Lagoon is the Malibu Colony, home or second home to most of Hollywood's richest movie personalities and idols renown throughout the world.

Santa Monica/Venice Beach

The next point, which the Lord had initially given only as Santa Monica/Venice, was a little confusing as I and several of the people familiar with the area had identified several locations along about a three-mile stretch of the coast line that appeared to be gateways. Each of these had some physical monument marking those gateways. Some clarification came as I drew the lines on the map and the line connecting several of the other points passed through only one of these monument/gateway locations. That location was a namesake statue of Saint Monica that stands at the end of Wilshire Boulevard in Santa Monica. Wilshire Boulevard passes through the financial and political heart of Los Angeles and is where most of the influence over the Los Angeles Area lies.

This statue had already been identified by a prophet in the area as having the appearance of being a phallic symbol when viewed from the beach several hundred feet below the bluff on which it stands.

A Gate Keeper Changes Sides

This prophet had also met a former warlock who had a coven in Santa Monica and who used to come to this gateway marker to access the astral planes of the demonic realm. From this point, he would cast sexual and financial spells over the financial and entertainment industry of Los Angeles/Hollywood. (See further definition of a gateway in APENDIX A) This former warlock stated in a video-taped interview, that one day he came down to this statue to connect up with his demonic gate keepers. He found a group of Christians standing in a circle around this idol and worshipping with guitar led worship (they were not worshipping the idol; they were worshipping there to overcome or break the spiritual authority given to that idol in that location). The warlock stated that this spiritual music had the effect of shutting down the gateway to demonic communication. He said it was like trying to talk on a party line phone with someone playing music on a third line that was completely drowning out the conversation between the other two parties.

As he was pondering this dilemma, it occurred to him that what these Christians were doing through their worship in that gateway was more spiritually powerful than his attempt to contact the demons associated with that gate. From that realization it also occurred to him that maybe he should find out more about what they were doing that was more powerful than what he was doing. Pursuing that logic, he became a Christian a short time later and now ministers to others trapped in witchcraft and Satanism. From this man's testimony and a phone conversation with him, I learned that this particular location was a very powerful gateway to the astral control over the financial and entertainment industries in Los Angeles.

Wayfarer's Chapel

The next point was a puzzle to me because the Wayfarer's Chapel is a very beautiful little chapel on a hillside overlooking the Pacific Ocean. It is on the tip of the Palos Verde Peninsula just to the North of the Long Beach and Los Angeles Harbors. It is also just a few miles from the sites where Cabrillo, who was likely the first white European to set foot on the West Coast of what is now America, landed in San Pedro Bay and Santa Monica Bay in fall of 1542. On a clear day, it also overlooks the tiny island where Cabrillo was reportedly buried in January 1543 having died from an infection of a broken bone received in a fall while going ashore on one of the Channel Islands a few miles up the coast.

However, at the time, I was looking for more directly related clues as to why this point had been given to me by the Lord. I always assumed that this was a Christian church and I had even participated in a wedding there as best man in 1968. This is in fact a very popular church for weddings with a full schedule of them every Saturday and Sunday of the year. Many of Hollywood's best known stars have also been married in this chapel by the sea. That should have given me some clue as to the false impression of the Christian roots to this chapel.

The chapel was designed by Frank Lloyd Wright and is famous throughout the world simply for that fact. But as I visited the Chapel in 2002 and gathered information about it, I would learn that this chapel is also home of a sculpture of the Tree of Life. Not the one in the garden you may be familiar with from Genesis and Revelation, but the one I mentioned a few chapters ago as being the key to astral understandings and the pathway to esoteric knowledge. It was then that I learned from the brochures about the chapel, that this religious institution held to and was the Los Angeles educational center for the Philosophy of Swedenborg.

I had heard of Swedenborgism before but I had no idea of what this religious philosophy consists. I went back to the Internet for more research. Emanuel Swedenborg (1688-1772) developed and wrote about a philosophy toward God, of which he claimed he was made knowledgeable through a visit to heaven. His philosophy, somewhat related to universalism, also holds that the angels are those who have died to this physical life here on earth or on other planets. Of salvation, he writes, "…even though there are many false concepts in the seemingly endless forms that religion takes, to get into heaven you need only two:

1. A belief in God - or at least a belief in something higher than yourself, and . . .
2. A desire to live a good life according to what you believe."

Swedenborg acknowledged that Jesus through His death became once again one with the Father and thus the only one true God. Swedenborg does not hold to the significance of Christ's death as the only means of salvation and eternal life. He also holds that there is no second coming of Christ in that we are the second coming when we become one with God in our god consciousness. There is much more to this philosophy that varies from what could be considered at the core of Christianity. It is not my purpose here to completely examine this aberrant theology, but to simply point out that it is outside the scope and definition that most of us would identify with as orthodox Christianity. That said, the next entry on the Internet search I was doing to understand what this philosophy believed, and for which this chapel was a teaching center, was a letter written in the 1920's by a Grand Mason of the State of Washington:

> "Swedenborgism, however, has so interwoven itself with the "high degrees" of all systems, and by this I mean those degrees above that of Master Mason, and below the Knights, that it cannot be passed over lightly or explained in a few words. It must be understood to understand this so-called part of Freemasonry. (By Bro. BURTON E. BENNETT, Sc. D.
> The Master Mason - January 1926
> Former Park Commissioner of the city of Seattle, former Pan-American Commissioner from the State of Washington, former United States District Attorney for Alaska, member of Ionic Lodge, No. 90, F. &AM., of Seattle, etc)

Now I understood the connection of this point with those other locations throughout Los Angeles County as representing a false worship. I would discover that there is a geometric pattern in the Masonic Lodges that surround this high place and gateway of Los Angeles, and that much of the control of finances and the economy of not only Los Angeles but of much of this nation is connected through this high place overlooking the harbors where thirty four percent of this nation's commerce passes. On the map of that area of Los Angeles County there is a corridor through which that commerce flows that is in geographical alignment with the Masonic Lodges, and passes through locations identified on the map as the "Harbor Gateway" and the city district of "Moneda" (the goddess of money).

Other intercessors and prophets that I had not yet met in the fall of the year 2002 also had identified the strong witchcraft presence on this peninsula and the massacres and suicides of whole Tongva villages that occurred in this area, centuries ago.

Directly off the coast the Palos Verde Shelf, was one of the richest fishing grounds in Southern California until extremely high levels of DDT pesticide were discovered to have totally contaminated these waters in 1970. This is the result of discharges from a manufacturer in Torrance. There were also found to be very high levels of PCB's (a cancer causing substance present in the oil used in large electrical transformers) being discharged through the White's Point outflow very near to this chapel.

A Village Called Puvugna

The next point on the map was the once site of the Tongva village of Puvugna. This site is now on State owned property that comprises part of the campus of California State University at Long Beach. It was identified by and brought under protection by the decedents of those Tongva people when the State attempted to develop the site into a shopping center. The Tongva identify this site as the location of the once sacred village of Puvugna where an "ethereal entity" appeared to them perhaps around 700AD. A Franciscan Monk documented the story of the appearance of this entity at Puvugna during the early 1800's, as he was interviewing Tongva elders regarding their creation and religious legends. As the legend goes, the people had just killed their god, which they called their "captain." Shortly after this act of murder, this ethereal entity appears to them and transforms through three appearances or segments of time, each of which had a different name attached to it. The name of this entity Chinigchinich signifies "all-powerful" or "almighty" and it is believed by the Tongva, that he was ever present, and in all places: They believed he saw everything although it might be in the darkest night, but no one could see him. This entity informs the people that he is stronger than their former captain and that now he is their captain. Chinigchinich was known under three distinct names, as follows: *Saor, Quaguar,* and *Tobet*. Each name possessed a particular signification, denoting diversity or a difference of times. (We will look at the altering of time in a later chapter dealing with Tibetan Buddhism) Tobet was the final state or time of Chinigchinich during which he taught the people to dance and then disappeared into the heavens.

Tobet may be significant because of a character by a very similar name in the Apocryphal book of the Bible Tobit. The story in that book of Tobit is mostly off the subject of this chapter so I will not go into detail. However, a couple of parts of that story relate to an angel Raphael that appears to Tobias, the son of Tobit, as a man that joins him on the journey in his quest to find a wife and also instructs him to catch a fish and carry it with them. Later in the story, parts of the fish are burned to drive off a demon named Asmodaeus.

This demon also appears in another book of the Apocrypha, the Wisdom of Solomon and in the end of that book flies off to the "highest mountain where he ever rests." The other significant issue regarding the fish is the use of the fishes gall to heal the eyesight of Tobit. The points of significance are that the creation legend of a nearby tribe speaks of a fish creator and of the need of the breaking open of a sacred stone to release gall into the waters of the earth to make them again sweet for the fish to survive. Most of us would identify gall as bitter not sweet and the sea as bitter salty to us but perhaps sweet to the fish of the sea, the dwelling place of Leviathan. Again, remember the teaching earlier in this book about how having our senses trained through practice helps us to distinguish between good and evil. This fish creation legend may relate to the religion of Dagon (2500BC) the Fish god, Father of Baal.

Also the implication of the story in the Wisdom of Solomon is that this high level demon whose name Asmodaeus means bringer of anger, bringer of wrath, sits on Mount Everest, (I find this quite a coincidence between the demon ever resting on the highest mountain and the mountain being named in 1865 after Sir George Everest, the British surveyor-general of India) between the two highest lands and nations in the world, Tibet and Nepal. The name of the mountain in Nepal is Sagarmatha (means: goddess of the sky) and in Tibet is Chomolungma: (means: mother goddess of the universe)

Linguistically the word Tibet could easily be misunderstood and pronounced Tobet. This may have something to do with why the religious practices taught to the Tongva by their "lawgiver and teacher of their shamans" Chinigchinich, are so similar to Tibetan Buddhism that archeologists have theorized that the Tongva were visited by Tibetan Buddhists long before Europeans came on this shore. There is no historical record to indicate that this happened in the physical.

Having discovered a number of instances within the last two centuries when founders of religious movements including Helen Blavatsky (The Theosophical Society), Aleister Crowley (The OTO and Magick), Alice Bailey (The Lucis Trust and World Good Will) and John Roger (Ascended Traveler cult in Los Angeles) have all had visitations from "Ascended Tibetan Masters," it seems purely logical to me that a similar demonic manifestation may also have been the source of the Chinigchinich religion. This religion became the first missionary movement on the North American Continent and the predominate religion among most of the tribal peoples throughout the area we now call Southern California.

The Ley of the State

Among the other things that the Lord revealed about this general location is that the ley line through Frazier Park from this point goes directly to the California State Capitol, Sacramento. There is also another mysterious tie to the City of Long Beach. The State of California and the City of Long Beach both have the Roman goddess Minerva on their respective seals. On the State seal, there is a bear at Minerva's feet. In the

Mythology of Minerva, she is a friend of the Roman goddess Dianna of the Ephesians, which we also know as Artemis in Greek mythology. (Minerva becomes Athena in the Greek mythology) Artemis lived in the mythical land of Arcadia. (The name of my hometown at the time I was discovering all of this. Maybe I am just living in a mythical land after all?) Artemis had a handmaiden named Calisto. Calisto was assaulted by one of the Greek Gods and became pregnant. When Artemis discovered this, she turned Calisto into a bear. Hence, though many in the State would say that the bear on the State seal and the State flag is because of the commonness of the bear in the California territory, the appearance in the State seal next to the feet of Minerva would suggest a more mythical connection to Artemis or Dianna of the Ephesians.

Other evidence pointing to this is that one of the very popular tourist locations in California's early years was the town of Calistoga, the hot spring "spa capitol of the world." Artemis discovered the pregnant state of Calisto, when Calisto was invited to bathe with her in a hot spring.

Since many citizens of the previous centuries had much more training in classical mythology then we do today, the tie of the bear to this mythology seems more likely than the general explanation given of the abundance of bears in California. It is also likely that the lone star on the state flag, is more related to the identical star of the goddess Babylon, another and earlier manifestation of Artemis, brought together with the bear Calisto on the flag, then it is to the supposed link to the Lone Star Texas Territory.

Nevertheless, back to Long Beach and its tie to Sacramento through Minerva on both seals. The Minerva in Long Beach is more linked to another aspect of the Mythology of Minerva, that being her battle with Poseidon the god of the sea (Neptune to the Greeks) and the constant struggle between the two. In the Long Beach seal, an octopus tentacle reaches out of the ocean and wraps around the leg of Minerva where the bear Calisto appears in the State seal. Minerva, though she had defeated Poseidon for control over the land, still calls upon the power of the god of the sea to create storms to destroy her enemies or drive them back to the shore so she can deal with them. Here we see the root of the linkage between the demons on the land and those that inhabit the waters that will show up as we deal in a later chapter with Tibetan Buddhism. This also relates to the actions of Jack Parsons who conjured up a storm at sea to drive L. Ron Hubbard back to shore in 1946, and the worshipping of a goddess of the sea creating a storm and possibly affecting the closing of seaports all along the West Coast in the fall of 2002.

The primary Tibetan center in Southern California moved to Long Beach in 1994 when their building in West Los Angeles was damaged by the Northridge earthquake. Long Beach has also become a strong center for witchcraft in recent years.

The Tongva, were sea goers, whose, principal religious site was on Catalina Island, twenty-six miles off the coast of Long Beach and the Palos Verde Peninsula. From that Island location, it is believed that they created sand mandalas in order to place curses upon and bring destructions upon their enemies, a form of geomancy that has been practiced in Tibetan Buddhism for hundreds of years.

In the past decade, the primary visual feature on the Campus of California State University at Long Beach has become the huge one hundred and ninety-two foot high blue Pyramid built as an athletic facility. This Pyramid is located just a quarter mile from the site of Puvugna and has become a most visible anchor point for the ley line to Sacramento. This huge building has also been used for musical and dramatic presentations according to a musician friend of mine. In fact, the "God and King of Tibet," the "Prince of Peace on Earth," the Dalai Lama was in attendance at one presentation in this building at which this friend was playing in the orchestra. My friend described the particular opera being performed as so vile and violent that the conductor stopped the orchestra and warned the actors on stage that if any more of the blood being liberally splashed around was splattered on the orchestra, the orchestra would leave immediately.

Somehow, I was beginning to get the drift of why the Lord had identified these particular points and singled them out as locations from where we were to establish His presence through worship and lift a canopy of prayer over the entire County.

IN FAVOR OF THE SAINTS

East of Whittier

The next point on the Lord's list was "East of Whittier." Directly East of Whittier is the Hsi Lai Buddhist Temple in Hacienda Heights. Hsi Lai Temple was built in 1988 by the Taiwanese Buddhist organization of FoGuang Shan. Located on 15 acres of land in Hacienda Heights, the temple was built in the fashion of Ming and Qing dynasty architecture. Hsi Lai, which means "coming to the West," was built to spread Buddhism in the West by the FoGuang Shan order. The area of Hacienda Heights is very heavily populated by Chinese Buddhists. This temple was the location of Al Gores' famous and investigated fundraising lunch before the 2000 presidential elections. This was the event that he "didn't know was a fundraising lunch" and was linked to the illegal financial political contributions and conviction for those illegal contributions, of a Chinese businessman.

This temple was in 2002, also the spiritual center for Buddhist worship in the Western United States.

A mountain peak very close to this temple is the site of pagan witchcraft circles and a street corner just a short distance below the temple is where the body of a Christian woman was left at a gas station, having been dragged there behind a car after a ritual blood sacrifice somewhere on the mountain above.

On the maps the Lord led me to draw, it lies on a spiritual ley line to San Jose and San Francisco (more about that in the next chapter) through the Pasadena convergence[1] and through the Frazier Park convergence. It is in direct East -West alignment with Marina Del Rey (home to many actors, directors, and producers of Television and Motion Pictures), Loyola Marymount College (A Catholic College that has strongly supported Tibetan Buddhist activities in Southern California), Florence Avenue (the trigger point of the 1992 L. A. riots after the Rodney King incident) and Mt. Rubidoux in Riverside County (a known spiritual high place). It is also on the ley line between the Wayfarer's Chapel and the Claremont East Gate or Base Line, which I will describe next.

SPIRITUAL MAPPING THIRTEEN POINTS OF UNDERSTANDING

Claremont on the Base Line

The next point that the Lord gave me in that prayer meeting in September 2002 was also a little vague, "over Pomona at the East end." Over or to the North of the City of Pomona at the East end of the County is the town of Claremont. Primarily known for its exclusive Claremont Colleges cluster and the Claremont School of Theology (perhaps the most liberal protestant "Christian" theological think tank in the U.S.) these schools are located on either side of route 66 at the East end of the County.

The phrase "over Pomona" could also be interpreted to refer to the founding of this town around its seven colleges. The Santa Fe Railroad provided the impetus for the creation of a community named Claremont in January 1887. It was one of about thirty town sites laid out between San Bernardino and Los Angeles in anticipation of a population explosion resulting from the arrival of the railroad. However, the real estate boom was short-lived and Claremont would have become one of a long list of local railroad "ghost towns" if not for the decision of the local land company to transfer its Hotel Claremont and 260 vacant lots to the recently founded Pomona College in 1888.

The founders of Pomona College wanted to establish a school of "the New England style" and the community that grew up around it also reflected the founders' New England heritage. Even the form of local government they used, the Town Meeting, was brought with them from their hometowns in the East.

The original college and the city located just south of Claremont are both named after the Goddess Pomona who also is the prominent goddess in the center of the Los Angeles County Seal. I find it interesting that the ACLU recently forced the County to remove a very small cross from the Seal. That cross was there to symbolize and acknowledge that this county's original settlers were Spanish Catholic Monks. It was these monks led by Franciscan Junipero Serra who established the San Gabriel Mission as part of the system of twenty-one missions that made up the first governance of the California territory in the 1700's. Thus, this cross does not signify the establishment of religion by the

County Government, but simply acknowledged that this county owed its existence to the founding work of a religious system and that most of the name of places around the county, come from that root. I am surprised that the ACLU did not seek to change the name of many of the counties in the state which are named after Catholic Saints, and the name of Los Angeles which is a shortening of its full official name translated, "The Town of Our Lady the Queen of Angels of the Little Portion."[2] Apparently, the ACLU does not seem to see any "religious" significance to leaving a most prominent "goddess" image on the seal. Pomona was the Roman goddess of the orchards and the harvest, and her feasts consisted of apples, nuts, grapes and other concord fruits. To the Romans, the apple was the symbol of love and fertility. Her feast day was celebrated on November 1. Hence, when the Romans invaded the Celtic lands whose inhabitants celebrated the feast of Samhain or what we today call Halloween; Pomona was incorporated into their October 31st festival and also became the goddess over the occult and witchcraft. Perhaps there should be little wonder of the degree to which witchcraft is present in the areas of Claremont and Pomona with one of the better-known witchcraft stores in Southern California, the Crystal Caldron located in Pomona. You will also find books on witchcraft authored by various faculties of the colleges and seminars on witchcraft held in campus facilities.

In 1942, Japanese-American citizens who had been rounded up from all over Southern California were temporarily housed at the nearby Los Angeles County/Pomona Fair Grounds until being disbursed to other internment centers around the country. In 1945 and 1946, the fair grounds were also used as a prisoner of war camp for Germans and Italians captured in the European campaigns of World War II.

The particular point at which we were to meet for the Canopy was on Baseline Road. Baseline Road follows the San Bernardino Baseline, which was established in 1852-1853 as the baseline for U.S. land surveys, and approximates the course of a wagon road blazed in 1856 by the Mormon settlers of San Bernardino. The first contemporary building inside the Los Angeles County line on Baseline Road is a Mormon Church, standing as gatekeeper at the East gate of Los Angeles County.

SPIRITUAL MAPPING THIRTEEN POINTS OF UNDERSTANDING

This particular point was indicated on my maps by the convergence of a number of ley lines from the other points specifically designated by the Lord. This makes sense, as Baseline Road was the surveying layout line that was used in mapping for most of the Southwest United States. The East-West ley line from this point connects to the Westlake point passing through the Pasadena Convergence point. It also is in direct alignment with the Wayfarer's Chapel point through the Hsi Li Buddhist Temple. That ley line also passes through the Claremont Colleges and the Claremont School of Theology. A ley line through the focal point of Frazier Park, anchors in the City of Monterey, once a capital of California. A ley line to Balboa Watergate crosses the 210 Freeway in Lake View Terrace at the point that Rodney King was beaten and arrested. It was this incident with Rodney King that led to the release of chaos, death and destruction over Los Angeles in the riots of the spring of 1992. Do these so-called gateways and opening of portals, marked by ley lines have anything to do with the release of chaos and destruction on the earth and over our cities? I have come to believe they do. Do you remember the literal meaning of Shalom from Chapter Five? Destroys the authority that builds or establishes Chaos is the meaning from early Hebrew. Sounds like a pretty good reason to put on your "shalom shoes" and get walking around some of the sources of chaos in your community.

Of the remaining seven points, six are in somewhat remote locations with only small populations of people currently living nearby. They do not appear so much related to religious movements, witchcraft and practices on or nearby their locations, but instead appear to be gateways representing theft, deception, discrimination, and seeking answers to life other than in and through the God of the Bible. Since there is only very small populations around these areas, there is less written about the specific locations and the Lord led me to look more particularly at what the gateways represented by looking at what passes through them and the associated unrighteousness of those things.

Lake Los Angeles/Saddle Back Butte

As I looked at the map of Lake Los Angeles out in the Antelope Valley at the North East corner of the County, the next point on the Lord's list, Saddleback Buttes State Park popped out at me. I thought that perhaps this was some type of spiritual high place. Seeing that there is a State Park with a Native American Museum right next to this at Paiute Butte, I went out there to see if it were likely that the Saddleback Butte could have been a spiritual high place. At this point, I am confident it was and may still be, lying at the Northeast corner of the County.

The Kitanemuk people are believed to have had villages in this area. They are of Shoshonean language group and Paiute culture. As Saddleback Butte was the highest peak in the area and has a mesa top, I believe that it was used as a spiritual high place. Going back to somewhere around 700AD the religious practice was similar to the Chinigchinich religion practiced by the Tongva and the nearby Serrano peoples. There is a Native American museum nearby at Paiute Butte, which is believed to have been the location of the principal village. This area would later become known as Lake Los Angeles by developers in the 1900's, and was an oasis in the desert with many artesian wells.

In the 1950's, developers dredging to create a lake for development of a home community uncovered fifteen bodies in a mass grave that dated to early native times. UCLA took over the archeology and was said to have removed the bodies and taken them to UCLA. This has been an act that appears to be in violation of state law, and has been greatly protested by native peoples. As I knew none of this information prior to this word from the Lord indicating this as one of the prayer/praise points, there is likely more spiritual significance to this location then I have been able to uncover up to now. On the map, the ley line through this point to the Wayfarer's Chapel passes through the Pasadena convergence and bisects Catalina Island. The ley line to Santa Monica passes through UCLA. The ley line to Westlake passes through the Balboa Water Gate. I believe this point represents the destruction of the native peoples, and spiritual authority over land and water.

SPIRITUAL MAPPING THIRTEEN POINTS OF UNDERSTANDING

The North Gate Highway 14

Next on the list is the extreme North end of the Antelope Valley and of Los Angeles County, Avenue A and Highway 14. This is the North Gateway. It is also the West gate of Edwards Air Force Base and all of that connection to the space program.[3] It is the gateway to Red Rock Canyon, a native sacred place, the Mojave Desert, where Jack Parsons did part of his 1946 ritual and evoked Babalon. In and near the town of Mojave, you find the home of the mothball fleet of most of the airlines, Rutlan aviation, aviation speed and altitude records and flight-testing of bomber designs. This North point is also the gateway to the Owens valley sites of the fraud and theft of water and land during the early 1900's for the City of Los Angeles, the internment of the Japanese during WWII, the highest and lowest points (Mt. Whitney and Bad Water, Death Valley) in the lower 48 states, Radio Telescopes searching for life in space, and the list goes on.

The North-South ley line from this point to Puvugna passes through the Pasadena convergence point. The ley line to Wayfarer's Chapel crosses Mount Washington the location of the Hollywood sign and another witchcraft high point. The Ley line to Santa Monica crosses the 210 freeway to converge with other ley lines at the point of the Rodney King Beating. The ley line to Malibu passes, appropriately enough, through the Balboa Watergate. I believe this point represents discrimination, theft and deception for economic gain. Its connection with the space program and the electronic telescopes in the Owens Valley represents seeking to find another source of life other than God. Its connection to the theft of water represents seeking life from the physical rather than the spiritual.

More About Frazier Park

The next point, Interstate Highway 5 at Frazier Park is the funnel through which Northern California is connected to Southern California. This is the main North-South route for nearly all transportation and commerce on the entire West Coast. As I drew lines between points on the map, it is also the focal point for all the ley lines connecting major cities to the North. A ley line from Malibu through this focus goes to Lake Tahoe. The ley line from Wayfarer's Chapel passes through the points of Santa Monica, the Santa Suzana Pass and through Frazier Park to Fresno, the center of California agriculture and gateway to the Sierra National Parks of Yosemite, Sequoia and Kings Canyon. A ley line from Puvugna, passes through Hollywood, through the Balboa Watergate and runs along the pipes and aqueducts carrying water from Shasta lake, but also as focused by the Frazier Park focal point runs to the current state capitol of Sacramento. The Ley line from the Buddhist Temple passes through the Pasadena convergence and focuses through Frazier Park to San Francisco. The ley line from Claremont focuses to Monterey, a former capitol of California and the center of fishing, postgraduate military training and language training for the diplomatic corp. I believe this point represents a key spiritual focal point over all of the commerce, transportation and agriculture of California. It is also representing the spiritual authority connection over Hollywood and government. This connection is anchored in the false worship of other gods, idols and materialism.

The Balboa Water Gate

Moving back down Southward along Interstate 5, we enter the greater Los Angeles area at the North end of the San Fernando Valley with a man made waterfall on the East Side of the Freeway at Balboa Boulevard. This waterfall is an aeration device for the water flowing out of the Los Angeles Aqueduct from all over Northern California and into the Los Angeles Department of Water and Power Van Norman Reservoir. Just West of I-5 on Balboa is one of the main L.A. Department of Water and Power facilities for processing the water entering Los Angeles. I have called this point the Balboa Watergate, as this appears to be the understanding that the Lord gave this point. This is the entry point of all of the Northern California waters into the City of Los Angeles. William Mulholland on behalf of the Los Angeles City Department of Water and Power bought these water sources and even the land, on which many of the reservoirs stand, through deception and unrighteous dealings. This story was portrayed in the 1974 movie Chinatown starring Warren Beatty. This unscrupulous dealing has been the source of continued contention, bombings, gun battles and political battles since the early 1900's and goes on today. The St. Francis dam built about 12 miles North of this location by Mulholland, and where much of this water was stored in the early 1900's, collapsed on March 12, 1928, releasing a 15 billion gallon flood that was one of the greatest civil disasters in American history. The water began as a 75-foot high wave and scoured a path to the sea 2 miles wide and 70 miles long. In its wake, it left much of Ventura County under yards of muck. The final death toll was nearly 500. Weeks later, bodies continued to wash up on beaches as far away as San Diego. This point represents spilling of innocent blood, deception, unrighteous authority over land and water and the false source of living water.

Santa Susana Pass at Rocky Peak

From the Balboa Watergate we move to the West Gate in Santa Susana Pass at Rocky Peak. This location at the North West corner of the San Fernando Valley is very literally a gate to the West as hundreds of Western movies were filmed in these unusual rock formations. The rocks were the hideout of real bandits in the 1800's and early 1900's and the home of the Charles Manson Family for a time before the infamous murder of Sharon Tate, the wife of Director Roman Polanski. Polanski's movie directing credits include Chinatown in 1974 and Rosemary's Baby in 1968. The latter, I will mention further in the chapters on prayer/worship walking Venice Beach. This also was the location of Rocketdyne where the Saturn V rocket engines were tested in the early part of the space program and used to regularly light up the sky over and shake the entire Los Angeles Basin during the tests that were done here during the 50's and 60's. It is through this pass that the Ronald Reagan freeway runs out to his Presidential Library in the Simi Valley. All those living in the Simi Valley pass through this area to enter Los Angeles County. This point I believe represents power, deception and violence.

The West Lake

The next location, given by the Lord as simply the West Lake, was a bit of a puzzle. Westlake Village is a development that lies right along the Los Angeles and Ventura County Line where El Camino Real (the Kings Highway known today as U.S. Route 101), passes out of Los Angeles County. The Franciscan Monks pioneered this roadway as a wagon trail that joined the twenty-one missions of California. I suspect that this is the primary reason for this point being in the list, as when population followed the settlement of these missions, it also leads to the demise of most of the Native peoples. This was not the intention of Father Junipero Serra whose stated purpose for his work was to see the salvation of these native peoples. He often complained to his superiors about the type of people that were being sent to settle the areas around the missions. He complained that they were lazy, took advantage of the natives by forcing them to do their work for them, and that they were corrupting them with their tobacco, alcohol and gambling. Perhaps this why the Native Americans of California are now paying us back by corrupting us through their tax free tobacco sales, and casinos with alcohol and gambling?

This Westlake point lies on the East West ley line from Claremont West through the Pasadena Convergence point. It is at the North West end of a ley line from Wayfarer's chapel through the Malibu Lagoon. A ley line from Puvugna passes over Los Angeles International Airport, Marina Del Rey and the site of the newly constructed SRIVENKATESWARASWAMY (say that name three times fast!), Hindu temple on Las Virgenes Canyon Road. This temple faces East and lies in perfect East – West alignment with Santa Monica Blvd through West Hollywood (the center of Los Angeles' homosexual community) and the straight portions of Route 66 from San Gabriel to

San Bernardino. A ley line from Westlake to the Buddhist Temple in Hacienda Heights passes through the UCLA convergence point. The Ley line from Westlake to Saddleback Butte Peak passes through the Balboa Watergate. I believe this point represents spiritual deception from the Asian cultures to the West and the corruption and lawlessness from the European cultures to the East.

A Center Pole on Mount Wilson

Finally, we come to Mount Wilson. The Lord gave this to me as the center pole to the canopy of prayer and praise. It is here where most of the communications antennas for all of Los Angeles are located. Most of the Television and Radio seen and heard in Los Angeles County, at some point passes through the antennas and transmitters on Mount Wilson. The Mount Wilson Observatory run by Cal Tech in Pasadena is also here with the 100 inch Keck Telescope and new construction of a radio telescope. The ley lines from this point seem to be more directly related to Pasadena as they cross the gates and boundary points of Pasadena. Overall, I believe this point represents spiritual authority and control of the air over all of Los Angeles County.

I have not covered every detail relating to every point, for to do so would take many more pages. It is not the point of this book to simply point out every evil and sinful connection to every location in the world. If you look even slightly below the surface in the world around us, the connections to the demonic and to activities that point away from the God of the Universe are very evident. There is a tendency in Spiritual Mapping in this day to simply look for all of the millions of evidences of demonic activity and then find oneself overwhelmed and clueless with what to do about it. I am not saying that the answer is always to create a canopy of worship and prayer over the whole mess. What I am trying to point out in this chapter is that it was first of all the Lord who pointed to these particular locations and then had me understand some of what these particular ones might represent of the sin of this territory called the County of Los Angeles. It was the Lord, who before I even knew what these points might represent instructed what was to be done as a prophetic act over this county from these particular points. Back to my oft-repeated statement, you must hear from the Lord, what to do, when to do it, how to do it and then you must follow Him in exact obedience in the battles of this spiritual war in which we are engaged. It is only when we lift His authority, and begin taking possession of the Kingdom, that the Ancient of Days will, "rule in favor of the saints."

In the next chapter, we will look at when and how the protective canopy was raised over Los Angeles County from these thirteen points and what some of the affects of that canopy have been in the past several years.

Endnotes

1. Convergence points seem to be spiritual portals or gateways where numerous ley lines cross. This is related to the occult practice of "path working" and "astral projection."
2. As of 2004 the foolishness of changing all those names is actually being looked into according to a World Net Daily news article from June 13, 2004.
3. Edwards Air Force Base is the alternate landing site for the space shuttles which were built in Palmdale just a few miles to the South. The shuttle pilots are trained to fly the shuttle at this location using a specially modified aircraft that can be programmed to respond and glide just like the shuttle which is in an unpowered rapid decent glide on re-entry landings.

CHAPTER 14

A PROTECTIVE CANOPY IS RAISED

In the first week of November 2002, I now heard from the Lord to go ahead and set a date for the Canopy prophetic act. The Lord did not give me a date and the roads were still closed in the National Forest areas, but the Lord said for me to set a date. I still did not even have thirteen people who I thought might want to be a part of this, and I also recognized that it would take some additional time to prepare information for others so that they could ask the Lord if they were to be involved. So, I sat down with a friend and we prayed about a date and then arrived at the date of January 4, 2003. We recognized that we were coming into the holidays and getting someone to commit to giving up a whole day to participate might be difficult before Christmas. Getting to some of these locations might involve driving one hundred and fifty miles each way. For some people it would be a whole day to drive to a location, spend about two hours there and then drive back. We scheduled the Canopy for the first weekend in January recognizing that most people who had traveled for Christmas would be back by that time, and would not yet be into the busy schedule of the new year.

This friend and I also talked about how we would get information out to people so they might pray whether they would be a part of this act. Even more importantly, how we would get specific information to people about exactly where these locations were, how to get there, how long it would take, and what to do when they got there. Since this friend was an Internet developer, he put together a web site and added this project to a Southern California Christian Events calendar on another of his web sites. We were cautious though about how much information to put up on a public web site. This because on other occasions both he and I had experienced spiritual attack and opposition from those involved in witchcraft. Therefore, he also created a non-public website on which we could place detailed information for those who would respond by email as having interest in the project. This worked great and by the first part of December we had been receiving a number of inquiries.

Shortly after having set the date and started up the web site, the Forest Service lifted the road closures to the National Forest sites (Which they originally had said might be for a whole year!). We would now have access to all of the locations. I spent the first couple of weeks of December driving to all thirteen sites. I determined where people could park, where they could actually gather to do the worship and prayer and created maps with directions to each site. We then put all of this information as well as background on each site up on the non-public web site. In the last week of December, I wrote up a guide document for what was to be done at each site and began contacting some of the individuals who believed they were to be involved. By several days prior to January 4, we had at least three people for ten of the sites. I made some cold calls to churches in the other three areas and raised a few more people.

Preparing the Way

On January 2nd and 3rd, I again drove out to every site but one. I placed an eight-foot pole with ropes, stakes and a hammer hidden at each location. The poles were used at each location to represent the poles and cords supporting the canopy that we were supernaturally constructing through worship and prayer. I have found that it often helps to have some physical props when conducting prophetic acts. It helps people connect their physical senses to the supernatural act. As witnessed by some of the comments from those participating, this not only became a tangible evidence of what was being done in the spiritual, but it also brought focus, and the establishing of a memorial marking of the event with scriptures written on the poles and stakes. I received a report in November 2005 from one of the participants who said that the pole they had erected was still standing. He reported that a brush fire had just gone through the area and burned all the brush around the pole, but the pole was still standing untouched by the fire. At another site, the pole became the fulfillment of a vision that one of the participants had seen several months prior. However, this person did not know the meaning of the poles with cords or ribbons that she had seen in the vision until she got to the site and they were putting up the pole I had hidden several days before.

Establishing Order Through Instruction

I had never met many of the people who participated in this Canopy of Prayer and Praise on January 4, 2003. I did not even know some of the people who would be leading at the various locations, so I wrote a protocol for guidance on that day. I had even less knowledge about each person's experience with prophetic acts, or anything about their spiritual background. I am very thankful that the Lord guided me to put together a protocol that seemed to be just enough direction to bring a unity of purpose and spirit at each location, but left opening for each location to interpret and flow with what the Lord would show them.

Here is the instruction that I gave via emails and the Internet site:

> There is no formal program for these gatherings to raise a canopy of prayer and praise over Los Angeles County. But here are some scriptures, thoughts and songs that I believe the Lord has put on my heart with regard to this gathering of his people at 13 points to **together and simultaneously lift a canopy of prayer and praise**. An intercessor from the Alta Loma area saw a vision during a time of prayer a week before she heard about this canopy of prayer and praise. In that vision, the Lord

gave her a picture of something rising up out in her area that was hindering break though in LA. **After a time of prayer, they felt that the Lord was granting a season of grace, the month of January**, and saw a white fleece like a blanket being pulled over the mountain of black. Two of the locations of this canopy relate to one of the issues that is seeking to rise up in their area. I know some of you live or work outside of Los Angeles County and I thank you for hearing from the Lord and joining with us for this day. You have heard the horn calling the army of the Lord and have come from your own homes to join in this battle, that is not ours, but the Lords. May you be blessed in your help, as I believe that the effect of this day will spill into the surrounding counties and even the whole State of California.

I would suggest that during the first ½ hour you spend time greeting one another as there may be people at your location from several different parts of the body and you may never have met them. Spend the time between **10a.m. and 10:20a.m. warmly greeting each other and praying blessings over each other**, your families, and your churches or ministries. Be careful, be sure no one is left out from having blessing said and prayed over them. There may be people of different church backgrounds and different interpretations of some doctrinal issues, but that is not the point on this day. It is that we give thanks for the whole body of Christ and for the role of every part of it. If you are part of the predominate group that is gathered at a particular location and your tradition does not speak in tongues or dance in the Spirit, fine, you pray and worship in the Holy Spirit as you know and warmly bless others who do it differently. I have been in gatherings all over the world with brothers and sisters from all different denominations and doctrinal leanings, worshipping together and blessing one another as they together lift up our chief shepherd and pastor, our Lord and King, Jesus.

At **10:20 take ten minutes to put on your armor by reading together Ephesians 6:10-19**, I would suggest one person read or take turns reading verses to take into account the difference in translation of individual verses. I in particular like to visualize the effect and covering of each of these pieces of armor. The belt of truth holds everything in place and is like a mooring point for a ship as it holds together the various pieces of armor. It is like the belt of my trousers, which keeps them from falling down and causing me embarrassment. It also keeps me from the temptations of the world. The breastplate of righteousness is the covering of Christ's righteousness over all that is unrighteous within me. It is within my torso that I experience the feelings of anger, hurt, fear, anxiety and many other emotions. These are feelings that grip our heart, wrench our gut, and chill our spine. It is to these that Satan loves to point an accusing finger at our unrighteousness, so we must put on this armor piece of Christ's righteousness so that the enemy cannot stir up those things within us. The ancient Hebrew script for the word **Shalom** or peace was made up of 4 symbols or pictures that were read literally to mean, "**destroys the authority which establishes chaos.**" Can you picture your feet being covered with shoes that are prepared to spread the good news that in Christ we are destroying the authority that is establishing chaos? I see the shield of faith as actually taking up by faith Jesus as my shield. He is before us, behind us, to the right and to the left, He is above us and below us, completely surrounding us with His presence as we by faith lift Him up. He has and is taking upon Himself the blows of the enemy intended for us, and extinguishing every flaming missile of the evil one. (Some missile defense system! It doesn't cost $100 billion dollars, just one life, and it is already fully operational.) Then we have the helmet of Salvation, a covering of healing, deliverance, rescue, redemption, over our mind, our eyesight, our hearing, and our words. Moreover, taking up the sword of the Spirit that is the Word of God, we can now pray with all kinds of prayers and petitions, at all times in the Spirit with this view in mind, to be on the alert with all perseverance and petition for all the saints.

During the second ½ hour from **10:30 to 11a.m., have someone read or jointly read together II Chronicles Chapters 19 and 20.** Pay particular attention to Jehoshaphat's response to this crisis of being attacked. Beginning with Chapter 20 verse 3, spend some time together relating this story in II Chronicles 20 to the present situation. We are being attacked on every side by forces that are challenging the Lordship of Christ over our County and our State. I don't know about you but this has caused me to be afraid at times, for my family, for brothers and sisters in Christ, and for the salvation of the lost in this county and state. During this half hour project yourselves as a group into this situation as written in II Chronicles 20. Note that one of the things Jehoshaphat does is to recount to the people the position of God and how He delivered them out of Egypt, drove out the inhabitants of the land, but sparing the peoples who are now marching against them. Remember how in John 17 Jesus prayed, "I do not ask Thee to take them out of the world but to keep them from the evil one."

Spend a few minutes **sharing how various ones in your group have experienced God's answers to prayers and deliverance from situations in the past**. Be thoughtful of others and keep your individual sharing brief. This is a faith building exercise, as we now come before the Lord and present to Him this

A Protective Canopy is Raised

present situation of finding our land filled with false gods, witchcraft, immorality, and idolatry. We have the expectation by faith of His deliverance even in this day. Now together read from verse 12. "O our God, wilt Thou not judge them? For we are powerless before this great multitude that is coming against us, nor do we know what to do, but our eyes are on Thee." Spend a few moments in silence painting this picture in your mind as described in verse 13, "And all Judah was standing before the Lord, with their infants, their wives, and their children." Lift your eyes up to the Lord also at this time in expectation that you will hear from the Lord concerning this great battle that is before us.

I as one having heard from the Lord to lift this canopy, am proclaiming as did Jahaziel on that day, listen all Christians and the inhabitants of Los Angeles County, thus says the Lord to you, do not fear or be dismayed because of this great multitude, for the battle is not yours, but God's. We have come down today against our enemies. You will not fight in this battle, **we have stationed ourselves to stand and see the salvation of the Lord on our behalf. Do not fear or be dismayed, for today we have come out to face them, for the Lord is with us.**

At 11a.m., I am asking each group to erect the pole provided, as symbolic of the 13 poles of this canopy over the county. The group at Mount Wilson will be erecting the center pole. Feel free to write on these poles words or scriptures that the Holy Spirit may give from the Lord.

Now let the celebration of worship, praise and prayer begin with the focus on acknowledging our Lord Jesus as our salvation and welcoming His rule, His reign, His Dominion, His Kingdom to come into place over Los Angeles County. Let it be here on earth as it already is in heaven.

I would suggest that the hour **between 11a.m. and Noon include a reading of the 10 commandments as found in Deuteronomy 5:6-21, the Lord's Prayer, and songs such as Joy To The World and Great Is Thy Faithfulness.** Listen to the words as you sing and pray them out in song. As this is a time of praise to the Lord, listen to the Lord and praise Him as he directs. Praise as the Lord has given you expression, both individually and corporately, using dance, flags, instruments and voices. Be inclusive of one another and bless one another as you together glorify the Lord. Yield to one another in leadership, as the Holy Spirit would direct.

At 5 minutes to noon, greet one another again warmly and speak blessing over one another, pray on their behalf that utterance may be given to them in the opening of their mouth, to make known with boldness the mystery of the gospel. (Ephesians 6:19)

Some groups may have come prepared to share communion at this or an earlier point in the day.

You are welcome to stay and continue as the Lord leads, but also feel free to leave at Noon. We will leave the poles in place as possible.

Thank you for your help this day in honoring the Lord.

Reports of the Impact on the Participants and in the Heavenlies

If what occurred in the heavenlies was half as profound as what occurred in each of our lives that morning I know that a great shift took place. I in fact do believe that a great shift took place in the heavenlies as I continued to hear comments from people that were not even aware of what we did. I have heard about changes that happened in their lives and ministries in the following months and years. I will share a few of those stories as we continue on in this book, but first I want to share some of the email reports that came in the afternoon of the canopy from participants at some of the sites. These are exact copies of the emails, so I have not cleaned up the spelling and grammar, but I have removed the names of individuals mentioned.

Claremont East Gate

Most everyone arrived before 10, except one gal who got there at 10:15, so we had already introduced ourselves and were ready to start at 10. We began by assigning tasks as the Holy Spirit led...someone to read each Scripture, and then two to lead us in communion at the end. The entire first hour, as the Lord led, various individuals wrote Scripture on the pole. At 11, we erected it. Just before that, the Lord gave me this picture of this HUGE canopy suspended in the air, it was quite awesome! _____ and _____ taped the entire morning, as well as took some pictures at the end. The Lord gave one of the intercessors Is 61:1-4.

> The Spirit of the Lord GOD is upon me,
> Because the LORD has anointed me
> To bring good news to the afflicted;
> He has sent me to bind up the brokenhearted,
> To proclaim liberty to captives,
> And freedom to prisoners;
> 2 To proclaim the favorable year of the LORD,
> And the day of vengeance of our God;
> To comfort all who mourn,
> 3 To grant those who mourn in Zion,
> Giving them a garland instead of ashes,
> The oil of gladness instead of mourning,
> The mantle of praise instead of a spirit of fainting.
> So they will be called oaks of righteousness,

The planting of the LORD, that He may be glorified.
4 Then they will rebuild the ancient ruins,
They will raise up the former devastations,
And they will repair the ruined cities,
The desolations of many generations.

As she proclaimed it over LA County, I saw a huge mouth on the map of California...the mouth was LA County. I really felt like LA was to be a mouthpiece for the Lord. We followed the protocol you sent...it was a huge help...thanks! During the prayer time, some of the themes were confession, asking for His mercy upon the county. Over Claremont and then the rest of the county, we prayed regarding intellectualism, and asked the Lord to bring alignment...Spirit over the mind. We prayed for the schools, all the way up through the universities. The gal who is on staff at the Claremont Colleges repented for the sins and invited the Lord to visit the campus afresh. We prayed for a spirit of worship to descend upon the churches...the manifest presence of the Lord. We prayed for the generations, for healing and the diversity of His creation. We also asked that heaven would meet earth over LA County, that there would be a release of the miraculous. It was almost like heaven was being unzipped.

Before we started, one of the men saw a huge evil face and he wanted to bind it before we started. Hopefully this is Okay...but I asked him not to. I felt that this was a distraction from the enemy...trying to get us off task. I told him that by focusing on Jesus and inviting His presence...it would leave...it did.

Right before we took communion...a blimp passed before the sun...causing it to be dark and then light. I thought this was very prophetic. It also brought back the memory of a reoccurring dream that one of the intercessors has been having. It was of a group of people in a dark cave...each one holding a lit torch.

We ended by blessing the other groups and asking the Lord to seal His good work and praising Him for what He was doing...looking forward in excited anticipation...

What a wonderful day! :) -_____-

As another note of the results at this particular point, one of the persons there is an administrator at one of the Claremont Colleges. On Sunday, January 5, there was a very strong windstorm throughout Los Angeles County. (I will talk a bit more about this in the next chapter.) In Claremont and on the campus that this particular person worked at, this wind uprooted a tree near the entrance gate to the campus. Now this campus had been closed to Christianity but some changes were beginning to happen as a result of this person's ongoing presence there. When the administrator went to work on Monday morning, the tree that had fallen had caused the gatepost at the entrance of the campus to be lifted up and the gates swung open on their own accord. Immediately this person's first thoughts were Psalms 24:7-10.

> 7 Lift up your heads, O gates,
> And be lifted up, O ancient doors,
> That the King of glory may come in!
> 8 Who is the King of glory?
> The LORD strong and mighty,
> The LORD mighty in battle.
> 9 Lift up your heads, O gates,
> And lift them up, O ancient doors,
> That the King of glory may come in!
> 10 Who is this King of glory?
> The LORD of hosts,
> He is the King of glory.

Back to some of the other E-mails:

Hacienda Heights

> We were able to see Mt. Wilson and the entire East SG Valley from this hill.
>
> As we prayed, I felt a wonderful connection with the people there as well as other Christians praying in other locations that I could not see. The Latino man held up the tent pole like a sword and staked it in the ground. We ended by forming a circle around the pole holding hands thanking God for what He has accomplished through our prayers that day and prayed for protection for us and our family. -_____-

The group at Hacienda Heights went out to lunch together and then four of them went to pray over a house that the Lord had been putting on the heart of one of the men every time he drove by. This house is right in line with the apparent ley line that I drew on my map that goes from the Buddhist Temple to the center of San Jose and San Francisco. It also passes over the convergence point of a number of other lines in Pasadena.

Anyway, they go to this house. The front door is open and there is a car for sale in the front yard, so this group of four went up to the door. The man invites them in to what has been described to me as a museum of the occult and the cults, with pictures of every god (including Jesus) Skulls, weapons, demonic masks and all sorts of other objects. It turns out that this guy is a psychic healer who has a radio broadcast in San Francisco, which he broadcasts via phone hookup from the studio in his house there in Hacienda Heights. So now, we have physical evidence of this spiritual ley line, one of those divinely revealed when God gave me the thirteen locations for the canopy back in September.

Finally after they had been there talking with this guy for quite a while one of the team says, "look, you know we are all Christians as we have been talking openly with you, but there is one thing greatly troubling me. Some day you and I are going to stand before the judgment seat of Christ and I cannot in good conscience stand there unless I say clearly to you now that Jesus in the only hope for salvation and you are someday going to have to make a choice whether you believe that or not. But for me, I cannot leave here today without making known this fact and choice to you." Following this testimony, the man allowed the group to pray for him. He prophesied that one of them had a problem with their leg and offered to pray for that one, but they all declined indicating that none of them was aware of a problem with their leg. They left having opened relationship and with openness from the man for them to return at another time.

This divine encounter was a real revelation to us in understanding some of how these spiritual highways, "power" lines, or "phone" lines, that we have called ley lines, function. I had previously received teaching on this in Argentina during the 1990's, but now with the witness of the young former warlock from Santa Monica and this demonstration by the Lord in Hacienda Heights, I could relate more clearly to the information I had been told before. According to former practitioners of witchcraft and astral workings, one builds a pathway along these lines between gateways by getting permission to travel or use a segment from the demonic gatekeepers that are positioned at the various intersections or convergences of these ley lines. This man was using his psychic demon empowered abilities over this ley line to conduct business through the radio show in San Francisco using the physical path of the phone lines between the two locations along a spiritual ley line. It would be interesting to know if his same level of power was still functioning after the canopy we constructed over his house and a large portion of that ley line. It appears that his ability to discern on that day had dropped some, as there was no one in the group with a leg problem.

Puvugna Village Site, Cal State University Long Beach

Today's Canopy of Prayer and Praise was awesome! God's presence was strong today. I wish that we were still there! We started greeting each other and there was a tremendous sense of unity between all of us who were there. My Pastor prayed and blessed us, God's power fell and

I could barely stand! As my Pastor-Pastor _____ was praying, it was as though God, at the blast of His nostrils, just swept every unclean thing away. R_____ and the rest of us just flowed together as we read scriptures and worshipped the Lord.

There was a purity and holiness felt, and the atmosphere was very light and free. I believe that God did much damage to the enemy and we are victorious! Glory to God! I still feel His presence and that peace that all of us left with when it was said and done. We are totally blessed and excited Jesus is Lord over L.A County! –_____-

Wayfarer's Chapel, Palos Verdes

There were just three of us at the Wayfarer's chapel- _____, _____ and myself _____. We had a blessed time worshiping the Lord and writing scripture on our pole and each putting in a stake. Two interesting things for me that were confirming what were happening were visions or pictures the Lord had given me previously. One was that the Lord showed me lights going up to heaven that I believed were gateways to heaven that were around Los Angeles. When I saw the picture on the web site of the lights going up to heaven, it reminded me of this. Second, while I was in Kansas City during the Call, the Lord was showing me poles with cords or ribbons attached. I thought they were May Poles, but couldn't figure out why I was seeing them. When I saw the poles you had for us to erect, I knew this was from the Lord and what I had seen. I'm interested in how you came up with this idea and what you believe these poles represent. I felt like we were claiming the territory for the King of Kings and inviting Him to come reign on this earth and take the land that is His.

Followed the Suggested Protocol you sent. That was great. Erected the pole at 11:00, wrote scriptures on it, worshiped, etc. We also did communion. _____ took some pictures. We left there around 12:45. We left the pole standing. -_____ and _____ -

Malibu Lagoon

We had 14 people 13 that fully participated following the suggested directives and it was a sweet time. –_____-

Balboa Water Gate

D_____, her husband _____ and I met for prayer at Balboa. It was wonderful and the Lord said and did some unexpected things. We prayed Ezekiel 47 over the Valley and LA.

There was a clear word that came forth as we prayed at the Balboa Site.

Hebrews 4:9, "There remains therefore a rest for the people of God." Also Josh 21:43-45

43 So the LORD gave Israel all the land, which He had sworn to give to their fathers, and they possessed it and lived in it.

44 And the LORD gave them rest on every side, according to all that He had sworn to their fathers, and no one of all their enemies stood before them; the LORD gave all their enemies into their hand.

45 Not one of the good promises, which the LORD had made to the house of Israel failed; all came to pass.

The Lord distinctly said, "My people must learn to rest in Me. Lives are full of frenzy, hurriedness, impetuosity, and snap decisions. Yet, I am calling My people to rest in Me; to know My rest, to trust in Me in all things. Many things will occur in the natural that will be disconcerting and alarming, but those that rest in Me, will know My peace and My peace will abide in them. It is this "rest" that will draw those unto Me that do not know Me and they will meet Me and come to know the depth of My abiding peace. So, walk through your days in My rest (shalom: wellness, goodness, well-being, health, grace) and I will cause you to possess the petitions that you have brought before Me." (January 4, 11: 30 a.m.) –_____-

Frazier Park, North-West Gate and Focal Point of the Lines To The North

I was at Frazier Park with a Pastor _____ and his wife _____ from Ojai. We were just the three of us but also had a wonderful time of prayer and worship. We prophesied blessing over each of the other 12 groups and called for angels to join you. We called for the glory of the Lord to descend over Los Angeles County and shine through the darkness and blindness that the enemy has sought to hold many in. We called for salvation of all of those who have been held in the captivity of that darkness. Since we were at the focal point of the ley lines or pathways of communication, and commerce with the cities of the North, we prophesied the enlarging of the communication channels with God's spirit and the flow of the Lord's economy between the North and the South.

L_____ observed that three stakes at each of the 13 points represented the 39 blows that Christ received upon himself for our salvation. I observed that the enemy was in chaos trying to figure out what was going on today. I saw images running around trying to figure out which way to go and where to attack, as they were being hit from all sides and blinded by the light from above. We also prayed that the tent pegs set today over Los Angeles County would be stretched to the North, South, East and West, bringing the covering of the Lord's Kingdom over Ventura County, Kern, San Joaquin, San Bernardino, Riverside, Orange and San Diego Counties. We left the pole standing. –_____-

I was at this location. I can only describe what I was seeing in the spiritual realm as chaos. Initially as we set the pole in place I saw what looked like huge golden ropes about one foot in diameter go shooting out from each of the thirteen locations toward the center pole on Mount Wilson, then ropes connected each of the other points to one another. As this happened, I saw images of horses rearing and spinning, throwing their riders who had an absolute look of terror on their faces. It appeared that the riders were trying to get their horses under control and form an attack force against the points of worship, but they did not know which point to attack first and in the confusion were bumping into one another and falling from their horses. The sense I had was that the unity present at all thirteen locations surrounding them, was something that they had never experienced before.

I would learn a couple of days later, that all together there were seventy-six people spread over these thirteen locations. Among the seventy-six there were twenty-six different churches and ministries involved. For two hours on the morning of January 4, 2003, these seventy-six people representing 26 different churches and ministries came together in perfect unity for one purpose, to erect a canopy of prayer and praise over Los Angeles County and it was throwing the enemy, under that canopy of the Lord's presence, into utter chaos.

Here are a few more of the reports from that day:

Highway 14 and Ave A North of Lancaster

Canopy support #8 reporting in. We were three at the site instead of five but I have learned to expect some to be taken out before a happening. What a tremendous worship time we three had.

IN FAVOR OF THE SAINTS

We pretty much followed your protocol. I had prepared pages of praise verses from the Psalms and for the first half hour we recited those to the Lord along with other praises. We did read the scriptures suggested and erected our support pole with selected scriptures written on it.

We worshipped, praised and spoke the Word. We know that it is God's desire to save, heal, prosper and bless so that we may all live in his presence and peace. So, we asked for nothing except God's Kingdom come, God's will be done in all of Los Angeles County and the blessings to be spilled over to the surrounding areas. We had the most wonderful time of worship and thank you for inviting us to be a part of this canopy raising. I, in the spirit did see the canopy being raised to cover all of L.A. and saw that the darts of the enemy were being repelled by it. At 3 p.m. we had our normal prayer time at Lancaster and during that prayer, I saw the intercessors coming in under the canopy to minister prayer to the people of L.A. (Good cover, thanks.) -_____, ____ and ____-

Saddleback Butte Peak, Lake Los Angeles

Arrived 9:45 waited until 10:00 no one else showed up greeted one another and followed protocol and time for each step while hiking 1.6 miles to mountain top. Arrived mountain top at exactly 12:00 give or take 5 min. And on time with protocol as well. Thanks for everything, me and one partner experienced no warfare, except some personal minor afflictions with me, but really nothing. Awesome time worshiping speaking the word as well as scriptural reading by the word of God and anointing the mountain top with oil, being led prophetically by the spirit of the Lord over

A PROTECTIVE CANOPY IS RAISED

the North and South, East and West as well as seeing Him stand before us. Great time of prayer and blessing over one another anointing one another as well as the flags which were spread out around us on the rocky peak, also Anointing rocky peak in a circle like fashion as well as anointing LA county stamp on mountain, also survey seal embedded in rocks on peak. Also a divine appointment with one gentleman who resides in Lancaster, who's daughter and son-in law are Pastors in the area. He was led by the spirit to hike up to the peak. We personally felt that the spirit of the Lord led him to agree with us in the final prayer before leaving the mountain peak, at 3:30 pm to begin to hike down which was allot easier. HALLELUJAH!!!!!!!!!!!!!!!!!!!!! AMEN. In the physical on the way up at exactly 12:00, I heard drum beats thinking it was my heart because it was in sync with my heart rate, then I began to listen more closely and said to my prayer partner do you hear that drum beat coming from below the mountain valley, or is that my heart beat and she said yes I do hear something and we listened and then continued. The last hundred feet to top of peak, beat was gone. We listened to the beat for approx. 5 to 10 min. It was a steady beat. Going down hill after completing the task the spirit of the Lord quickened me to the Northeastern area in the valley, a rather large tall angel lowering and raising a sword. I asked, what is the angel doing Lord? Replied, he's speaking forth orders. Two warring angels in the North, approx. 10 min. later walking down the path discerned healing anointing type wave coming down the north coast into Santa Monica beach coast area. Also, a stirring around us as well, prayer partner witnesses to some of the discernment of angels stirring us. We continued to enjoy the rest of the day with the Lord and fellowshipping. Thank you for this opportunity to raise the Canopy of Praise Over LA County. –_____-

I met the man who covered this point with his prayer partner just the day before the canopy. I had not yet heard from anyone who had indicated a willingness to drive to this farthest away point and hike the 1.6 miles and a thousand feet climb in elevation to the top of this peak. I prayed and asked the Lord to bring someone who would be willing, as I did not think that I could make this hike myself. I had a serious accidental fall off a ladder six months prior and was not able to do much walking yet. On the day before the Canopy, a friend and I just happened to bump into this man and talk to him about the Canopy. He immediately asked if he could participate and asked where he should go. I told him that I still had this one point not covered, but that it was the farthest point and also involved hiking 1.6 miles up a thousand foot peak carrying the eight-foot pole. He said give him the directions and he would go. We met later that day and I gave him the pole with the cords, pegs, hammer and the directions. What a warrior, he and his prayer partner made the climb not only with the pole, but also took an assortment of praise flags and used them to dance and pray in worship on top of the mountain as the Lord led them.

Mount Wilson Center Pole of The Canopy

We were 8 praise participants at Mount Wilson. 3 men and 5 women. We found a perfect spot, a little further away from the main street, right under the highest communication tower on Mount Wilson.

The view was spectacular and we were able to see the Mountains just before Malibu, Santa Monica, Wayfarers Chapel at the Portuguese Bend, behind it we could even see the mountains of Catalina Island, we saw Long Beach, Hacienda Heights, the Claremont East gate. Right in front of us was Pasadena, Los Angeles

Downtown and Hollywood. Behind us, we knew about the groups of Saddleback Butte, Antelope Valley and Frazier Park. To our right we saw the vicinities of Balboa Watergate, Santa Susana pass and Westlake.

We blessed and anointed each other, put on the armor of God, worshiped, praised, read scripture and sang songs to the glory of the Lord. We wrote blessings and scriptures on the pole and then the three men anchored the pole in the earth, while the women covered them with songs and prayers and worship. Right at that time when we started to pound the pole into the ground, we saw in the direction of Wayfarers Chapel a very strong light that stayed for about 4, 5 minutes. We saw that as a wonderful sign from the Lord that His Light is prevailing over the darkness.

We continued to praise and about 15 minutes before 12:00 we started to receive the praise from each and every location and with our hands we collectively gathered all the praises from the other groups. We did not yet release the praise, but only received the praise and stored it. After we had received the praises of all 12 groups, we added our praises to it and about two or three minutes before 12, we released ALL PRAISES TOGETHER AT ONCE up into the heavens. It was a wonderful and powerful experience. One of the participants saw in the center of our circle strong currents and flashes of light being released. Another participant was feeling that the number of participants on Mount Wilson (8) was of significance, as 8 signifies a new beginning. We felt the peace of the Lord his acceptance of our prayers and His joy that His people love, worship and praise Him. He is certainly going to move on their behalf. Expect things to happen! God bless you. –_____ and _____-

A week and a half after the Canopy day, many of the people involved met as part of another event and we were able to report to all what had occurred. Everyone who participated felt that he/she personally had gained something in their spirit from being a part of this prophetic act, but more than that, it illustrated to many for the first time in their life, the concept that they could somehow cause change in the spiritual dominion over a territory. It increased their faith, opened their eyes and helped to deliver them from the feelings of helplessness to be able to cause any change in the spiritual climate over their churches, neighborhoods, and cities.

Shortly after this event, I was asked to go help a team in Washington, D.C. put on a Canopy event. However, after talking with those involved, it appeared that this was not something that God had specifically asked them to do, it was just a copycat event because they saw how powerful what we had done was. I declined their invitation, as I explained to them that we cannot just go out and copy what has been effective in one area, and apply it to another area. We must see what Jesus is doing and come into agreement with that. That is not to say that this type of canopy should not be done in other locations. It is to say as I have emphasized over and over, it should only be done in response to clear direction from the Lord when, how and from what locations. I personally have been led to do several smaller canopy prophetic acts, one of which I will cover in a later chapter. I am also aware of several occasions where a canopy such as this has also been lifted over a whole nation.

Continuing to Enthrone the Lord on the Praises of His People

Even as I am writing this in January of 2006, there is a Canopy being done in the United Kingdom for England, Wales, and Israel. The format is a little different from what I have described here, because they are following what the Lord has revealed to them as they create a canopy of the Lords presence over these three countries through worship and prayer. The important point I want to make here about the concept of a Canopy of Prayer and Praise is, that its general purpose is to change the spiritual dominion over a location. It is to remove the dominion of Satan as having the primary influence and authority over an area.

Through our prayer and worship, carrying out the office of priests to our God[1], we are bringing the habitation or presence of God, enthroned on the praises[2] and placing the area in subjection to the Lord[3]. In this way we, who have been made to be a kingdom and priests to our God, are reigning on the earth. We are having widespread influence and prevailing on the earth. [4] Even though Hebrews Chapter Two tells us that all things have been made subject to Him, verse 8 tells us, "But now we do not yet see all things subjected to him." Why do we not yet see all things subjected to Him? Because we who have been made to be a kingdom and priests to our God have not yet used the keys to the Kingdom[5] to enter into all of the realm, to take possession and to occupy till I come.[6] The word "occupy" in the King James Version is translated in other versions as "conduct trade" or "do business" and comes from the parable of the "ten minas," which were given to servants to conduct business with until the master returned.

We must see that it is our responsibility on this earth to be about "doing business," taking possession of the Kingdom with the resources and keys that have been given to us. In later chapters we will see how absolutely essential it is for us to be about this business of taking possession of the Kingdom. Only when we do so, will the wearing down of the saints, the overwhelming of the saints, and the overpowering of the saints described in Daniel Chapter 7 be brought to a halt as the Ancient of Days comes and passes judgment "In Favor of the Saints."

In the next chapter, I will continue with how I believe this particular Canopy of Prayer and Praise brought about a covering and protection over Los Angeles County in 2003. How it demonstrated the Ancient of Days ruling in favor of the saints, over events prophesied and actual. I will also talk about the biggest fear that keeps some from doing acts to take possession of the Kingdom. That is the fear of "retaliation" from the enemy.

Endnotes

1. Revelation 5:10, and Numbers 16:46-48
2. Psalms 22:3
3. Hebrews 2:8
4. Revelation 5:10
5. Mathew 16:19
6. Luke 19:13 (KJV)

CHAPTER 15

RETALIATION? OR EVIDENCE OF VICTORY?

For years, I had heard discussions and teachings on issues surrounding spiritual warfare that always carried cautions of or fears about retaliation from the enemy. Many people, through fear, have not prepared for or entered into an offensive state of spiritual warfare out of fear of what the enemy might do to them or to others around them if they did. As a result, they have taken a very passive role in their Christian walk. They do not want to rock the boat or cause any waves in the society around them. They don't want to do anything that might cause the demonic realm to consider them a threat to the dominion of Satan over their city, and even over their family. They are kind of just hiding out in a very quiet personal form of religion to get through this life and into heaven without the demonic realm noticing them.

Others have used terms such as horizontal warfare versus vertical warfare and have emphatically stated their refusal to be involved if we were doing vertical warfare. They would state that we have authority to deal with demonic oppression of individuals and ourselves on a horizontal level. However, to deal with principalities over regions and cities was vertical warfare and that was work only for Jesus. I actually would go one-step further. I would see both what they define as horizontal and vertical warfare as work only for Jesus and His power. Nevertheless, we are his agents here on earth to direct the weapons of warfare. I personally do not see the distinction between horizontal and vertical warfare. In the physical battle zone of war, you aim your weapons in whatever direction the enemy is attacking. On the other hand, if you are the one attacking, you still aim them in the direction of the enemy. It is more important to understand what our weapons are and how to use them. A knife or bayonet might be sufficient for hand-to-hand combat, but you might need some big guns or missiles for the bombers at 20,000ft. So too in spiritual warfare on any level it is very important to understand that we just aim the weapons in the direction our commander Jesus directs us and we pull the trigger. It is the divine power (Greek "dunatos," from the root dunamai from which we derive the word dynamite) or powder, as I called it in an earlier chapter, which propels the ammunition in our weapons to cause destruction of the enemy and his fortresses.[1]

I have heard others argue against engaging in any form of "spiritual warfare" because they deny it exists or proclaim that, "Jesus has already won the battle so we should just be rejoicing in the victory, the war is over." Some of these same people just accept the destruction of their marriages, finances, their family's lives and their health as identifying with the sufferings of Christ. Or else they become bitter and start blaming luck or God for their misfortunes.

Understanding the Issues

That brings us back to the basic unbelief and lack of understanding of the Bible and of God that is prevalent throughout this country and much of the "civilized" world. It is also a lack of understanding that the nature of a Kingdom is not just a place, but is instead an authority structure, a domain, or sphere of influence, where the king's authority is dominant.

I also find that few understand and distinguish between the Kingdom and authority of the Christ, and the Kingdom of the Father. It is the Kingdom of the Father to which all the Kingdoms (authority and power structures) of this world, when they have been brought into subjection to the Christ, will be delivered.

Then comes the end, when He (*Jesus*)* delivers up the kingdom to the God and Father, when He (*Jesus*)* has abolished all rule and all authority and power. For He (*Jesus*)* must reign until He (*Jesus*)* has put all His (*Jesus*)* enemies under His (*Jesus*)* feet. The last enemy that will be abolished is death. For He (*The Father*)* has put all things in subjection under His (*Jesus*)* feet. But when He (*The Father*)* says, "All things are put in subjection," it is evident that He (*The Father*)* is excepted who put all things in subjection to Him (*Jesus*)*. And when all things are subjected to Him (*Jesus*)*, then the Son Himself also will be subjected to the One (*The Father*)* who subjected all things to Him (*Jesus*)*, that God may be all in all.[2] **My Insertions*.

Bringing this World into Subjection to Jesus

It is my firm belief, based upon scripture and upon experience, that in this day we are part of the process of bringing all things in this world into subjection to Jesus. This is not just an evangelism process of bringing people into relationship to Jesus. It also involves the warfare of reclaiming this world from the authority or dominion of Satan and bringing it back under the authority of God. This involves various acts of prayer, worship, reconciliation, healing, prophetic acts and deliverance over peoples, over lands and regions. These are acts done in faith, believing that they will have effect, because the Lord has revealed or disclosed them to us as acts that will change the dominion or authority structure over the people or place where we are being obedient to do them.

Act of Righteousness

These acts are acts of righteousness, because they are actions to fulfill a covenant we have with God over this world. The word righteousness in the Hebrew has to do with a covenant or contract between two people.

Righteousness is one party fulfilling their obligation to the covenant whether or not the other party does so. When God made a covenant with Abram in Genesis 15, God counted or accounted Abram's act of faith to believe Him as righteousness or Abram's part in fulfilling the covenant.

So too when we believe and act in faith to do what God has shown or asked us to do, it becomes an "act of righteousness." We, through our "acts of righteousness" which we can only do through faith, believing what is disclosed to us through the holy spirit and acting on it, are creating a garment of fine linen, "bright and clean" as a covering for the bride.[3] The bride is clearly defined in Revelation as the: "holy city, Jerusalem, coming down out of heaven from God, having the glory of God."[4] And as, "the holy city, new Jerusalem, coming down out of heaven from God, made ready as a bride adorned for her husband."[5]

Come I Will Show you the Bride

The word Jerusalem is a composite of "Jeru," which means founding or establishing and "salem" a form of the word "shalom," which means, "destroys the authority that establishes or builds chaos." New Jerusalem could be defined as the "new founding of an authority that is without chaos," bringing things back to the way they were, "in the beginning." If the fine white linen, the garment or outer covering of the bride, is the "righteous acts of the saints," this would mean that the things that the saints do in faith, believing in Christ, are the adornment or what gives beauty and honor to the authority structure that comes down out of heaven from God. The bride was betrothed to Jesus when He declared, "All authority has been given to Me in heaven and on earth."[6] The "marriage supper" occurs in Revelation when the bride (New Jerusalem) has clothed herself completely with the righteous acts of the saints and "The kingdom of the world has become the Kingdom of our Lord, and of His Christ; and He will reign forever and ever."[7] Note I said Kingdom and not Kingdoms. The Greek word used here is singular which is in agreement with the usage in Revelation 1:6 and 5:10 when the text says "and thou hast made them to be a kingdom." As they "reign" (have widespread influence, prevail) upon the earth, they are taking possession of the Kingdom, bringing all things (dominions, authority structures, powers) into subjection to the authority of the Christ such that the "kingdom" of this world becomes the Kingdom of our Lord and of His Christ.

Taking Possession of the Kingdom

What are the saints doing? I believe the righteous acts that we are to be about, through faith and in the righteousness of Jesus consist of the bringing of everything into subjection to the authority, the dominion, the Kingdom of Jesus. He is disclosing those things to us through the Holy Spirit and we are acting in faith to do and say the things He discloses.

Remember that Jesus went about preaching the "gospel (good news) of the Kingdom" (Look it up yourself!). Personal salvation alone is not the gospel that Jesus was preaching. We, as Paul was instructed in Acts 26:18, have to be using some Kingdom power to get people out of the dominion of Satan to God, "so that" they have the opportunity to repent and have an inheritance among those being sanctified by faith in Jesus. We are doing this when we are bringing the Kingdom (the authority of Jesus' dominion) near and through the power of the Kingdom are opening people's eyes, bringing them out of the darkness into the light, out of the dominion of Satan, to God. We are taking possession of the Kingdom, which we have been made to be.

The process of doing so is warfare. We have to displace squatters, who are operating under a different authority, by using the weapons of our warfare and the authority of the Kingdom. We are causing and enforcing "Thy Kingdom come, Thy will be done, on earth as it is in heaven."[8] We are binding here on earth what has already been bound in heaven and loosing here on earth what has already been loosed in heaven.[9] But this is warfare and it can be a violent process. It can be violent worship, violent prayer, using the weapons of our warfare, which are divinely powerful for the destruction of fortresses.[10] The enemy is likely to fight back, but if we are in Christ, the enemy cannot prevail.

An Isolationist Stance Only Enables the Enemy

In World War II, the United States took an "isolationist" stance as Germany was over-running all of Europe and a good part of Russia. The United Kingdom was suffering greatly also from the bombing raids and on the verge of collapse. In Asia, Japan was invading China and much of Asia. The United States was selling food and war supplies to England, but the Germans were sinking many of the ships carrying the supplies. It was not until Japan attacked Pearl Harbor, destroying much of our naval forces, that the U.S. was finally provoked enough and jumped into the war. If we had waited much longer, England would have been destroyed and would not have been available as a necessary staging and jump off point for the forces that finally invaded German controlled Europe and defeated Germany. Isolationism does not keep the enemy from taking territory and enforcing his dominion. It does not prevent destruction and death, let alone establish and expand righteous dominion.

Surrender to the enemy does not prevent destruction and death either. Belgium surrendered to Germany knowing they did not have the forces to defend and protect their country. They thought by surrendering they would escape the destruction going on all over Europe. They were wrong! The Germans bombed and destroyed their cities anyway. Surrender did not enable the Jews to escape the holocaust.

We cannot hide from warfare in fear. We cannot just deal with some parts of it and not others. We cannot just deny it exists and rejoice in the victory. The battle is not over yet.

Yes the Victory is Determined but the Battle is Not Over

If the battle was over when Jesus arose from the grave and Satan no longer carried any ability to have authority in this world, why would Jesus have appeared to Paul after His resurrection and ascension, to instruct Paul to open people's eyes so that they would turn from "The dominion of Satan to God?"[11]

RETALIATION? OR EVIDENCE OF VICTORY?

If the battle were over when Jesus arose from the grave, why would Paul have found it necessary to give the following instruction?

"Put on the full armor of God, that you may be able to stand firm against the schemes of the devil. For our struggle is not against flesh and blood, but against the rulers, against the powers, against the world forces of this darkness, against the spiritual forces of wickedness in the heavenly places. Therefore, take up the full armor of God that you may be able to resist in the evil day, and having done everything, to stand firm."[12]

If the battle is over, and we are no longer facing spiritual warfare, where is the event in scripture or history that states this is accomplished fact? After the resurrection of Jesus, the instruction of scripture written during the approximately one hundred years following the resurrection teaches how to stand in the midst of this evil day and overcome Satan's dominion.

We find that scripture warns, on the occasion of what I believe is the ascension of Jesus into heaven in Revelation 12, "Woe to the earth and the sea, because the devil has come down to you, having great wrath, knowing that he has only a short time."[13] Why would it be necessary for the "they" in Revelation 12:11 to "overcome" if there was nothing left to overcome? "They" are no longer under the bondage and slavery to the fear of physical death[14] because of the inheritance of eternal spiritual life among those being sanctified by faith in Jesus[15]. Therefore, "they" are also able to "overcome" the wrath of the one who for a short time has been thrown down to the earth, by the fact that they do not love their (physical) lives even unto (physical) death. The evidence around us still strongly indicates the continuing presence of evil and great degree of authority by Satan in the world today. If Satan no longer has any influence in this world why would John have written, "We know that we are of God, and the whole world lies in the power of the evil one."[16]

What would be the purpose of Jesus giving the "keys to the Kingdom," to bind and loose if there were nothing for us to bind or loose here on earth that has already been bound and loosed in heaven?

IN FAVOR OF THE SAINTS

Satan the Usurper of Authority

All this to say, we are in the process of taking possession of the Kingdom that we have been made to be and there will be battles or warfare involved in doing so. We are taking back authority over parts of this world that Satan has no right to, but over which he has gained some measure of authority or dominion. This happens either because he or his demons have usurped the authority of men and women in this world who have not known of the true God or of the kingdom available to them. Or it is because humans of this world have yielded their authority and worship to Satan and the "gods of this world." I will illustrate this point further in the final chapters of this book.

Evicting the Squatter

Let me illustrate this whole taking possession of the Kingdom in another way. You have been given a house by someone, a title document has been issued in your name, and you have been given the keys to the doors of the house. Now you just put those keys in the drawer with the title document and sit back saying, "I own that house over on such and such street." Some months later you drive by that location and you notice that there are squatters living in the house you own! What's the problem here?

Well the problem is, even though you have the keys and you have the title, you have never used the keys to open the door, walk in, take possession of the house and occupied it! So, a squatter has moved into the unoccupied house. They don't own it, they don't have the title, they do not even have the keys, they entered through a back way, but they have possession of it, are occupying it and have usurped your authority over the house!

Now you will need to enforce your ownership and call upon the authority of the government that gave you ownership legally, to evict, perhaps even bind in handcuffs, and to remove the squatters from the house that you own. You have to take the key you have been given, which opens the front door, and "loose" the authority of the government into your house to bind and evict the trespassers. You have in the process, used the key of binding to subject the squatters to higher authority in order to remove them so that you may exercise your right to ownership and possession of the house. You have done this through calling on the same government authority that recorded your title. You have called upon them to enforce your ownership and possession of the house. You have now used your keys to open the door to the house and set foot inside. You have taken possession of the house. However, it is not enough to have just set foot inside and then to have turned around and left. You must occupy the house so that the squatters do not return.

Now we must also understand that we might not have been able to get the squatter out of our house by going over there on our own and politely asking, "Mr. Squatter, will you please take your belongings and your trash you have scattered all over my house and leave. And on your way out will you please fix that window you broke getting in?" More than likely, this lawless one would laugh at us and then beat us up or take out a gun and shoot us. In and of ourselves we likely do not have the power and authority to enforce our ownership, even though we might have the ownership title paper and show it to the squatter. Instead, we invoked the proper enforcement authority to come with the weapons and power to enforce the law and our right of ownership. In the name of and through the power of lawful authority the squatter is evicted.

In or By There is a Difference

The seven Jewish exorcists of Acts learned this lesson the hard way when they attempted to cast out a demon saying, "I adjure you by Jesus whom Paul preaches." The demon replied, "I recognize Jesus, and I know about Paul, but who are you?" "And the man, in whom was the evil spirit, leaped on them and subdued all of them and overpowered them, so that they fled out of that house naked and wounded."[17]

In the early 1970's, while I was in seminary, the original movie "The Exorcist" came out into the theaters. I was doing some study on the concept of exorcism in scripture and came across a subtle distinction between the failure of these exorcists in Acts 19 and the successes of Jesus, his disciples and others in casting out demons. The significant difference I found in the texts was the use of a simple preposition in the Greek New Testament that could be translated either "by" or "in" depending upon the context of the passage. The Jewish exorcists were calling upon a power and authority, which was twice removed from them. They were commanding the spirit to come out "by" the name of Jesus, but not a Jesus whom they knew, but Jesus "whom Paul preaches." On the other hand, the disciples cast out "in" the name of Jesus. As Jesus, who just about anybody agrees had authority over demons, was in them and they were in Him. They were simply exercising the authority of the Christ who was in them.

With the squatter, I show him a piece of paper and tell him to get out by the authority behind the piece of paper and he just rips up the piece of paper and beats me up. However, when I show up at the house in and surrounded by the enforcement authority of the government, the squatter will have to respond to that authority either by fleeing, submitting or being subdued by it.

Failure to Believe God

The "Promised Land" given to the nation of Israel by God did not come into their possession and they did not occupy it until more than five hundred years after it was promised to them. Even after God, acting through Moses to deliver the nation out of the slavery and bondage of Egypt, took them to the threshold or entry point of the Promised Land, they balked and refused to enter into the land and take possession. They sent spies into the land. The spies reported that it was beautiful and fruitful. They also reported that there were giants in possession of and occupying the land. The nation was afraid of these giants and refused to believe that God would enable them to take possession of it. They were afraid to engage in the warfare to take possession and change the dominion over the land from the dominion of the giants to the dominion of God. As a result, God sent them back into the wilderness for forty years until all of that generation, who had not believed God and had been unwilling to take possession of the land, were dead. The only two men who had believed God and had been willing to fight for the land, Joshua and Caleb, are now freed from that unbelieving generation and lead the next generation of Israelites in taking possession of the Land. Even Moses, who had led the people out of slavery and to the land, was not allowed to live and enter into that promised possession, because he failed in leading the people past their unbelief.[18]

Don't Give In to Bullies

So, also in this day people of every tribe and tongue, people and nation, have the promise of having been made to be a kingdom, but they have not known that they could actually take possession of it now, or they are afraid to do so because it involves warfare. I know people in this day who would rather just give up something that is rightfully theirs, then go through the battle, possible pain and wounding, to fight to take possession. I know because I have been one of those people. We are not just talking about personal possessions. We are talking about the authority structure or dominion over our families, our community, our nation and this entire world. We are talking about bringing the dominions, the authority structures of this world into subjection to the Kingdom of the Christ.

There's a Job for Everyone in this Army

Before I go on in this chapter, I want to clarify something. You may be reading this right now and feeling like, "this is all fine for you Don; it is obvious that you were called to be a front line warrior doing hand to hand combat with the enemy, but I am just not made that way." Ok, you are right, you may not be made that way and prepared jump out of a trench and run across the no man's land into the face of the enemy. But it takes a lot of people doing a lot of different jobs in an army for that army to fight a war. Some will never be out there on the front line with a rifle in one hand and a hand grenade in the other, but they will have a pen in one hand and a purchase order in the other to get the ammunition out there to the front line. Others might be manning the artillery located miles from the front, but accurately aiming their guns and missiles at the enemy's defenses to batter them down. Different roles, different responsibilities, but they are all in the same army fighting the same war.

What if the guy with the purchase order were to hear somewhere that the war was already over so he just put away his pen and stopped ordering ammunition and sending it to the front lines? What if the artillery commander was to say, "I don't see any enemy, so stop wasting this ammunition and let's go get some dinner and relax?" The body of Christ is the same way, there are many parts and many gifts, and they all have their individual roles and responsibilities in this war. Nevertheless, if they do not know there is a war, think that it is over, or refuse to do their part, the front lines will be over run, and all of us will suffer the consequences.

Having Widespread Influence and Prevailing

Being in the Kingdom involves an element of personal salvation and the inheritance of eternal life that takes place through personal repentance of our sin (which is rebellion toward the authority of God over our lives). However, it is also a much bigger issue than just the personal one. We were told in Revelation 5:10 that not only have we been made to be a kingdom, and priests to our God, but that, "they shall reign in the world." Remember "reign" can also be translated as having widespread influence or prevalent in the world.

Right now, as I look around the world, I do not see this to be the case. I see every foul dominion of murder, theft, terror, immorality and greed as having widespread influence and being prevalent (prevailing) in the world. I see many of those, who have been led out of the slavery and bondage of the fear of death, refusing to believe God or unaware that they must take possession of the Kingdom in this world. They are just huddled in small camps singing victory songs and complaining about the giants all around them. They are afraid to put on their armor, form a group of warriors, and engage the enemy. Instead, every time they step outside of the camp, bolstered by the once a week victory and pep rally, they get battered and wounded by the ones with dominion over and having possession of, all of the area outside of the protective circle of the camp. The next week, they somehow manage to limp back into the camp to have their wounds dressed and get pumped up to step back out the door.

This is not the way it is supposed to be. This is not the way it has to be. When we refuse to engage in battle against the rulers, against the powers, against the world forces of this darkness, and against the spiritual forces of wickedness in the heavenly places, it does not stop the war. It does not prevent us from being wounded, and it does nothing to remove these squatters from the Kingdom promised to us. It does not matter if you want to engage in spiritual warfare or not. The war is going on and either you are going to be killed, taken prisoner, or you must take up your weapons and fight.

You've Been Drafted into the Army

This last weekend, on Memorial Day, my wife and I watched an old black and white movie on TV. It was the story of Sergeant York, a Medal of Honor recipient and one of the most highly decorated soldiers of World War I. This man Alvin York grew up in the back hills of Tennessee, a simple farmer working a rocky piece of land. York was a drunkard and fighter through his early years until he falls in love with a woman and wants to buy a better piece of land so that he can marry this woman. He works very hard day and night to pay for the land only to be cheated out of part of what he had already paid and the land sold to another. He determines to kill the man that cheated him, but on the way to kill him, his mule is struck by lightning and as a result of a previous conversation with the local pastor, he gives his life to Christ that night. The fighting and drunkenness are gone. Alvin becomes a model Christian and a pacifist.

A very short time later, the United States enters WWI and the Draft is instituted, requiring all men to register for the Draft. At the encouragement of his pastor, Alvin complies with the law and registers for the draft, but with the assistance of the pastor applies for a conscientious objector exemption. The exemption is rejected. Alvin ends up in the Army. Because of his skill in hunting game, and teaching his fellow soldiers how to shoot and hunt, he is promoted to Corporal but is still not sure about killing men in war. Ultimately, on the battlefield he leads his small squad in capturing a German emplacement and taking prisoners. Then some other entrenched German soldiers in that location start to open fire and have his squad and the prisoners pinned down. York crawls through enemy fire to a point where he is able to use his excellent marksmanship to start picking off the German Soldiers one by one until over one hundred of them throw up their hands and surrender.

His commanding officer during a debrief about what happened asks him how many Germans he killed, he says he does not know, but he knew that if he did not kill the soldiers that were shooting at them, a lot more people would have died. His commanding officer questions, "So you killed not out of anger or to just kill the enemy, but to save lives?"

Sergeant York came to the realization that even though he did not believe in war and did not want to participate, it was necessary to stand up to the enemy to protect freedom and save lives because the war was real whether he wanted to participate or not.

When your eyes were opened, you saw the light of Christ, and you chose to come out of the darkness into the light. You were also rescued from the dominion of Satan, and entered into the King's domain. At that moment, whether you realized it or not, you became part of the army of the Kingdom of God. Satan's army is out to kill you and deprive you of any opportunity of expanding the dominion of your king.

Satan can no longer separate you from God for all eternity as he could when he held you in the bondage of fear of death under his dominion, but he can wound you making you an ineffective soldier. He can intimidate you with images of how big his giants are so that you will not engage in battle to take possession of the "promised land." He can cause so much noise and distraction, that you cannot hear the marching orders of your commander. He can dishonor God in your eyes, and cause you to be fearful of God, so that you, just like the people of Israel are afraid to approach and listen to God on your own.[19] He can also trick you into losing your physical life through taking foolish actions, which God did not instruct you to take.

If you are going to end up on the front lines of the warfare whether you choose to or not, would you rather be there with effective battle armor and powerful weapons and the training, leadership and communications to do some damage to the enemies camp, tear down his walls and repossess the Kingdom? Or, will you just stand there with your armor and weapons back home in the closet as you are being shot to pieces and run over.

The Issue of Retaliation

When it comes down to the issue of "retaliation," I would rather take a chance on a few sniper bullets coming at me from a retreating army which I expect and prepare for, then be in the midst of a constant barrage of bullets, missiles, hand grenades and suicide bombers that I haven't got a clue what to do about or why it is coming at me.

When I obeyed the Lord to lead the raising of a Canopy of Prayer and Praise over Los Angeles County, I experienced what I believe to be eighteen separate retaliatory attacks over the period of the week before and the week after January 4, 2003. I had to laugh at how obvious some of these were. They were serious and took time to deal with, but every one of them was able to be handled through prayer and then doing what it took in the physical realm to deal with the physical aspects of the attack.

As an example, I was struggling financially at the time, and two days before the Canopy, I received a $1500 electric bill for my business.

My normal bill was about $200. After praying, I called the electric company the following Monday, they said, "That does not sound right, do not pay the bill until we get back to you." They called back in a few days and apologized for having misread my meter not only for that month, but also for the two previous months. They said they would send me a new bill for $0.87. A bill of fifteen hundred dollars corrected to just eighty-seven cents!

The same thing happened with a bill from my Internet provider. The bill received the day before the Canopy was for over $900. I had just had a new high-speed service put in, but because of rebates and introductory offers, it was not supposed to cost me anything. It took prayer and four hours of being on hold on the phone to get that one straightened out, but it did not prevail! There were other attacks that were more personal in nature and even a physical attack on my throat, but all of these things the Lord prepared me for and led me through overcoming.

I have found that if we are closely listening to the Lord, we only do what He shows us and He tells us to do when it comes to offensive warfare, and if we obey Him exactly, we will be able to handle the enemies retreating pot shots. I have found in recent years that many times now the enemy does not even bother to try retaliation, because he knows that it will only bring more fire down on him.

One of the things that happened the day after the Canopy, I thought was retaliation. It actually turned out to be the destruction of an enemy stronghold that he could no longer hold. Let me tell you that story, as it is quite interesting.

Is This Retaliation

Sunday, January 5, 2003 a very strong wind came up at about noon Pacific Coast Time. The wind became stronger and stronger all afternoon and evening. It started causing some damage around the county. Late Sunday night, the wind caused a whole string of very large power poles to fall down in the city of Arcadia, California. This city of about fifty thousand people is right next to the city of Pasadena. My

RETALIATION? OR EVIDENCE OF VICTORY?

video studio was on Live Oak Avenue, having an Arcadia address, but actually outside the city, about a half block from the Eastern city line.

The power poles were not little ones, but the type that has three different levels of power lines with the top ones being in the tens of thousands of volts. The wind blew the first pole down at the Western city limit of Arcadia. Then in sequence, each pole from that one along Live Oak Avenue all the way to the Eastern city limit came down. Twenty-nine poles in all came down. The interesting thing is that they all fell across the roadway, and did not damage a single building, a car, or any persons. A few trees were broken, and several street signals were damaged, but that is all.

Of course, since these poles carried a major link in the electrical grid of the area, power was knocked out for almost a week as the poles were replaced. This had a direct impact on my business, as I was in the middle of some production work and had to buy a generator to complete some of it. As I looked down the street and saw how these poles had fallen in a line across the city to a point within a half a block of my shop I thought this was retaliation toward me.

Several nights later, I was doing some research for a friend that involved going back and looking over Jack Parsons' diary of the Babalon Working. Only at that moment did I realize that he started the "Babalon Working" ritual at noon on January 4, 1946. We had completed the Canopy of Prayer and Praise over the County at noon on January 4, 2003, exactly fifty-eight years to the minute later. (I probably could make something of the number fifty-eight, but I will leave that to some of you other prophets out there) This was also exactly one year after the Lord had started showing me the issues in Pasadena that were associated with Babalon. Now here is something even more interesting. Parsons' diary continues January 5, 1946. He describes a violent and destructive wind that comes up at noon on that day, and causes a lot of destruction throughout the County. "January 6, 1946, the strong wind continued but more erratic and dying down by the following morning." This was identical to the weather in January 5-6, 2003. I would observe in the next several weeks a lot of activity on the Internet that seemed to indicate that someone or some group was trying to repeat the ritual that Parsons' and Hubbard had conducted in 1946.

At this point, I was sure that this was retaliation, but that we had probably been prompted by the Lord to choose that particular date for the Canopy of prayer and praise to change the spiritual covering over the County and thereby weaken the ability of the ritual to be successfully completed in 2003. I don't have any proof of that, but other events that would happen over the next year definitely showed the protective nature of this canopy over the County.

A Different View of What Happened

That is not the end of the story. On Wednesday of that week, I was talking with a friend. She and her husband pastor a church just a block South in the middle of the stretch where the twenty-nine power poles fell. I was telling her how I thought that the poles falling was an act of retaliation following the Canopy. She stopped me and said, "Oh no, that is not what was happening, let me tell you what the Lord told me." "In October 2002, I had gone to bed early one Sunday night. The Lord woke me up at about 10p.m. and showed me that there was a "power line," a demonic structure along Live Oak Avenue. This demonic barrier had been a hindrance for years between the Christians living in the part of the city to the North of the line and those living on the South side of the line. This created disunity between the churches of the city." She then said, "On this past Sunday night, I had again gone to bed early and again the Lord woke me up at around 10p.m. and said, 'The power line is coming down'." "I prayed for a little while and pondered what had been said then went back to sleep." "Just a couple of hours later, twenty-nine power poles supporting a major power line along Live Oak Avenue came down. The line and poles came down only inside the city limits of the city, but every pole between the East and West city limits came down." She said, "This was not retaliation by the enemy, it was just God doing a little house cleaning under the Canopy you erected."

Whew, that was a lot to take in. Nevertheless, it made me start looking at some of the things around me a little different. I have come to see that this battle is not just about my possessions, my salvation, and me, but is about issues much bigger than even the loss of individual lives. I have now come to see that some of the things that I once would have classified as retaliation by the enemy for the spiritual warfare I was doing, were in fact just desperate acts by a retreating enemy or evidence of the victory won in the battle.

Endnotes

1. 2 Corinthians 10:4
2. 1 Corinthians 15:24-28
3. Revelation 19:8
4. Revelation 21:9-10
5. Revelation 21:2
6. Mathew 28:18-19
7. Revelation 11:15
8. Matthew 6:10, Luke 11:2
9. Matthew 16:19, 18:18 The Greek grammar of this verse tells us that whatever we bind here on earth is only coming into agreement with what has already been bound in heaven.
10. 2 Corinthians 10:4
11. Acts 26:18
12. Ephesians 6:11-13
13. Revelation 12:12
14. Hebrews 2:15
15. Acts 26:18
16. 1 John 5:19
17. Acts 19:13
18. God's stated reason that Moses would not enter into the promised land is found in: Deut 32:51-52 "because you broke faith with Me in the midst of the sons of Israel at the waters of Meribah-kadesh, in the wilderness of Zin, because you did not treat Me as holy in the midst of the sons of Israel. For you shall see the land at a distance, but you shall not go there, into the land which I am giving the sons of Israel." The incident over the giants in the land was not the first failure of Moses to demonstrate his faith in God and exercise his leadership to lead the people out of their unbelief.
19. Exodus 20:19

CHAPTER 16

SIZING UP A SPIRITUAL PROBLEM

During the summer of 2001, a friend and fellow warrior took me out to Venice Beach, California, on the first Sunday in August. This was the day of the annual Krishna Festival in Venice Beach. This had been a tradition in Venice Beach for over twenty years. The Festival would start with a parade of four huge hand-drawn oxcarts having four story high silk temples on them and drawn by Krishna Monks. The parade traditionally started at the Santa Monica pier (the Western end of Route 66) and followed the concrete boardwalk at the edge of the sand about two miles to the center pavilion of Venice Beach. Then a day long Festival of music, drama, teaching about lord Krishna, and free food would take place, centered in and around, the Pavilion area in the Center of the Venice Beach Boardwalk. I waded through the crowds that had swelled some from the forty-to-sixty thousand people, that normally came out to the boardwalk on a sunny Southern California Sunday Afternoon. I looked around me and saw the free food booths, which were all clearly labeled with the statement, "This Food Offered to the Lord" (*Krishna*) and then the name of the family or organization that was handing out the food offered to the idols associated with Krishna. I was saddened as I watched the devotion and intensity of support for this false religion based around a man who was being contrasted as more holy that Christ. Then there were the Idols in a number of locations.

Mocking Christianity

However, what really got to me was listening to and watching a drama, being performed on the main stage, which was a direct mockery of Christianity. A preacher man dressed all in black was working a pair of young people into a frenzy of stereotypic Pentecostalism and saying, "do you want to be filled with the Holy Ghost?" Finally, the preacher lays hands on them and they both fall dead (slain in the spirit) to the floor. The preacher turns to the crowd and walks away brushing his hands and saying, "There now, I killed their spirit!" I was incensed and determined that if even a hand full of spirit filled Christians had been in that place surrounding the stage with the presence of the true Lord, this mockery and ridiculing spirit would not have been able to sway such a large crowd.

During the fall, winter and spring of 2001-2002, the Lord was working on other things in my life and I did not think much more about that experience until the following summer. When the first weekend in August rolled around in 2002, again my friend invited me out to help him capture some video footage. At one point, he and I were standing in the midst of a tightly squeezed crowd of several thousand in front of the main stage. The speaker on the platform sounded like he was introducing some famous corporate executive or celebrity who was about to receive a life achievement award. He went on and on building up to a crescendo where he said something like, "And this person who I am talking about is none other than the LORD..." I couldn't stand it anymore, much to the horror of my friend standing next to me, I shouted out at the top of my lungs, "JESUS CHRIST." My friend quickly looked around and grabbed my arm as though getting ready to make a run for our lives before the crowd would turn in anger on us.

We might as well have been standing in a crowd of manikins, because I don't think that a single person heard me in the blindness and deafness that the enemy was working on that entire crowd of worshipers of a false god. Not a single person turned to look at me or seemed to hear my shout, even though the noise level of the crowd was very low.

Maybe it was just another case of God putting His shield around me like the waves that washed over my feet and legs on the evening of the witchcraft ritual on the beach that shut down the ports on the West Coast. Anyway, I had heard enough so I moved out of that crowd and began walking around to see what else was going on at the festival.

Influence over the Movie Industry

I overheard several conversations of movie producers talking to turbaned headed and robed writers about their latest scripts being incorporated into movies. No wonder there is so much Hinduism and Buddhism in the movies now days. These practitioners of the Eastern religions are hanging out in abundance among the stars, writers and producers many of whom live there next to the sea in Venice and Santa Monica. They are having a far greater influence than the Christians who will not go near the "wicked" movie industry.

I also listened to Krishna worship that was using guitars and applying new words to many very familiar "Maranatha Music" melodies. A prophet friend came down with his worship team and tried to set up in the same location where they had been playing every Sunday afternoon through the summer. They were politely escorted off the boardwalk because the Krishna's had a permit that covered the whole Venice Beach area for that weekend. Therefore, no one else could have amplified sound. Actually, it appeared it was only Christians who were not permitted to have amplified sound that weekend, because many of the other cult groups were still out there.

Anyway, I was so incensed in my spirit by what I observed that Sunday afternoon, that I found myself prophesying out loud as I was getting into my car to leave, "Before the Krishna's return, next August, five thousand Christians will have set foot on Venice Beach to take possession of the Kingdom."

All for One and One for All

I don't know how many Christians actually set foot on the sands and boardwalk of Venice Beach over the next year, but it was a significant number. I was not directly involved in all of the groups and individuals who I would hear about and on whose hearts the Lord had put it, to go out to Venice Beach, prayer walk, worship or just do prophetic acts, acts of righteousness. I cannot tell you all of their stories; what motivated them or even what they did, but I will tell you my journey of discovery and faith through the spring and early summer of 2003.

I had talked to a number of people about organizing some worship rallies, and evangelistic outreaches on the beach for the early summer of 2003. But it just was not happening. What I was envisioning was teams of people made up of prophets, intercessors, worshippers and evangelists who would work in harmony with one another to change the spiritual atmosphere over the area, bringing the presence of the dominion of the true Lord through worship and intercession. Then the prophets and evangelists would loose the conviction and repentance of those who had been freed of the dominion of Satan and whose eyes would be opened by the power of God.

See, I strongly believe that we do not go out to do worship just to attract people, and then beat them up with the convincing arm-twisting of some high-powered evangelist. I had several dreams and visions of situations where all of the gifts and ministries would function together, not to attract a crowd, but to create an atmosphere in the public arena. The presence of Christ would be so strong that people would be attracted to the peace that was markedly different than the chaos of the dominion of Satan that they were used to having all around them. The atmosphere would be created by the intercessors and worshipers, and when the dominion had been shifted from the dominion of darkness to the light of Christ and from the dominion of Satan to God, then the prophets would prophesy through the Holy Spirit to bring conviction in the lives of those to whom the Kingdom had been brought near. The evangelists would gently lead them in the path of repentance and receiving the inheritance of eternal life. The intercessors and those with discernment for deliverance and healing would also minister to the crowds.

The Attractiveness of the Spirit of God

I had seen a small realization of this experience during September 2002 when my friends and prophets Don Paul and Rapper Prophet Clyde Rivers, brought a worship team out onto the Third Street Promenade of Santa Monica on a Saturday evening. This is another location just a few miles from the Venice Boardwalk that draws tens of thousands of people on a summer weekend evening in Los Angeles. Along the promenade, there are several dozen locations where entertainers are allowed to set up for two hours at a time. At the end of two hours, everybody has to move to another location, so there is a brief mad scramble to claim another location within a block or so. Again, I came out that night as an intercessor and cameraman to capture this historic event.

It was amazing. People were drawn to the free flowing prophetic worship that moved through forms of jazz, Latino, and rap motifs. We were drawing quite a crowd even though the vocalizations to the music were blatantly Christian, speaking out the name of Jesus, God and the Holy Spirit repeatedly. But what really startled me was when Clyde started prophesying over people who were walking by and calling out to them. At first, they would just turn while still walking slowly by as if to say, "Are you talking to me?" Then they would be engaged and turn their steps toward and closer into the crowd around the team. Finally, as room was made for them, they would step through the crowd, end up on their knees worshiping God and being prayed over right out there in the middle of this public entertainment hot spot of Los Angeles. Through the power of God, His Kingdom was brought near to them, their eyes were opened, and they came out of the darkness into the light.

I also saw this type of partnering of different giftings on a larger scale the Saturday before the Krishna Festival of 2003, but I will cover that in the next chapter.

False Worship at the Beach

Through the early spring of 2003, the Lord was putting the Venice Beach area more and more on my heart. This was, as I puzzled over the strong influence of witchcraft over parts of Santa Monica and its neighbor to the South, Venice Beach. We had come to recognize that a number of art objects along the stretch of beach between the Santa Monica Pier and Venice Beach Pier had witchcraft and occult themes. There were a number of Asherah poles and nearby altars of Baal.[1] I cannot prove that this is what they are intended to be, but everyone to whom they have been pointed out, agrees with our assessment. After a number of these things begin to be exposed, it was reported in the local newspaper that five members of the cities' arts commission responsible for placing these objects were removed or resigned from the commission.

I had learned that this area between the two piers had been the birthplace of the Church of Satan as Anton Le Vey had worked as a carnival ride operator at the Pacific Ocean Park, while beginning the writing of the Satanic Bible during the early 1960's. Le Vey, in 1968, would also have a starring role in the first major "Satanic" movie produced in Hollywood, as the High Priest in Rosemary's Baby. Another friend of mine who grew up on the East Coast in a family of Satan Worshipers told me that she had been brought out to this area between the piers every other summer. She stated that this area, which was called Ocean Park at the time, was one of two-major satanic programming centers in the United States. She was brought out every other summer to undergo ritual programming.

Lord Open My Eyes that I Might See and Understand

The Santa Monica City library was about to be closed down for a two year remodeling job, and limited access to some of the reference material. I was led by the Lord to spend an evening there before the closure, reading some of the old newspapers from the early 1900's to see what the Lord might show me about why there was so much witchcraft in this area.

SIZING UP A SPIRITUAL PROBLEM

I learned a number of things that evening which I believe shed light on the principalities over this area of Ocean Park and Venice. The most significant discovery I believe was the spirit of competition that accompanied the development of this area and led, I believe, to conditions that introduced the witchcraft and Satanism into the area.

At the turn of the century into the 1900's, Santa Monica had become a very popular entertainment spot for Los Angeles residents. They flocked to the coast to enjoy the sunny beaches and a number of amusements from dancing to carnival rides on the Santa Monica Pier. In 1905, Abbot Kinney of a wealthy tobacco family, and now a West Coast Real Estate entrepreneur, opened his Venice America for a summer festival. He had taken over a section of land that was nothing but saltwater marshes a year earlier as the result of the split of a real estate partnership that had developed the Ocean Park area just South of Santa Monica. Kinney set about immediately dredging a canal, building Venetian style hotels and commercial buildings, and a pier with a restaurant and large auditorium. Because his development created competition with Santa Monica, he was unable to get a streetcar extension from the line running to Santa Monica and had to convince a different rail company to bring in a separate line from Inglewood to the South.

In these early years of the 1900's, the competition for entertainment and the crowds was fierce. At one point between 1905 and 1920, there were eight separate piers and fourteen full sized roller coasters along this two-mile stretch of oceanfront. Other entertainments included the largest indoor heated saltwater swimming pool in the world, numerous dance halls, restaurants, amusement midways and performance stages. The economic competition was so great that there were also numerous arson fires that burned down whole piers during this period.

The Spirit of Economic Competition

In that evening at the Santa Monica Public Library, I believe I found the answer to two questions about this area. Why was the economic competition so great in this area even to this day, and what if anything does this have to do with the strong influence of witchcraft and Satanism over this area? As for the competition, I found a paragraph of historical material that I believe points to the root of the spirit of competition over this area. This was a paragraph in a series of articles on the history of the area published years ago in the *Santa Monica Outlook* newspaper, (I've lost some of my notes from that evening, so I do not know what year the articles were done). The paragraph pointed out that the Tongva peoples, who were the first natives of the area, used to collect a particular type of shell from the salt marshes in the area where Venice Beach stands today. Before Europeans first set foot on these shores, these shells became the monetary unit for commerce between most of the tribal groups of what is now Southern California. As a result, the Tongva were very wealthy traders until tribes in the inland areas begin to develop the manufacture of glass beads. These glass beads became the new system of monetary exchange. Competition was born! The Tongva were still wealthy as they also had other resources that they traded, but they no longer were able to control the monetary exchange unit. I believe that this established a root issue of competition over this area to which demonic principalities were able to attach. This resulted in the ongoing issues of economic attraction, and competition. This is manifest in recent years by the competition even for space by street vendors and entertainers along the boardwalk through the area.

With the competition of the early 1900's, some of the primary means of attraction were carnival rides and amusements. A large amount of them all gathered into one place. This area truly became the Coney Island of the Pacific, which is exactly what some developers were trying to create. Along with the many rides and attractions came workers to operate these attractions. It is my theory, and just a theory, that this brought an influx of Gypsies, fortune-tellers, and other "carnies" (carnival workers) from across America and perhaps even Europe, to appear in and operate the many amusement zones. I have not been able to find census data or ethnic data for the turn of the century Ocean Park and Venice to support this theory. So hear me, it is just a theory! Abbot Kinney, who had more educational pursuits in mind, non-the-less built an amusement midway that included freak shows, dancing girls and occult shows that proved to be more popular and profitable then the lectures and art exhibits he had planned. This also was the case along the entire two-mile stretch of piers and amusement zones. Along with the amusements of a public nature, there were also manifestations of lawlessness that included underground tunnels from the seashore to the basements of hotels in Venice that served to transport liquor during prohibition. Other lawlessness was manifest by illegal gambling in bingo parlors and gambling ships anchored in Santa Monica Bay. Bill Harrah the founder of the Harrah gambling empire moved to Reno, Nevada after his father's bingo parlor where he had worked in Venice was finally shut down for illegal gambling in the 1940's.

Satan's Influence Grows

The area of Venice and Ocean Park had become very blighted by the end of the 1940's and became a cheap rent district for beatniks and motorcycle gangs in the 1950's. The drug and alcohol culture was tinged with witchcraft and Satanism. It was in this atmosphere of pawnshops, liquor stores, general blight and pollution both physical and spiritual that an attempt was made to resurrect the glory of the earlier days. Popular orchestra leader Lawrence Welk was brought into the Aragon Ballroom on the Ocean Park Pier and televised nationally as a very popular show. In the last half of the fifties, CBS Television along with the Los Angeles Turf Club of the Santa Anita Race Track (in Arcadia, California) built the briefly popular Pacific Ocean Park to try to compete with the just opened Disneyland in Anaheim a few miles away. The Pacific Ocean Park was short lived as a result of the blighted nature of the surrounding area and the high maintenance costs associated with its location in the salt air and salt spray from the ocean underneath.

This period manifested the Satanic programming, and Anton Le Vey's rise out of obscurity. In the late 1960's, the city of Los Angeles, which had annexed Venice, began tearing down the piers and buildings and started cleaning up the beachfront. The invention of the polyurethane skate wheel popularized street skating in the 1970's and the miles of paved boardwalk turned Venice Beach into the skating capitol of the world. This began to bring back the crowds of tourists and beach goers and soon led to the sidewalk display of vendors, entertainers, religious and political demonstrators, fortunetellers, and religious gurus that marked out locations along the boardwalk every weekend.

Removing the Dominion of Satan

In the spring of 2003, having recognized the spirit of competition over this area and the strong presence of the witchcraft, Satanism and just about every other manifestation of false worship and demonically inspired oppression, I began praying how the spiritual atmosphere over this area might be changed. The Lord acknowledged my prayer by saying, "There are many demons in Venice Beach, but they have a perfect right to be there. They have attached themselves to the woundedness and immorality of the people in the city. They have been invoked in, and they have come attached to practitioners of darkness. But what does not have the right to be in Venice Beach is the dominion of Satan over the area which empowers the demonic to operate on the ground level." The Lord went on to say, "If you will simply walk down the boardwalk and worship Me, I will draw near to you. If you will refuse to acknowledge Satan's authority over this area, he will flee as you enthrone Me on your praises." This strategy given by the Lord in answer to my prayer is very similar to what we find in the book of James[2], "Submit therefore to God. Resist the devil and he will flee from you. Draw near to God and He will draw near to you." It also reinforced the concept of enthroning the authority of Christ as a result of lifting up worship and praise to him.[3]

In May of 2003 in partial fulfillment of my prophecy the previous summer about walking Venice Beach, a few likeminded friends and I set off to prayer/worship walk Venice beach for seven consecutive Saturday mornings. This was intended to change the spiritual dominion over Venice Beach before the Krishna Festival the first weekend in August. We also began planning a specific act of reconciliation involving Native Americans to break and remove the spirit of monetary competition associated with the shells from the wetlands of this area.

Root Issues Matter

This is a pattern in spiritual mapping. It is often necessary to identify the root issue that opened a region to a particular spiritual influence that is often characterized down through history by a similar spiritual manifestation. In this case, I believe this spirit of economic competition had its roots in the Tongva's attempt to control the economy of commerce throughout Southern California by using an object as a monetary unit that was only available in a territory over which they had control. This same spirit has been manifested in the same region since the beginning of modern development of that land in the late 1800's until the present. With that spiritual dominion in place, the door was now open for all other sorts of demonic attachment related to lawless competition for economic gain, including the use of witchcraft and Satanism to bring about power and influence over political and financial leaders. In recent years the economic competition in the region, was centered around the motion picture, television, and related music industries. Many of the current television programs based around witchcraft, vampires, and homosexuality are all coming out of this region or are influenced by this region.

What is Occupational Theology?

The prayer/worship walking we did in 2003, we know caused a shift in the spiritual dominion of the area as evidenced in a number of ways that I will describe as I continue. But we also know that for those shifts to remain permanent it takes a continuous occupation of the territory. We see in scripture Christ's teaching:

> "Now when the unclean spirit goes out of a man, it passes through waterless places, seeking rest, and does not find it. Then it says, 'I will return to my house from which I came'; and when it comes, it finds it unoccupied, swept, and put in order." "Then it goes, and takes along

with it seven other spirits more wicked than itself, and they go in and live there; and the last state of that man becomes worse than the first. That is the way it will also be with this evil generation."[4]

A few of my friends and I call this "Occupational Theology." This is because in this present age, we are not destroying the demons. They just seem to shift to a different territory that has not yet been taken possession of for the Kingdom by the saints in that area or is no longer being actively occupied. A friend of mine has coined the term "Displacement Theology" to describe these same phenomena.

I have found after experiences in a number of cities and regions that this returning to unoccupied space generally applies not only to individual people, but also to cities and regions. In a number of cities around the world, I have watched anywhere from a few individuals to numbers of churches come to a place of listening to the Lord and through prophetic acts, prayer walking and unity of purpose have stepped outside the walls of their churches to take possession of the Kingdom or spiritual dominion over their city. They have seen phenomenal change in the city and numbers of people being delivered and brought to salvation and amazing cooperation between the churches and the city government. Nevertheless, it has been discouraging to watch as after this has occurred many of the individuals, or churches satisfied with an increase in numbers or momentary experiences of unity have let slip their occupying of the newly possessed dominion outside their church walls. They have gone back to the old ways of isolation from others in the body of Christ and dominion over the city as a whole has slipped back into the possession of the demonic realm. They have not maintained and occupied that of which they acted to take possession.

Spiritual Authority vs. Man's Authority

In a few cases that I personally have been involved in, several individuals acted together to deal with issues of reconciliation or prophetic acts to remove demonic influences over an area. These acts of righteousness were done without the formal support of the local church, because the pastors and leadership were too busy to listen or to participate. It was subsequently interesting to listen as these same pastors reported on the new freedom that they were experiencing in worship and even street evangelism. Even when it was explained what had been done by individuals on behalf of the churches and the city, the pastors still refused to acknowledge the connection, find time to participate in other actions within the city, or further to take possession of the spiritual dominion of the city. In a few instances, I have also seen these same pastors and leaders be removed, or choose to move, from that city shortly thereafter. I believe that it is because they had not gained spiritual authority over the area and could not continue to stand under the pressure of the Satanic spiritual dominion over their city, their church and their own lives. It is a shame that most seminary and Bible training available to pastors and church leaders does not cover and does not understand the principals about which I am writing.

Experience Kingdom Theology

It is my hope that through this book, and writings and teachings by Dr. Peter Wagner, Ed Silvoso, Dr. Dutch Sheets, Dr. Bill Hammond, George Otis Junior, Alistair Petrie, Dr. Paul L. Cox, Bill Johnson, Arthur Burke and others, that "spiritual leaders" of this day will begin to wake up, learn and experience Kingdom Theology first hand. It is my prayer that they will start being equipped and equipping the saints for the work of the ministry of taking possession of the Kingdom. It is my hope that they will begin to understand the anointing as priests that comes from unity and begin to see their whole city as the church that includes all of the individual gatherings of Christians in the city. I pray that they will start seeking the Lord to understand His strategies to change the dominion over their city and not just to fill the pews with financial supporters of their own church and ministry. I pray that they will start working together to bring the Kingdom near to those people and parts of their city that are still under the dominion of Satan and do acts of righteousness to deliver the city and the people in it from the dominion of Satan, to God.

Right now though, it is time to hit the pavement in Venice Beach and obey what the Lord had been revealing for us to do in the spring of 2003. So, come on with me and let's take a walk on Venice Beach.

Endnotes

1. See for example Judges 6:25-27
2. James 4:7-8
3. Psalm 22:3
4. Mathew 12:43-45

CHAPTER 17

TAKING A WALK ON VENICE BEACH

A very sunny Saturday morning in May of 2003, five of us, two women and three men gathered at the corner of a parking lot in Santa Monica, to prepare for our first prayer/worship walk through Venice Beach. We parked in Santa Monica so that we could put on the armor and pray before actually entering into the territory that was our target. I had learned on previous walks that there is a distinct shift in the spiritual atmosphere in different areas that are controlled by a different principality or spiritual dominion. It is very difficult sometimes to do spiritual preparation for the walk when you are already under the canopy of that spiritual dominion. The boundaries of these spiritual dominions many times correspond to political and human boundaries though not always. The shift in spiritual dominion can sometimes be sensed by a spiritually discerning person who has their "senses trained through practice."

Don't Expect a Spiritual Welcome Wagon

In the spring in 2005, I was on a five-week trip in a motor home. On that trip, my wife and I were in a different spiritual dominion nearly every night. For the first several nights, it was quite interesting as both my wife and I was challenged (attacked) very dramatically in our sleep by the principalities in that region. We finally realized by the third night that we needed to pray over the city and over our home away from home each day to seal it from the harassment of the local principality. Some were more powerful than others, but we could feel the distinct change from one city to another. We now do this covering prayer every time we travel and enter into a new area.

Back to the Boardwalk

A lot of prayer walking and worship had already been done in Santa Monica by May of 2003, so we seemed to have the freedom to do our preparatory prayer, putting on of the armor and anointing of our feet with oil without harassment even though we were in a very public location with dozens of people passing by. We put on the armor in prayer as I described in Chapter Five, did prayers of forgiveness of each other and addressed any other prayer concerns in each other's lives. I then anointed each person's feet with oil and we set off walking toward Venice Beach several hundred yards to the South.

The instruction I had received from the Lord was that we were to be inconspicuous in dress and manner and that we were to keep our focus on the worshipping of the Lord. At least on this first walk we were not to pay attention to what was happening around us and were not to engage in evangelism. We would stop and worship around or near objects and people where we sensed a particularly strong presence of the demonic but not get caught up in attributing any power or authority to Satan in the process. As I described in an earlier chapter one person was assigned as an armor bearer to keep watch over how we were being affected by the surroundings and help us to keep the armor intact.

I had walked in Venice Beach a number of times and though I had felt the oppression there, it had never really felt threatening or directed at me previously. I guess that was in part because I had never come there before specifically to displace the spiritual dominion over the city. This time was different. Almost immediately after crossing the city-line we all felt the heaviness of the oppression that now seemed directly focused upon us. Very shortly after entering into the city, we had our first experience of a warlock coming up out of nowhere and speaking curses in our face in tongues (nose to nose). We just kept quietly worshipping under our breath and tried to ignore that first challenge to our presence in this spiritual dominion. It was several hundred yards further when the lady helping a young teen pick out a satanic tattoo distracted me, as I described in an earlier chapter. I thank you, armor bearer, for helping get the armor back in place.

About half way through the walk, we had a major disturbance as several warlocks managed to separate our group briefly and assault the two women with a barrage of curses before we could locate them. Unfortunately, the two women did not tell me that they had been cursed again before we left the area that day. I always make it a practice to do a cleansing at the end of a prophetic act, but I did not address this particular event against them because they did not tell me about it until two days later after two sleepless nights of demonic harassment. At that time by a conference phone call, we through prayer dealt with cleansing the curses off the two women and they were free. I learned to instruct the prayer walkers to do a complete debrief and talk about things they experienced during the walk so we could do a thorough cleansing in prayer before anyone leaves.

We were challenged a third time on our way back up the boardwalk toward Santa Monica. This was the third instance of a demonically oppressed and driven individual who was able to identify us in the spirit realm as not of the same spirit, running up, and cursing us to our faces. This also is typical of entering a demonically controlled territory in the spirit and for the purpose of changing the spiritual atmosphere. You don't have to be dressed in a way that identifies you as a spirit filled Christian. You don't have to say anything out loud or act in any way different from the people around you. Those humans with demonic watcher and controlling spirit attachments will be able to pick you out of the crowd. As you gain greater spiritual authority in the area and the presence of the Lord's authority becomes stronger in the area, the warlocks and watchers will have less ability to identify you, as their spirits become less empowered by the Satanic dominion over the area.

As we neared the end of this walk, the first of seven weeks we had committed to, we all felt like we had hundred pound weights tied to each foot. The smells, the taste in the air, and the noise, was causing us to be nauseated and our heads were pounding with pain. Stepping back across the city line felt like stepping into a cool shower. We took a breather sitting on the lawn, prayed a cleansing prayer and left to our homes. I had my doubts that day whether I would live through seven weeks of this, but I had learned that the Lord never instructs me to do something I am incapable of doing, so I planned for the next week.

Week Two

The next Saturday morning it was again just five of us, but it was a different five on this morning. This would be the pattern for the first five weeks of prayer/worship walks. There were some repeat people on various weeks, but every week was a different makeup of just five people including myself. This second week was a little easier. We started out the same way putting on the armor, addressing individual prayer needs, and anointing our feet. This time we only had two instances of being cursed to our face, and though that is always disturbing, we did not feel even touched by the curses uttered. Gone also was the heaviness of the feet, and the nausea. In addition, on the second week we encountered and met a Christian woman with a booth set up along the boardwalk and part of a ministry that would be touching lives of people along the boardwalk for the next two years as a bold and compassionate witness for Christ. We prayed over her ministry and continued our prayer/worship walk.

Week Three

The third week is when we really began to see the effects of our efforts and the beginnings of a change in the spiritual atmosphere. There were three other Christian groups out on the boardwalk that morning. They were all in fixed locations and offering up different types of presence. One consisted of two young teen boys playing the guitar and singing worship music. There was the woman we had met the previous week, handing out books and tracts. This week there was also a Campus Crusade group on their first week of a summer outreach. They were right in the middle of a location on the boardwalk that several others and I had previously identified as being used as a pagan temple representing water spirits. I identified myself to the leader and gathered his group around to pray over them and put on the armor. I then proceeded to tell them something another friend had taught me. This friend, Rick Heeren from Minnesota, had several years before coined the phrase Portable Arks of the Covenant. He would point out that each of us individually had become a portable Ark of the Covenant when we received Christ and allowed ourselves to be filled with the Holy Spirit. Here is how he would describe this.

Portable Arks of the Covenant

Actually, the Ark is called the Ark of the Testimony of the Presence of God in most scriptural references. Therefore, what we are talking about is being a portable Ark of the Testimony of the Presence of God. In the description in the Bible we are told that the Ark had within it, the tablets of stone on which were engraved the Ten Commandments of the Law. The New Testament of the Bible tells us that the Law is now written on the hearts of the believers.[1]

Also in the Ark was some of the manna from the wilderness in a golden jar.[2] Jesus says: "I am the bread of life. Your fathers ate the manna in the wilderness, and they died. This is the bread which comes down out of heaven, so that one may eat of it and not die."[3] Therefore, when we feed on this manna and eat this bread of life it forms us into a purified vessel just like the jar of gold in the Ark.

The third item in the Ark was the budded rod of Aaron signifying the priesthood. The rod, in the test of the priesthood in Numbers Chapter 17, sprouted green leaves, the sign of new life, just as we are to bring forth new life in Christ. It had blossoms giving off a sweet fragrance, as we also are to be lifting up the incense of prayer and worship as a sweet aroma before the Lord. Moreover, it had ripe almond fruit[4], as we are to be fruitful in our work as priests of the living God. We become a living rod representing the office of the priesthood we have been made to be.[5]

The box of the Ark was covered with fine gold, which was pure. We are to be covered with the breastplate of righteousness, which is the purity of the Christ and His righteousness. Above the Ark were the Cherubim whose wings spread over the Ark and the space between the wings formed the Mercy Seat were the presence of God rested.[6] We are told that the Angels are ministering spirits, and messengers[7], and cherubim are a covering over us and over the mercy seat[8]. Because of the mercy of God His presence now rests on us and in us. See you really are a Portable Ark of the Testimony of the Presence of God.

I then told the Campus Crusade group about the time when the Ark was captured by the Philistines, and they took it and placed it in the temple of Dagon. During the night, the idol of Dagon fell before the Ark of the Testimony of the Presence of God. In the morning, the Idol was set back up. On the next night, the idol not only fell again, but this time the head and the arms were broken off.[9] Often in scripture, the head represents authority, and the arms represent the power or the strength. So, one might deduce that on this occasion of the idol falling, it lost its authority and its strength or power. I then pointed out to the students that they, on this very morning, were standing in the middle of a pagan temple. I suggested that they watch to see what idols might fall in this day as a result of the presence of these portable Arks of the Testimony of the Presence of God.

Another God Falls Before the Ark

As we were leaving that location, there was a palm and tarot card reader setting up in the area directly next to the Campus Crusade group. She appeared to be in a trance. I suppose connecting with the demons that empowered her to carry out her occult practices. When we came back by that area about an hour later, the palm reader was now surrounded by four policemen who were explaining to her that she had violated the rules for using that space this morning and would have to leave. She had lost her authority and power to stay in that location next to these Portable Arks of the Testimony of the Presence of God.

You Are Sons of God Don't Kill Me

The other very interesting thing that happened on this third morning occurred just as we reached the end of the boardwalk and were turning around to head back. There was what appeared to be a homeless man in a wheelchair alongside of the boardwalk. I felt led that I was to pray for him. I asked him permission and then prayed for him for financial and relational issues. I gave him a twenty-dollar bill, which he gladly received though he had not asked for anything. As we turned to walk back up the boardwalk to Santa Monica, another homeless man about twenty yards ahead of us, in the center of the crowded boardwalk, pointed directly at us and cried out in a very loud voice, "You are sons of God, don't kill me." He just stood there looking at us as I walked up to him and wrapped my arms around him. He slumped in my arms and rested his head on my shoulder as I quietly prayed for him. I then released him and he turned and walked off into the crowd. That would be the last time that we were spoken to or cursed for the rest of the seven weeks. From that point on, we could visibly see the reduction of the power and authority of the demonic over the people along the boardwalk. We would see our authority increase as now we would begin to see visible evidence of our prayers directly affecting individual psychics and tarot readers as we would quietly stand near and pray for them.

Week Four

The fourth week there was another new group out on the boardwalk. It was a group of young people who were Survivors. They were an anti-abortion group that was made up of young people who were from mothers that had considered aborting or children who had actually survived a botched abortion. I found a number of them were Christians as we talked to a few of them, so I prayed for their whole group and put on the armor. They would need that armor as it turned out. They were out on the boardwalk just silently holding up three-foot by four-foot poster boards with pictures of actual fetuses from abortions. Boy did that make the demons mad. There were crowds of people around them screaming at them to get these obscene pictures off the boardwalk and out of the view of children. The demons don't like public disclosure of the fact that abortion is the number one means of shedding innocent blood to empower the demonic realm in this country.

Surviving the Riot

The Survivors were positioned next to a man who had a whole bunch of white boards out along the boardwalk with lots of obscene language and poetry written on them. He also is a dispenser of confusion through dialogue with those passing by, using the twisting of words and ideologies to mock politicians and other leaders. On this morning, he was in rare form with some twisted dialogue about how President Bush was for abortion or was it that Bush was an abortion or was he an anti-President. Anyway, his dialogue above the screams of the dozen or so people that were now on the verge of a riot, was feeding the confusion in the air. I said something to him about how I thought he owed these young people an apology. Much to my surprise, he looked at me and said, "You're right," turned to the young people and apologized. Then sat down and closed his mouth for the rest of the morning.

Meanwhile the rioters had drawn the attention of the police who were arriving in force. The rioters were demanding that the police remove these obscene posters and the young people holding them immediately. A very calm police sergeant just informed the rioters, that the Survivor group was in a designated location. Under the free speech rules that govern the boardwalk, they had a perfect right to be there. Now the sergeant told this vocal group of protestors who were blocking the passage along the boardwalk, that if they did not disperse they would be arrested. I smiled at several of the young people we had talked with and they managed a smile out from behind their posters and in the midst of the fear that had been griping them from the threats of the rioters. Our group of prayer walker/worshipers continued down the boardwalk.

A Psychic Can't Talk

As we were walking back toward Santa Monica this time, we did a couple of experiments. There was a psychic who has an apartment right on the boardwalk with a balcony whose rail is about seven feet above the boardwalk. She was sitting on the balcony with her back turned to the boardwalk and her client facing out toward the boardwalk. One of our prayer warriors stopped under the psychic with his back to the wall just hidden from view from the balcony. The rest of our group stood about twenty yards away and watched. As soon as he started praying over the psychic, she grabbed her throat and her face twisted. Something had happened and she could not get words out of her mouth no matter how hard she tried. Her client just sat there looking very puzzled at this strange behavior. This went on for about two minutes with the psychic making numerous attempts to speak to no avail. Finally, the prayer warrior stopped praying and quickly walked away. The psychic quickly turned around and looked out over the crowd along the boardwalk but apparently could not figure out what had happened and quickly turned back to speaking to her client. In subsequent weeks, she no longer sat with her back to the boardwalk. She had her clients sit in that seat.

On another occasion, one of the members of our group quietly sat on a park bench near a husband and wife team of tarot card readers. As he began to pray silently, a wind came up and blew the whole stack of cards off the table in front of them. They carefully picked them up, sorted them into a particular order, and placed them back on the table. Again, a breeze came out of nowhere and blew them off the table. This time they picked up the cards and said to one another, "it is time to leave." They folded up their chairs and table, and left.

Week Five

Week five we again had just five prayer/worship walkers, but an associate of my mine had come down with me and was doing some video filming at the water's edge along the beach parallel to our walk down the boardwalk. We planned to meet up at the South end of Venice. As we entered Venice, there was something very strange this morning. Normally, there were about fourteen different, psychics, fortune-tellers, and tarot readers spread along the boardwalk. On this morning, their tables, umbrellas, their signs and chairs were there, their materials were there on the tables, but no psychics, fortune-tellers or tarot readers were at their tables. None of them were there on the boardwalk during the entire time we were walking that morning until just before we walked back out of the city. At the last table about a hundred feet from the city line back into Santa Monica, the psychic normally at that table had returned, so I went over to her table and just casually said, "you all are back, was there some kind of convention this morning or something, because we missed you all?" She mumbled something about attending a class that morning and turned away. We were pretty sure that they were having a meeting to try to figure out what was happening in the spiritual realm on Saturday mornings and why they were losing more and more power. The next week would pretty well confirm that theory.

Five Weeks Five People Five Dolphins Five Hours

My associate shared an interesting story when we met back up with him. As he was walking down the beach, talking with people and filming some footage for a film we were working on, he said that there were five dolphins just at the wave break line playing in the surf and moving down the shore at the same pace as we were, all the way to the end of the city. Very interesting! Five dolphins, five weeks, five prayer/worship walkers on each of those five weeks, there seemed to be a pattern here.

On the Friday before the sixth walk, I took a worship day. I drove up to a friend's ranch retreat center near Bakersfield, about one hundred miles North of Los Angeles and spend part of the day just worshipping by myself in an old barn on the property which has been put into service as a church. Several of the women at the center have a worship dance ministry and that old barn seems to have an anointing on it so I came to this place to spend some time before the Lord. I danced before the Lord, read scripture and prayed. At exactly five hours after starting this time of worship the Lord very clearly said to me, "That is sufficient!" All of a sudden, I understood that what He was saying to me is that His grace is sufficient. The number five has the meaning of grace I am told. I had been concerned because of only having five people participating in this prayer walking to change the dominion over Venice Beach and I now understood that all of the fives were the various ways the Lord was saying, don't be worried about the number of men, my grace is sufficient. That also was a very timely message to me personally, because the following eight days would be the most spiritually and emotionally challenging days in my life up to that point.

Week Six

The next day, Saturday morning there was a YWAM (Youth With A Mission) team to do the prayer walk with me. As we met at the corner of the parking lot in Santa Monica, several older women sitting around the area where we met were carefully watching us. This was the first time that there were more than five doing the walk, so we actually split into two separate groups. We put on the armor, prayed, anointed the shoes and set off. I had specifically briefed everyone that this was not an evangelistic outreach, but taking dominion through our quiet worship and prayer as we walked.

The assistant leader of the YWAM team was leading the second group that morning and that group kept getting distracted both by shopping opportunities and the desire to engage various vendors of religious articles in dialogue. After having been spoken to several times, she became very discouraged at her lack of leadership and ability to stay on focus that morning.

I was able to sit down with her later and explain that this was not an issue with her, but like the time I was distracted on the first walk, it is just the way the enemy gets under our armor and we need to readjust it. It was really my fault as the leader of this prayer walk that I did not explained this armor bearer concept earlier and assigned someone in her group to carry out that role. I think that it is really important to have an armor bearer the first couple of times that you are operating in a new situation and dominion with which you are not familiar.

Who's Covering Your Back

I was involved with another ministry that does an Internet broadcast every Sunday. This broadcast is able to do interactive video via the Apple® operating system and tools. As not everyone in the groups we connect with around the country has appropriate hardware and a fast enough connection to the internet, many of us have Wi-Fi accounts that we can connect with at a chain of very popular coffee outlets. Since these are public locations and we were doing a show that is about spiritual warfare, it was not too uncommon to have some demonized person break in and disrupt while any one of us was doing a live video uplink. This is another place for the armor bearer. Someone with their spiritual antenna up and monitoring what is going on around the group. They can act through intercession to block the enemy's use of these people to disrupt and distract at the very least, or place curses at the worst. On one occasion in New York as a man in our group was attempting to talk over the interactive connection, a man walked up and placed a drawing of a man with his mouth sewn shut in front of him as he was talking. That ended the interview, because now our man could not talk. A curse had just been placed on him.

Ok back to California and the sixth walk in Venice Beach that I was describing before I took the armor bearer tangent. It was obvious on that Saturday morning, that we had been identified by the witchcraft community of Venice Beach, and we were being carefully watched the whole time we were on the boardwalk. I think that they were trying to see what it was that we were doing that was having an effect on their power and ability to operate in the city. It was almost funny. There were people in second story windows along the boardwalk with binoculars watching every move we made. There were also a number of people making several passes by us and bumping into us each time. We were being followed. Yet, because all we were doing was silently worshiping the Lord in song, in scripture, in tongues, and in our spirit, all without opening our mouth or making any kind of an outward show of it, they were utterly baffled. But the power had gone out of the city and the witchcraft community would take desperate steps in the next week to re-empower that which they had lost.

On Tuesday night of the next week, I met with a couple of spiritual mappers, a Native American Christian Prophetess of the Tongva peoples and a Christian Native American Chief who leads a ministry to deal with territorial issues. We met to discuss dealing with the issue of the shells from the marshes where Venice now stands, and to put together a prophetic act to break that spirit of competition over the land. We planned an act of reconciliation that would involve over one hundred people, and be carried out in the middle of a very public place, the week before the 2003 Krishna Festival. I will talk more about this prophetic act in the next chapter.

Changing The Lock and a New Key Issued

On Wednesday morning, I participated with a group in Pasadena to deal with the key of authority in the city that had been given to the Dalai Lama. The Dalai Lama had on several occasions tried to construct mandalas in the city, which is an invoking of demons from the abyss. As I explained back in the chapter about the city seal, the key of authority was vested in Babalon for control over access to the abyss. The honorary key to the city had been presented to the Dalai Lama a number of years before and he made several attempts to use that spiritual authority in the city to open up the abyss. Fortunately, at that time a group of Christians stood in the way and when the Dalai Lama got out of his car and looked around at the crowd, he turned, got back into the car and left. We recognized that the key in the city seal was for a time under the control of Babalon, but eventually as the Lord revealed in January 2002, it was the key and a chain in Revelation 20 in the hand of an angel which would be used to bind the dragon and lock him up in the abyss for a thousand years.

One of the intercessors in the city had been pondering for months on how we might remove the symbolic authority over the abyss that the Dalai Lama held through the key to the city that he had been given. One day in the spring of 2003, this intercessor had a houseguest who was robbed of her purse while walking down the street. In the purse was a key to the intercessor's house. Realizing that the thief had a key to the house, the intercessor called the hardware store, ordered new locks and keys, and changed all the locks in the house. All of a sudden, it dawned on her that the Dalai Lama had the symbolic key to the abyss, so why not symbolically change the lock to the abyss and give the new key to Jesus.

This type of prophetic act may be new to you and may stretch your belief system a bit or a lot! However, let me reassure you that it is just such seemingly silly acts of faith that have tremendous power in the spiritual realm. Remember that Jesus made mud out of saliva and dust, and put it in a man's eyes to heal him. He also said that if you had the faith of a mustard seed that you would be able to say to the mountain be moved and it would move. Both of these things seem incredible and silly in our normal realm of understanding, but the Bible also tells us,

> "For My thoughts are not your thoughts,
> Neither are your ways My ways," declares the LORD.
> "For as the heavens are higher than the earth,
> So are My ways higher than your ways,
> And My thoughts than your thoughts." [10]

This is why it is so important to hear from the Lord what we are to do, how we are to do it and when we are to do it.

Anyway, on this Wednesday morning the group in the city brought a lock and a special key given to a local prophetess in Israel. We symbolically changed the lock on the abyss and gave the key to Jesus so that it would be available in heaven at some future time when that angel comes down with the chain and the key to bind and lock up the dragon.

The Audacity of Faith

You might ask what gives you the audacity to claim having a part in such a thing foretold in the Bible? I would answer, why not. Abram believed God, did what he was told and it was counted to him as righteousness. Remember the discussion a couple of chapters back about the righteous acts of the saints being the clean, white garment that adorns the Bride? You also might ask how do we know that this had any actual affect in the heavenlies? Remember the storm after the Canopy of Prayer and Worship that blew down the twenty-nine power poles? Do you remember the black column of clouds that formed over the witchcraft ritual when the ports shut down? Well on this morning in June 2003, it had been a bright, sunny, calm morning. Immediately as we finished this prophetic act, a not previously forecast strong wind came out of nowhere and great clouds began moving rapidly across the sky. Joel tells us that, "And I will display wonders in the sky and on the earth"[11] and Jesus says, "Do you know how to discern the appearance of the sky, but cannot discern the signs of the times?"[12] Sometimes the sky reveals changes and turmoil in the spiritual realm just like the meteorologists look at the clouds in the sky to discern changes in the weather.

That afternoon, a long time covenant relationship in my life would be broken by another person and a conjured accident would occur on the other side of town to attempt to re-empower the witchcraft in Venice Beach.

A Conjured Accident

I had heard of the concept of a conjured accident only a few months before from a man speaking at the church I attend. He related how when he was in Africa, he had read a newspaper article about a witchdoctor in a village in Africa. The witchdoctor sat by the side of a road and conjured up a vehicle accident, which occurred directly in front of him. Four people were killed in the accident. The witchdoctor crawled into the car and started harvesting body parts from the dead victims to use in future rituals and curses. In this case, if I am remembering the story as it was told, the villagers were so upset by the death of the four in the car crash that they dragged the witchdoctor out of the car and stoned him to death. The point of the story was that the witchdoctor conducted a spell or ritual to cause the accident to happen supernaturally. Sure, someone was driving the vehicle but the action of the demons called upon caused the vehicle to crash in such a way that the four occupants were killed.

On that afternoon in 2003, between the sixth and seventh prayer walk to change the spiritual dominion over Venice Beach, a vehicle driven by a person, inexplicably turned the wrong way into a barricaded street market and accelerated into a crowd of people killing ten. I believe that the driver of this vehicle was a mere victim of forces beyond their control. This was a conjured accident to spill innocent blood, which had the effect of empowering the demonic realm. If you look around the news headlines of the world, you will see other examples of these large life loss accidents that seem totally unexplainable in terms of what occurred. Minutes after this accident occurred, I received a call from a very reliable high-level intercessor I had been introduced to only a few days before. This intercessor, living in another city called me on their way home many hours away and stated, "This is a conjured accident which is intended to re-empower the witchcraft in the area where you have been changing the spiritual dominion. You will need to deal with the innocent blood of this accident before you do your seventh prayer walk in the area on Saturday."

Oh Lord, how am I to deal with this one?

Endnotes

1. Romans 2:15
2. Hebrews 9:4
3. John 6:48-51
4. Numbers 17:8
5. Revelation 5:10
6. Exodus 25:22
7. Hebrews 1:14, 2:1
8. Exodus 25:20-22 – As an interesting side note to this passage, it is this place under the wings of the cherubim that God says: And there I will meet with you; and from above the mercy seat, from between the two cherubim which are upon the ark of the testimony, I will speak to you about all that I will give you in commandment for the sons of Israel.
9. 1 Samuel 5:1-8
10. Isaiah 55:8-9
11. Joel 2:30
12. Mathew 16:3-4

CHAPTER 18

INNOCENT BLOOD AND BREAKING THE NECK OF WITCHCRAFT

I asked the Lord, "How do I deal with the spilling of innocent blood that others may have conjured to counter our actions to change the spiritual dominion over Venice Beach?" Innocent blood is sacrificed daily around the world in ways that most do not associate with witchcraft or Satanism. Most Christians do not understand or believe that the kind of ritual sacrifice spoken of in the Bible and portrayed in the movies still goes on in this day. Sometimes it is done in very secret and hidden rituals, but more often, the necessary spilling of innocent blood takes place out in the open in the form of seeming unexplainable accidents, murders and by the greatest abomination in this country, the killing of babies through abortion.

I say necessary, and you probably are thinking necessary for what? To explain why blood sacrifice is still done in this day to empower evil would take more space in this book than suits the purpose here. Just a study of blood in the Bible is more than I care to try to explain here. So, I ask your forgiveness for not providing all of the documentation and sources that the Lord led me through in the past several years to give me this understanding. I am going to make just several statements that I believe I have from the Lord and then move on with dealing with this incident in Santa Monica.

The Life is in the Blood

First, we have very clear statements in the Bible that the life of a person or animal is in the blood.[1] Jesus takes this one step further in John to say that unless we eat of His flesh and we drink His blood we cannot see eternal life, because eternal life, is only in His blood.[2] I find it interesting that many of the Universalist's and those teaching Christ Consciousness, specifically go out of their way to teach against this interpretation of the statements of Jesus and teach that Christ's blood had no power in sacrifice, but that He was just symbolically saying that we are to be in the same stream of consciousness with Him.

The spilling of innocent blood causes a defilement of the land and the land curses the one who spills the blood so that they no longer have authority over the land.[3] God states that it pollutes the land, and no expiation can be made for the blood on the land, except through the blood of the one who spilled it.[4] Because of this principle, those under the authority and dominion of the demonic realm are deceived into believing that they gain power over other men and over the land by defiling the land with innocent blood, blood sacrifice or actually drinking blood. God instructed the nation of Israel to set up refuge cities where those guilty as a manslayer (accidentally having caused the death of another) would be protected from his blood being innocently shed on the land through the anger and grief of the relatives of the one accidentally killed until the matter could be judged.[5] Israel is also told to purge its land from the innocent blood, through delivering the killer to the avenger of blood so that it might be well with them.[6]

The Lord revealed to me that the shedding of innocent blood is constantly necessary for the empowerment of demonically driven evil, because Satan is no longer empowered through the authority of God as he and his fallen angels once were. He has lost his place before the throne of God and the empowerment that comes from there. Therefore, he is instead empowered through the life and the authority of men. His authority structures are based upon separating men from the life that only comes from God. He usurps the authority given to men by God, by giving them a form of power over the life and authority of other men through the bondage of the fear of death. When there is a shedding of blood in this evil dominion structure, there is a temporary release of power and authority within this earth realm that can be accessed to empower evil. But since this is the shedding of unrighteous blood, the power released is only temporary, and the sacrifices must be continually be repeated to keep empowering the evil.

The Christ's sacrifice of His own righteous blood was sufficient for all time to empower eternal life and to destroy the fear of physical death and separation from the life of God. However, it must be accessed through our eating of the flesh and drinking of the blood of Jesus, taking His life into our very being.[7] This as explained in John was very difficult for His disciples to understand even as it is for us today. But it comes down to the fact that we must see as our only source for feeding our mind and spirit, the life that comes from God and that is only found in Jesus. Thus, Paul explains in Romans and the book of 1 Corinthians, that as death came through the first Adam, now life comes in Christ[8]

Blood Sacrifice Through Abortion

One of the primary means of continuing to empower demonic authority in the United States is the shedding of innocent blood through abortion. That is why the demonically driven rioters we saw in Venice Beach were so irate at abortion being portrayed as murder of human life rather than a necessary medical procedure to rid the body of unwanted tissue that is not yet a human being.

I recently had a conversation with a man who told me about he and his wife's recent experience over the birth of their first child. They did not have much money, so could not afford a doctor but instead went to a midwife at a women's clinic. The woman did a number of tests and told the couple that the child had a serious condition that would result in a malformed child who would live only a short time. This midwife then did everything she could to try and convince the couple to have an abortion. The couple refused and refused to receive further advice or treatment from the midwife when they heard clearly from the Lord that the child was fine and would be born healthy. They learned shortly of this woman's association with witchcraft in the local area and it became very evident that she was seeking to shed the innocent blood of a child of two Christians. The baby was born just fine, and is now a very healthy two-year old.

Dealing With the Conjured Accident

So back to the day of prayer, as I asked the Lord what to do about this conjured accident and the shedding of innocent blood during the middle of this week between the sixth and seventh walk in Venice Beach. The Lord instructed me to take several others with me and carry out the priestly function of worship and prayer over the area of the killing, making atonement over the sins of the people through the blood of Jesus Christ.[9] As I have described earlier in this book, this is the function of the priests that we have been made to be.[10] We were also instructed to spread salt on the land for healing similar to what was done by Abimelech after the destruction of the city of Shechem as described in Judges 9:45. This prayer/worship walk, making atonement through the blood of Jesus for the sins of the people and spreading of salt we planned to do early Saturday morning before going on to our seventh walk in Venice.

Authority to Establish Chaos in Santa Monica

Friday night, I drove out to Santa Monica to drop something off for a friend. As I was driving the hour across Los Angeles from my home, I kept hearing reports of violence and chaos out in Santa Monica along Ocean Avenue and in the Palisades Park along the West side of Ocean Avenue. The police were warning over the radio of thousands of people gathered in the park near where the deaths had occurred on Wednesday afternoon. As my friend lived on Ocean Avenue, I had to go right through this area to get to his home. What I saw was a gathering of homeless, witches and warlocks numbering in the thousands all gathering on the Western edge of the death scene. They were absorbing the empowering resulting from the shedding of the blood of ten lives two days before. It was a scary scene as violence and chaos was indeed being generated out of this empowering of the evil.

Salt in the Wound

I returned to the area early the next morning with three other men as we set out to make atonement over the area through the blood of Jesus Christ. There were still hundreds of witches and warlocks gathered at the end of Arizona Street where the conjured accident had occurred, two blocks to the East. As we looked at the area where the accident actually occurred it was crowded with people preparing for a memorial service later that morning. There were news people with TV cameras, and a makeshift memorial of flowers, candles, pictures, and whatever being built by the crowd. We broke into two groups of two and walked down either side of the street quietly praying, worshiping and sowing the salt stealthily under the very lenses of the TV cameras and all along the street.

We reached the intersection on the West side of the "accident" and crossed over still pouring a trail of salt. As we crossed the intersection, we could feel the flow of energy that was moving down the street toward the crowd of witches and warlocks two blocks away. Apparently, the line of salt and the atoning prayers cut off the flow, because when we got back to the car and drove by the park thirty minutes later, there was no one there. The flow of empowerment had stopped and they had left. We went on down to wait, at the starting point for our walk, for the others who would be joining us that morning in Venice Beach.

Week Seven

As we arrived at the place where we had been gathering for the past six weeks to pray, put on the armor and anoint feet, there was a change. The older ladies, who had been watching us so carefully the previous two weeks, were not there or anywhere along the wall where they had been. It was though we had been taken care of through the witchcraft of the previous week and their guard was down. As we walked from the car to the walkway along the beach, I noticed something moving out on a telephone pole next to a lifeguard stand on the beach. This was a couple of hundred feet away and I could only see what looked like a bird struggling with something black. I thought perhaps it was a bird entangled in a black plastic trash bag, but my distance vision is not as good as it used to be, so I asked one of the men with me to run back to the car and get my video camera with a telephoto lens. Before he returned with the camera, the black object fell to the sand at the foot of the pole and the bird flew off flying in a figure eight over the pole. It then made a wide circle and flew directly over my head while looking straight at me. The bird was a Peregrine Falcon, which after flying over my head then flew down the beach about a half mile to pole just opposite the beginning of Venice Beach. It remained there on that pole for the whole next four hours that we were walking that morning. I walked out on the beach to the pole where the black object had fallen and found a pure black pigeon with its neck broken but no other signs of injury, trauma or blood.

The Neck of Witchcraft Broken

Here is the interpretation of this event that the Lord gave me that morning and which was confirmed through several other intercessors, when I described what I saw. Peregrine Falcons are normally mountain birds and are rarely seen that close to the ocean. Pigeons are often used as watchers, assigned by practitioners of voodoo and witchcraft. Pure black pigeons are very rare, and I have never seen one in this area before or after this event. The Lord said, "I have sent my predator and have broken the neck of witchcraft over Venice Beach this morning because of your righteous act to deal with the spilling of innocent blood." The way was now cleared for the seventh prayer walk.

7 Waves of Worship

The instruction the Lord had given me that morning was specific as to how we were to do this walk. If I had not asked the Lord and listened to Him, I probably would have been inclined to act on the suggestions of many others and followed the pattern given to Joshua when He walked around the city seven times on the seventh day. But the Lord gave a different instruction for this day and this city. He said that we were to be like seven waves of worship washing over the city and that we were to do so like persons with a cervical collar around their neck, looking straight ahead and not turning to the right or to the left. As it "happened" that morning, we had twenty-three people present including me. We did our putting on of the armor, prayer, and anointing of feet and then the Lord had me instruct the people that we were going to be split into seven groups of three and one group of two. Each of these seven groups would start out at three-minute intervals just like the timing and interval of the waves on the nearby Pacific Ocean. The last or eighth group of two would represent unity (2) and a new beginning (8) being the eighth group.

As I explained what we were going to do, one of the intercessors present asked if I had read the Los Angeles Times that morning. I explained that no I had not, as I had not had time before driving out to deal with the conjured accident. He then proceeded to tell the group that the LA Times feature article that morning had been about Venice Beach. It seems that there is a concern that because the land was sinking, the waves of the ocean might wash over the city! If the city managers and the Times writer only knew that in fact waves would wash over the city that very morning, waves of worship.

More Eyes Are Opened

As we all lined up in our groups of three prepared to step off into the city, the Lord gave three more instructions. The first was that it would not be necessary to sing and pray under our breath on this morning and we could feel free to sing and pray out loud, which we did at various points along the walk. Secondly, we were to walk all the way to the Venice Pier, not just the business portion of the boardwalk on this day. Thirdly, he told me to tell the group that there were several in the group that needed healing before we started and we would deal with that right now. Immediately, two women dropped to the ground weeping and several of us ministered to them individually as the Lord directed. Mind you, this was not in a church. It was not even in a building, but was on the grass of the park along side of the beach walkway between Santa Monica and Venice, with hundreds of people passing by.

Actually at this point, there were dozens of people who were not passing by, but were standing there watching us. To my mind, this was real church, spiritual reality in a real world setting. Emotional and physical healing was ministered by and through the power of Jesus. Instead of being offended by this display of the presence of the Kingdom, some of the onlookers actually cheered and clapped when the two women stood up filled with joy and we launched the first wave of worship. People in the real world are not offended by the power of the presence of the Kingdom. They are only offended by a powerless show of religious bigotry and hypocrisy such as they are used to seeing on television and through some of the street ministries that often come down to this area to pour out "condemnation on them sinners."

Freedom to Worship Aloud

As we worshipped down the boardwalk that morning, past the mediums, the purveyors of various aberrant religions, the idols, the satanic symbols and practitioners, we were struck first with the understanding of where the thousands of witches and warlocks had gone when they left the park at the end of Arizona Street earlier in the morning. They were all here along the boardwalk. It was a sunny and hot morning and one of the largest crowds I have ever seen in Venice Beach, perhaps sixty thousand people that morning. Yet, there was absolutely no sign of demonic power being able to manifest against us

INNOCENT BLOOD AND BREAKING THE NECK OF WITCHCRAFT

or in any other way. Though we often sang loudly as we walked, no one looked at us. In fact, no one even seemed to be aware that we were there. I think that somehow we were operating in another dimension of heaven that morning.

When the first group, which I was with, arrived at the end of the city next to the pier, three things immediately came to our attention. We looked up at the street sign, which is Washington Boulevard, and the Lord said to us, "You have been washing a ton of sin from the city this morning."

Next, our eyes came to rest on a three story high mural on the building across the street. The mural is called "The Angel of Unity" and is illustrated with an angel flying low over a wave, which is breaking over the sun. Now the Lord said, "Your unity has brought the angels as your waves of worship have brought the Son in place."

The Bride Was Adorned

The third thing that came to our attention was just off to our right on the sand. There was a wedding party gathered on the beach and the wedding was just beginning. There was the bride gloriously adorned in her fine white dress, and the groom dressed in his best, and an Episcopal priest in white robes administering. As I explained earlier in this book, I believe the bride of revelation represents the marriage of the perfect authority of God to the bridegroom Jesus. Revelation explains that the garment of the bride, which is pure white linen, is the righteous acts of the saints. This garment of righteous acts forms the perfect adornment for the bride, the New Jerusalem, or new founding of "authority without chaos" to which the Christ becomes wedded.

As we, the first group, arrived the wedding had just begun. As the eighth group of two representing unity and a new beginning arrived, the bride and groom kissed. We understood that as we had carried out this righteous act of walking the city for seven weeks, now Jesus was established in a new founding of authority without chaos over Venice Beach.

It had been oppressively hot as we had walked down the boardwalk with the wind at our back, just like the waves coming in on the beach with the wind behind them. Now the Lord instructed that we were to walk back into the wind like a rip tide or undertow that occurs when a strong wind is building up the waves. This strong reverse wave is that which rushes back out from the beach and washes everything out to sea including unwary swimmers that do not know how to float on the surface of the water and not fight the current.

We stopped at the Asherah Pole out near the end of Windward Avenue, and after anointing the pole and praying over it, rested there for a while. Then we did some rhythm together, clapping our hands in a unity of spirit creating a dance. This drew the attention of many around us. We ended that rhythm clapping by standing to our feet and shouting in unity "Allie, allie, oxen, free, free, free, proclaiming the hiding was over. We continued the rip tide back to our starting point in the Ocean Park area of Santa Monica, near where we would meet again the following week for a different prophetic act.

Doing Church Jesus Style

We spent an hour or so debriefing with cleansing prayer and soaking in the spirit as God ministered to and through various ones of the group, right out there in the open with people walking by. Doing church, the way Jesus did, after taking a ministry walk with His disciples.

The following Saturday was a prophetic act involving Tongva and other native Americans to deal with the spirit of competition over the area where the Tongva used to gather shells that were the unit of money among the natives of what is now Southern California.

Drums of Reconciliation

The plan was for the use of a Native American ministry called One Hundred and Twenty Drums of Reconciliation. I gathered over a hundred people to come and participate with the Native American leadership team. We met in front of the twin Asherah Poles at the end of Ocean Park Boulevard, where the witchcraft ritual of honoring the Goddess of the Sea had taken place the previous fall when all of the ports on the West Coast shut down. Again, we were in the open, in public, on a Saturday morning. We dramatized the historical story of the use of the shells until glass beads were made and how both of these monetary systems were destroyed when the white settlers began to invade. Then we worshipped and danced, Native American style to the thunder of the One Hundred and Twenty Drums to bring reconciliation to the land.[11] After we had been doing this for about two hours, a policeman rode up on a bicycle and informed us that we could not play drums on the beach by Santa Monica Ordinance, but unless someone complained, we could continue. Since we had just finished our prophetic act and worship, I thanked the officer and we dispersed. It was shortly after this gathering that we read in the paper that several members of the arts commission, who had been responsible for many of the spiritual "art objects" around the city, including these Asherah Poles, had resigned the commission.

Preparing the Atmosphere Before the Krishna Festival

The following weekend was the first week in August and would be the annual Krishna Festival in Venice Beach. This as you might recall was the whole motivation for the prayer walks and the prophetic reconciliation, so we were anxious to see what the effect might be. The festival actually takes place on the first Sunday in August and begins with the "parade of chariots," four huge hand drawn oxcarts with four story high silk temples on them. The parade for twenty-five years had started at the Santa Monica Pier and proceeded down the boardwalk past the Asherah Poles where we had just done the drums and on down to the center of the festival at the Venice Beach Pavilion area.

We planned to cover the area of the pavilion with worship on the Saturday before the festival while the tents and booths were being set up. I invited prophetic worshipers to join us for the day on a grassy hill in the pavilion, and we would worship with CD music, flags and dance. Meanwhile, another team specializing in "prophetic evangelism" would be ministering along the boardwalk. There were also other teams in the city, who would just be prayer walking on that day. We gathered on the hill at nine in the morning. There was even a group of worshipers who came that morning from over a hundred-and-fifty miles away in Bakersfield to join in and support. As we began to worship, a strange thing happened. The wind, which had been blowing from the South East, shifted around to the North West, but only in the Northern half of the city. Flags on the top of a building several hundred feet South East of us were still blowing from the South East, almost one hundred eighty degrees out of sync with the flags on a building just to the North across the street. This continued all day until three o'clock in the afternoon.

Most of the morning we were led to play a CD that is called "Grace" and is a very quiet, gentle worship. This seemed to bring calm over the whole city except to the South East where two police helicopters and several news helicopters were flying all day. But on the boardwalk and on the grassy hill it was absolute peace. Many who were not a part of our group just came and sat or lay on the grass and soaked in the peace.

About noon, a city official came and told us we could not have amplified sound there on this morning as the Krishna's had the permit for the area for this weekend. The permit specifically prohibited anyone else from having amplified sound in the area. We obeyed and turned off the amplifier, but kept quietly playing worship on a portable CD player and dancing. The Prophetic Evangelism team, who knew of our presence, reported an unusually successful morning on that day. This furthered my theory and vision from the Lord that street or public evangelism should involve teams of worshippers, intercessors, evangelists, and prophets, working together.

Shifting the Wind

At about 3p.m., we found out what the helicopters were about. There were two separate barricaded and armed suspect incidents going on just a few blocks apart in the South East section of the city. When we learned this, one of the prophetic worshippers suggested that we should directly address this incident in prayer and worship. We lined up the worshippers in pairs with flags in a line from the top of the hill where our sound system was, down the hill toward the South East. We turned the sound up a little and began to dance with the flags. Immediately the flags on the building to the South East, which had been blowing from the South East, all day, swung around and were now blowing in the same direction as the ones on the building across the street to the North had been blowing all day. The helicopters left at the same time. We later learned that at that very time, the incidents had both ended peaceably with no shooting or injuries.

Peace and the Peace Officer

At five o'clock as we were leaving, I was standing waiting for another person alongside the boardwalk. As I was standing, there were two police officers standing and talking about five feet from me. I overheard one of the police officers say this was one of the most peaceful days out on the boardwalk he could remember, despite the incident in the South East part of the city. As they finished talking, I walked up to the officer who had made the comment and introduced myself as a former Los Angeles County Fire Battalion Chief. I explained I had overheard his comment about it being peaceful and told him that there were approximately one hundred Christians out on the boardwalk on this day praying and worshipping and that perhaps this had contributed to the peace. He asked how long that had been going on because there sure seemed to be a difference in the city over the last several weeks. I told him that a few, not the one hundred present today, but a few had been praying along the boardwalk for eight weeks and then asked if I could pray for him and his duty there in Venice. He consented and I briefly prayed for him.

More Evidence of Change

The other piece of news that we heard about on that Saturday morning was an article in the local paper announcing that for the first time in twenty-five years, the "Parade of Chariots" would not be permitted to start at the Santa Monica Pier and would not be permitted on the boardwalk in the City of Santa Monica. Instead, they would have to move several blocks inland to start at the Santa Monica Auditorium (the same auditorium where the Dalai Lama was invited to appear on his first public ritual in the United States) and that the parade would travel on surface streets until inside the Venice area where it could go back to the boardwalk. The parade would not be passing in front of the Asherah poles this year!

On Sunday morning, my team from the conjured accident walk, met early, prayed over and salted the entire route of the chariots. Later in the morning, I met with a YWAM team that had just finished a street evangelism school and were going to practice what they had learned on the boardwalk. I worshipped with them for a while, put on the armor and sent them off to an eye-opening day in the real world. We all planned to meet up again at 4p.m. for a time of worship down just opposite the main stage at the Krishna Festival. The Festival was much smaller this year, partially because the city relegated them to the area on the ocean side of the boardwalk and they were not in the center of the boardwalk as in previous years.

Earned Authority

At four, I went to our meeting location and immediately sensed in my spirit that we needed earned authority to be there that day.[12] This again has to do with righteous acts of the saints that establish authority in the spiritual realm. What I sensed I was hearing from the Lord was to deal with the litter left behind by the many people attending the Krishna Festival and sitting on this hill to eat their free food "offered to idols." I instructed each person as they arrived to help pick up all of the paper plates, cups and trash scattered about the hill. One of the men who had come with me, went down to the police station right next to the hill and rolled the trash can by the front door up the hill so we could dispose of the litter. He then rolled it back to the front door of the station where the police officer I had prayed for the previous evening was standing watching him bring the trash barrel back. The policeman smiled and said, "Thank you"

On this afternoon we were again intending to use amplified worship from a live team even as the Krishna's were still performing on their stage about fifty yards away. We did turn our amplifier away from them toward the sea, but I expected that we would be shut down pretty quick. Much to my surprise, a number of policemen came out of the station in pairs and walked by us without even a glance. About fifty of us worshipped there on higher ground than the Krishna's for several hours. We were joined on that afternoon by several people who had just given their lives to Christ on the previous day through the ministry of the Prophetic Evangelism team.

Significant changes occurred in Venice Beach shortly after this time, including a change in policy regarding the free speech area, which now requires the purchasing of a permit (eliminating some of the chaos in claiming locations each morning). This has eliminated some of the more off the wall, obscene and contentious persons and some of the Tarot readers. The power of the witchcraft has also been significantly broken. Unfortunately, most of the churches in town still do not get it. Without the maintaining of a strong spiritual warfare presence over the city, the demonic power seems to be growing again.

I have learned over many years that we must not only take possession of the Kingdom, but we must occupy until He comes. Until the Church comes to understand this, I fear that we will continue to be overwhelmed and overpowered by the kingdom that is waging war against the saints. Somehow, masses of the body need to understand, be equipped and march out to take possession of the Kingdom. Then an occupying force must be established to maintain the dominion of Jesus over the land. This is going to require a change of focus, from the equipping of a building to the equipping of a people, and from just doing church on Sunday mornings in that building to putting on the "shalom shoes," setting foot on the land to take possession of the Kingdom and changing the spiritual dominion throughout the city.

In the next chapter, I will begin to talk about why I believe the forth kingdom of Daniel 7 is present in the world today and how it is waging war against the saints.

Endnotes

1. Genesis 9:4, Leviticus Chapter 17, Deuteronomy Chapter 12
2. John 6:53-54
3. See for example Genesis 4:10-12
4. Numbers 35:33-34
5. See Numbers Chapter 35
6. Deuteronomy 19:11-13
7. John 6:53-64
8. Romans 5:14, 1 Corinthians 15:20-22
9. Numbers 16:46-48
10. Revelation 5:10
11. These drums were constructed in accordance with a vision by a Native American Christian and are used in reconciliation ceremonies all over the world, guided by a group of Native American elders from many tribes across the nation.
12. Arthur Burke of Plumbline Ministries in Anaheim, California has some interesting teaching on this concept of "earned authority." You may wish to contact that ministry to get the tapes on this subject.

CHAPTER 19

TIME FOR A MANDALA TO CHANGE THE LAW OF THE WORLD

It was almost midnight on Saturday October 4, 2003. I was exhausted from a day of moving into my new home, a fifth-wheel trailer. I was rushing all day doing the move and setting up the trailer so I would have a place to shower and sleep that night other than a cot in my office. I also had spent a number of hours on the phone that day as I was briefing and preparing a team that would be doing a prophetic act at 5a.m. the next morning out at the Los Angeles County Museum of Art (LACMA). The museum sits in the middle of Hancock Park in Los Angeles, which is also the site of the La Brea Tar Pits. What was happening at the museum the next morning was the consecration and beginning of a large sand mandala to be constructed inside the museum by Tibetan Buddhist monks. More about that in a minute, but right now back to the trailer and the lesson I was about to learn and have reinforced by the Lord.

I was exhausted as I prepared for bed knowing I had to be up and on the road in less than four hours to meet the group out at the museum all the way on the other side of LA. As I was getting ready for bed, I very clearly heard the Lord telling me to put worship music on the CD player in the living room of the trailer. The music was to play throughout the night.

Big Mistake!

I dug the CD player and my worship CD's out of a box and began setting up the player. It was then that I realized I was missing the speaker cables to the CD player. I must have left them in my studio a few blocks away. It was late. I was exhausted. I didn't want to get dressed, drive over to the studio and search for the cables that I was not sure where to find. I decided the worship music could wait until tomorrow. Big mistake! I proceeded to get ready for bed. The phone rang. It was one of the team checking on final details for the morning. We talked briefly. I said good night and hung up the phone. As I turned to place the cell phone on its charger, I accidently stepped sideways off a step in the bedroom I was not familiar with yet and fell down the step onto the floor.

The left leg and the hip joint that had been replaced in 1997, was extremely painful. I could barely move. I was able to crawl slowly close enough to where I had put the cell phone and I called my team member back. He assured me that he would take care of meeting the team at the museum and told me to get off the phone and call the paramedics. I did. Now I had another problem. I had locked the only door into the trailer and all of the windows were also locked. I was in great pain and could not get down into the other part of the trailer where the door was to unlock it. I finally thought of the broom in the closet right next to me and was able to use the broom handle to reach the door lock latch and unlock it before the paramedics arrived.

A Hospital Bed as a Command Post

After several hours in the emergency room, an unsympathetic doctor who could not see anything on the x-ray was intending for me to call a taxi and go back home. I managed to convince him that if I could figure out how to stand-up on the leg without collapsing from the pain, I would be more than happy to leave and go home. He relented and admitted me to a hospital room until the Orthopedic Surgeon who had done my hip replacement could look at the x-rays later that morning.

Lying in the hospital that morning I directed and encouraged our small "commando" team on site at the museum from my bed via cell phone. Meanwhile the Lord and I had a one to one conversation about obedience and about allowing myself to get too exhausted to follow his instructions exactly, including when to do what He was telling me. The worship music was intended for my protection that night, not the next day!

The Orthopedic Surgeon came by later in the morning and confirmed that I had a lengthwise fracture of the femur at the top where the pin from the replacement hip is inserted into the femur. He explained that this was a big deal and would be much harder to recover from than the actual hip replacement. I would have to remain in the hospital for several days and then move about carefully with a walker for weeks to allow the bone to heal and not split from the pressure of the pin. When they do a hip replacement, you are encouraged to be walking on it immediately, but not so with this injury. Putting weight on the hip and walking could cause much more serious injury and the need for surgical repair.

Remember when I mentioned the book *"Needless Casualties of War."* Well this was one of them. I had allowed myself to become exhausted just before entering onto the battlefront and I had not obeyed exactly what the Lord had told me to do.

Learning From Others' Mistakes

When my oldest son was in high school, we had visited the Air Force Academy and several of the other military academies, as he was interested in applying to one of the academies. He eventually did apply to and graduate from the Coast Guard Academy. On this visit to the Air Force Academy, we had picked up a small embroidered plaque with the picture of an airplane flying upside down. The caption on the plaque stated: "Learn from others mistakes, you may not have time to make them all yourself." I am encouraging you to learn from my mistakes, I have thus far lived to tell you about them, but you may not have time to make them all yourself. Don't go into heavy spiritual warfare when exhausted, and do obey exactly everything the Lord tells you! I will go so far as to say that I do not believe you should go into heavy warfare when you have been on an extended fast. I know this goes against the counsel of some, but the Lord's instruction to me has been, fast for spiritual insight not as preparation for or during battle. Remember the story of Saul who was fighting a battle against the Philistines, and put the soldiers under oath to eat nothing until the battle was over? Jonathan, his son did not hear his father's command and ate some honey he found in the forest. He tried to encourage the others to eat some of the honey also before going back into battle, but they were afraid of the curse pronounced by Saul so went back into the battle hungry. They were so hungry that as they started killing the Philistines and their livestock, they ate the flesh of the livestock with the blood still in it and broke a command from the Lord. Saul swore to kill any person who had disobeyed the vow not to eat until the end of the battle, even if it was his son Jonathan. The people stood up for Jonathan because he had been strengthened through the honey to lead them to victory and they prevented Saul from killing him.[1] I am not telling you not to fast before a battle if you are sure that this is what the Lord is telling you. I am just telling you that this is not the instruction I have received from the Lord. Again, the point is, don't go into battle exhausted, and do obey exactly what the Lord tells you to do, in the timing He tells you to do it and with the people that have been told by the Lord that they are to participate.

The Lord Sends Help

Now back to the Mandala at LACMA. About nine months prior, another intercessor and warrior had told me about this coming event to be held on County owned property at the museum. I knew almost nothing about Tibetan Buddhism other than what I had run across when the Lord had me do my two-week graduate program in mythology, witchcraft, etc., regarding the "U" we had found next to the watcher symbols in Pasadena. During that study, I kept coming across these appearances of "Ascended Tibetan Masters" who had dictated to Helen Blavatsky, Aleister Crowley, Alice Bailey and John-Roger. Then there was the issue of the key of authority to open the abyss that had symbolically been given to the Dalai Lama in Pasadena.

Shortly after learning about this upcoming event, I would meet another warrior by divine appointment who had actually been a Buddhist for 15 years prior to coming to the Lord 15 years ago. He now operated a ministry that did research and was seeking to educate Christians to understand Buddhism, and specifically to understand the distinct and dark nature of Tibetan Buddhism. This man became a friend and consultant over the next nine months as we tried to figure out exactly what was going on at the museum.

A Short History of Tibetan Buddhism

Let me give you a little history and background on Tibetan Buddhism that you will not find in the newspaper articles and books praising and exalting the Dalai Lama. There is much too much information to include in this book so I will only touch on some of the more pertinent information to give you a feel for what Tibetan Buddhism is all about and why it should concern Christians. To give you some of the historical background I am going to be briefly paraphrasing from Chapter 7 of a book entitled *A Guide to New Religious Movements*[2]. This particular chapter entitled "The Dalai Lama and Tibetan Buddhism" was written by James C. Stephens, a friend of mine who has helped me greatly in understanding the Buddhist mindset and interpreting the rituals and purposes that are being carried out in every corner of this country.

In short, the Tibetan Buddhist history goes something like this. Tibet had not always been Buddhists and had practiced an indigenous faith centered on shamans who worshipped fierce mountain gods and other demonic spirits. Remember the story about Asmodaeus in chapter 13? This was the demon mentioned in the Apocrypha as having flown off to the highest mountain where he ever rests. His name means bringer of anger, bringer of wrath. Could this be one of the fierce mountain gods worshipped in Tibet before it even became Buddhist?

In A.D. 642 the Tibetan king granted his Chinese and Nepalese wives' wish to introduce Buddhism into the land. Monks were brought in from India for this purpose. In A.D. 745, an Indian named Padmasambhava came to Tibet teaching that humans could reach enlightenment in one lifetime. He introduced tantric practice to the Tibetans, using mantras (chants intended to invoke divine power), mandalas (circular sand paintings of deities), deity yoga (symbolic sexual union with deities), mundras (occult hand gestures) and magic. The Tibetan king a Buddhist, requested this man to use his tantric skills to wage war against and conquer all of the malignant gods in Tibet. This led to a period of time in which the Buddhists sought to wrest control of Tibet from the indigenous religious rulers by overcoming the power of the local gods. They built altars in the capitol city but someone always tore these down.

The Buddhists decided to consult their oracles as to how to accomplish this. (The oracles are monks possessed by demons, who are consulted to gain direction over spiritual battles) They were instructed by the oracles to locate spiritual power points all over the nation, build altars, and to make offerings to local gods on mountain peaks, valleys, rivers and lakes. Looking at a map, they saw that these points formed a constellation-like image of a demoness, who was nailed to the ground by their altars. They built an altar at the place of the woman's heart and through this action gained authority over the kingdom of Tibet. The location of this altar is the City of Lhasa. This process is called geomancy, it is a systematic geographic practice of witchcraft over the land to gain spiritual authority.

In A.D. 1206, Genghis Khan led the Mongols in a war to establish his kingdom across China and Mongolia. The Tibetan lamas took the opportunity to convert Khan to Tibetan Buddhism before he became emperor of China and the Tibetan Grand Lama became a vassal ruler of Tibet and spiritual advisor to the emperor Khan. This led to the office of Dalai Lama as the god-king of Tibet.

TIME FOR A MANDALA TO CHANGE THE LAW OF THE WORLD

The Office of Dalai Lama

Dalai Lamas since that time are said to be reincarnations of a previous Dalai Lama carrying the same spirit (demon?). In the 1300's a new school of Tibetan Buddhism was developed as a reform movement. These monks are recognized by their yellow hats. This school is led by the Dalai Lama and focuses on study of tantric texts such as the Kalachakra Tantra. (Tantra is a philosophical system that includes many elements of ritual, meditation, magic or witchcraft, sacrifices, etc.) Kalachakra is the time god and this tantric system revolves around shifting the age or time. In particular, a key component of the time shifting agenda is the creation of Shambhala, a global Buddhist empire. This is to be done through many of the same practices used to establish spiritual and political authority over Tibet, namely through geomancy.

The current or 14th Dalai Lama has a monk who serves as his oracle. The current oracle to the Dalai Lama is a monk who allows himself to become possessed by a demon called Pehar who is said to have been the chief demon of the Red Mongol's and who was captured by the Tibetan Buddhists. The Oracle goes into a demonic manifestation and speaks in tongues, which the Dalai Lama then interprets. This process is illustrated in the 1997 movie "Kundun," directed by Martin Scorsese. It was at the counsel of this oracle in 1959, that the Dalai Lama fled Tibet and established his government in exile in India.

A High Level of Spiritual Technology

Over a period of nearly 1300 years, Tibetan Buddhism has been relatively isolated from the rest of the world. In this isolation they have through intense study and their tantric practices developed what I call, "a very high level of spiritual technology," centered in the development of a symbiotic relationship with the demonic realm. I say symbiotic relationship because of the need of the demonic realm to usurp human authority over this earth or gain the worship of men to be empowered to function in this world. The demons in Tibet have done both. In turn, the humans are able to exercise power through the demons that they worship.

Tibetan Buddhism continually uses both the terms "deities" and "demons." They may place some distinction between the two terms, but I have not yet heard or understood that distinction. It may relate to various aspects of the demons as they appear in different manifestations. Scripture tells us that Satan disguises himself as an angel of light.[3] The Tibetan religious art illustrates many of the deity/demons in several different manifestations or aspects. Some forms of the same name are called "wrathful," while other forms are called "healing" or "compassionate" or illustrate the sexual relationship of this deity with its consort.

What is a Mandala?

In the early spring of 2003, I had very little understanding about Tibetan Buddhism, but I was quickly coming to understand that the construction of a mandala involves creating a symbolic palace into which these deity/demons are invoked using mantras (magical chants accompanied by drums, horns and cymbals). I also understood that different mandalas called upon different deities for different purposes and then all of the sub deities/demons of that deity also were invoked to carry out the purposes of that particular mandala. Each of the demons is assembled into one of the four gates of the mandala according to their particular function. When each gate is activated through ritual, the demons in that gate are released to carry out some function. In many cases the function is destructive!

The 2003 LACMA Event

The event scheduled at LACMA for the fall of 2003 and lasting from October 5th through January 4th of 2004, was billed as an exhibit of Tibetan Buddhist art to be accompanied by the live demonstration of the construction of a mandala. It was to be an educational presentation of culture and art. Some of the people I would meet in the spring, having had previous encounters with these Tibetan "cultural experiences" knew better and relayed warnings. Additionally I was starting to have warnings relayed to me from obscure prophets around Southern California. These were people who for the most part are not known outside their immediate circle of friends, but of whom it is the witness of their friends that these people have been right on a number of times regarding things that the Lord has shown them before they happened. What I was hearing from these prophets, (several of them who did not know each other or have any connection with each other) was visions of a destructive event involving the explosion of a dirty nuclear weapon in the Los Angeles and Long Beach Harbors, and that this was somehow related to the Mandala.

This was pretty wild stuff to me at the time, even after the Revelation of the Seal and the Canopy over Los Angeles County. Now even I was having visions and dreams from the Lord about what was to take place. One of the things the Lord impressed on my mind and spirit was that I was to meet with a very senior county official and tell them about the spiritual and physical implications of this coming "art exhibit on County property." I had no idea how that meeting would take place, but apparently the Lord did.

A Miraculous Meet Up

In May, I was invited to a prayer breakfast at the last minute by a confused friend who thought they were inviting me to go to the City of Pasadena prayer breakfast. When we arrived at the address she had, we discovered that it was a City of Los Angeles prayer breakfast. We arrived and purchased our tickets at the door just before the doors closed. Much to our surprise we were seated at one of the front tables just in front of the head table. Our table mates were all current members of the Los Angeles City Council. An additional surprise was that the County Official that the Lord had been urging me to contact was seated at the head table. At the end of the prayer breakfast, I jumped up immediately, went to the stairs coming down from the head table, and greeted the official as he came off the platform. I introduced myself as a retired LA County Battalion Chief at which time he asked me where I lived in the County. When I told him Arcadia, he asked if I had been to the Arcadia prayer breakfast this year. I confessed that no, I had not gone because the one the year before was pretty secular and the speaker was a county officer who was a Buddhist. To that he agreed, but said that this year they had the Salvation Army Choir and band and the message was much more decidedly Christian. With that, I told him there was something God was prompting me to talk with him about, but I did not know how to get an appointment to do so. He gave me the phone number of his secretary and told me to call her and tell her that she was to set up an appointment with him. I thanked him and left.

Three weeks later, an appointment had been made for 5p.m. just as the office was closing. For the next three hours the official and I talked until he had to leave for a dinner engagement. I told him all about the religious ritual nature of the event scheduled at the museum and the issues regarding destructive gate openings. As I sensed his understanding, I also shared with him the prophetic words regarding the LA and Long Beach Harbors. When I asked him if there was anything he could do in his executive capacity to block the event at the museum and prevent the possible associated destructions, he shook his head. He said that unfortunately the museum was run by an independent board that does not even really answer to the County, that all of his fellow executives were secular humanists, and that he had very little sway with them. He then asked me this, "Can't the churches in the city do something about this?" I said, unfortunately most of the churches are so into themselves that they don't even have a network of communication between each other. All of the ones that I had tried to talk with were oblivious to Tibetan Buddhism and did not see a problem.

I did tell him that there was a small band of us who were trying to stand up against this spiritual assault, but that if something did happen in the harbors in the fall, he would understand and would be able to share with others what had happened. We prayed with each other and I left.

Deconstructing the Mandala Explained

When the mandala has been constructed, and the demons been invoked into the symbolic palace, the gates are ritually opened to release the demons to their function. With that work now complete, there is another ritual through which the demons are called back into the palace and the mandala is deconstructed. This starts with the senior monk carefully lifting out specially placed seeds in different parts of the sand painting. Each of these seeds represents a deity or principality associated with the particular mandala. The seeds are placed in a vase, the sand is swept up and also placed in the vase, though sometimes small vials or bags of the sand are given to the spectators to take home to bless their home. What do you know, demons to go, take one home with you today!

After the deconstruction ceremony, the monks dress in ceremonial headdresses, take their long horns and the vase of sand with the principalities and pour it into a nearby body of water. This is supposedly to bring healing to the water. However, when a warrior friend in Ohio asked a participant at this part of the ceremony for a mandala in Ohio, why they were pouring the sand and seeds representing principalities into the water, she blurted out that the reason was "to appease the water demons."

I had a very vivid dream in June of 2003 in which I saw the monks pouring the sand from this LACMA Mandala off the Santa Monica Pier. I will talk more about that in the next chapter when I also explain what the Lord showed to do.

The Time God is Coming

All summer and up until late September, it was advertised that the Mandala to be constructed was a Kalachakra Mandala. Kalachakra is the time god, and is also the "tantric" system of the fourteenth Dalai Lama. This "tantric" system consists of philosophical world view and view of the universe than includes, manipulation of politics and societies, ritual subjugation of local gods and "mother earth," and the practice of sexual magic intended to direct the practitioners into shifting time and bringing into being the Shambhala Buddhist Empire over the whole world and possibly the entire universe. This extremely complex multi layered sand painting incorporates 722 deities, demons and sacrificial females into a symbolic microcosm of the entire Kalachakra Tantra and understanding of the universe.

A number of Kalachakra Mandalas had already been constructed all over the U.S., so we pretty much knew what to expect. My friend James referred me to a website containing the English translation of an 800-page book by two Buddhists in Germany who had converted to Tibetan Buddhism and then been instrumental in bringing the Dalai Lama to Germany for the first time. Because of the great deal of time they spent with the Dalai Lama and the study they did for their conversion, they learned more than they wanted to know about the politics, the manipulation, and sexual magic (witchcraft) associated with Tibetan Buddhism and with the Dalai Lama in particular. Here are some comments and teaching from these Buddhists on the meaning and purpose of constructing a Kalachakra Mandala:

> "The *Kalachakra* sand mandala thus serves not only to initiate adepts but also likewise as a magic title of possession, with which control over a particular territory can be legitimated. Accordingly, the magic power of the diagram gives its constructors the chance to symbolically conquer new territories. One builds a magic circle (a mandala) and "anchors" it in the region to be claimed. Then one summonses the gods and supplicates them to take up residence in the "mandala palace". (The mandala is so to speak "energized" with divine forces.) After a particular territory has been occupied by a mandala (or cosmogram), it is automatically transformed into a sacred center of Buddhist cosmology.[4] Every construction of a mandala also implies — if one takes

it seriously — the magic subjugation of the inhabitants of the region in which the "magic circle" is constructed."

"In the case of the *Kalachakra* sand mandala the places in which it has been built are transformed into domains under the control of the Tibetan time gods. Accordingly, from a tantric viewpoint, the *Kalachakra* mandala constructed at great expense in New York in 1991 would be a cosmological demonstration of power which aimed to say that the city now stood under the governing authority or at least spiritual influence of *Kalachakra* and *Vishvamata*. Since in this case it was the Fourteenth Dalai Lama who conducted the ritual as the supreme Tantra Master, he would have to be regarded as the spiritual/magic sovereign of the metropolis. Such fantastic speculations are a product of the ancient logic of his own magic system, and are incompatible with our ideas. We are nonetheless convinced that the laws of magic affect human reality proportional to the degree to which people *believe* in them."[4]

"Scattered about the whole world in parallel to his *Kalachakra* initiations, sand mandalas have been constructed for the Fourteenth Dalai Lama. What appears to a western observer to be a valuable traditional work of art, is in its intentions a seal of power of the Tibetan gods and a magic foundation for the striven-for world dominion of the ADI BUDDHA (in the figure of the *Kundun*)"[5]

This Time Change the Law

Suddenly we learned a few days before the October 5 consecration ceremony that instead a Chakrasamvara Mandala was to be constructed. We scrambled to find some information on this Mandala, which had never before been constructed in the Western World. The Chakrasamvara

Mandala that was about to be built in Los Angeles is referred to as the "Law Mandala." Its purpose is to alter the law of the world by initiating the world rule of the Chakravartin. The 800 page expose' by Victor and Victoria Trimondi is entitled,

"THE SHADOW OF THE DALAI LAMA - *Sexuality, Magic and Politics in Tibetan Buddhism."*[6]

The book available on the internet gives us some understanding about the Chakravartin. Here are a couple of excerpts about the Chakravartin:

> "The Fifth Dalai Lama, who combined in his person both worldly and spiritual power for the first time in the history of Tibet, was also still careful about *publicly* describing himself as *Chakravartin*. This could have provoked his Mongolian allies and the "Ruler on the Dragon Throne" (the Emperor of China). Such restraint was a part of the diplomacy of the Tibet of old; or rather, since the Dalai Lamas were during their enthronement handed the highest symbol of universal rule — the "golden wheel" — they were the "true", albeit hidden, rulers of the world, at least in the minds of the Tibetan clergy. The worldly potentates of neighboring states were at any rate accorded the role of a protector."
>
> "We shall come to speak in detail about whether such cosmocratic images still excite the imagination of the current Fourteenth Dalai Lama in the second part of our study. In any case, the *Kalachakra Tantra* which he has placed at the center of his ritual politics contains the phased initiatory path at the end of which the Lion Throne of a *Chakravartin* rears up."
>
> "The *Chakravartin* was referred to as the "King of the Golden Wheel". This is the title given to the "Emperor of Peace", Ashoka (273–236 B.C.E.), after he had united India and with great success converted it

to Buddhism; but is also a name which the Dalai Lama acquires when the "golden wheel" is presented to him during his enthronement."

"As "king and politician", the *Chakravartin* is a sovereign who reigns over all the states on earth. The leaders of the tribes and nations are subordinate to him. His epithet is "one who rules with his own will, even the kingdoms of other kings" (quoted by Armelin, n.d., p. 8). He is thus also known as the "king of kings". His aegis extends not just over humanity, but likewise over Buddhas, Bodhisattvas, wrathful kings, gods, demons, *nagas* (snake gods), masculine and feminine deities, animals and spirits. Of his followers he demands passionate devotion to the point of ecstasy."

"The *Chakravartin* also represents the *Kalachakra* deity, he is the bearer of the universal "time wheel" and hence the "Lord of History"."

"As *lawmaker*, he monitors that human norms stay in keeping with the divine, i.e., Buddhocratic ones. "He is the incarnate representation of supreme and universal Law", writes the religious studies scholar, Coomaraswamy (Coomaraswamy, 1978, p. 13, n. 14a). As a consequence, the world ruler governs likewise as "protector" of the cosmic and of the sociopolitical order."[7]

Change the Law and Rule the World

We now knew that we were not just dealing with the spiritual take-over of a city or region, but the intent of this Mandala was the spiritual and political overthrow of the world. Oh boy! Now what do I do Lord? I spent a lot of time over the next several days asking the Lord that question. I was also asking a lot of questions like: "Is this for real?" "Why me?" "Who do I talk to about this?" That last one was because every attempt to talk to most pastors and church leaders about any of the things I have described in this book, were either just brushed aside as not important, or led to getting looks that said, "How hard did you hit your head when you fell off the ladder in 2002?"

The whole event at the museum was being presented as an educational, cultural and art experience. Many schools throughout Los Angeles brought busloads of students to tour the exhibit and witness the construction of the Mandala. There were film screenings scheduled, receptions and private dinner parties associated with the event. Additionally the Monks were meeting in other locations with business leaders and Hollywood personalities. A sub agenda of some of these meetings was to raise money for the Lord Maitreya project, but more about that in Chapter 21. Though this was an art exhibit, part of the exhibit was designed as instruction and an experience in meditation.

As with most museum special exhibitions, a book catalogue was produced to describe the exhibit. Most catalogues of this type contain prints of the art pieces in the exhibit along with lengthy articles on the history of the piece, information on the artist, and materials used, etc. But this 800-page large color book selling for over $100 dollars contained none of the information about history, artist, or materials used to construct the pieces. It was instead a detailed description of the deities, demons and rituals expressed in the pieces including the Mandala. Not only the rituals expressed though, but also the concept that the whole exhibit was a ritual in totality. I bought the book, and my former Buddhist and now consultant and I began studying to understand what was going on. One thing was clear to us and even to the LA Times reviewer of the exhibit, Christopher Knight, this was not just an art exhibit, it was a religious ceremony being carried out in a Government owned and run building.

As soon as I was able to get back on my feet from the fall in my trailer, I visited the exhibit and prayer walked the buildings and the park area around them. We did not yet know how this Mandala was supposed to accomplish its cosmic and demonic purposes, but we got our first big clue on October 22 when a brief ceremony was held at the Mandala to open the first of four gates of the symbolic palace, the fire gate.

Endnotes

1. 1 Samuel 14:24-46
2. Enroth, Ronald. <u>A Guide to New Religious Movements</u>. Downers Grove, IL: InterVarsity Press, 2005
3. 2 Corinthians 11:14
4. http://www.trimondi.de/SDLE/Part-2-08.htm as each of these chapters or segments of the Trimondi's book are created as individual documents, there is no way to give a page reference to further refine where in the chapter these excerpts were taken from. But there are sub-headings in the chapter and these excerpts come from the sub-heading entitled: **"Mandala politics"**
5. http://www.trimondi.de/SDLE/Part-2-08.htm Sub-heading entitled: "Mandala politics"
6. http://www.trimondi.de/SDLE/
7. http://www.trimondi.de/SDLE/Part-1-09.htm Sub-heading entitled: **"The world ruler: The sociopolitical exercise of power by the ADI Buddha"**

CHAPTER 20

GATES OF DESTRUCTION FROM THE ABYSS

A call came in late Wednesday afternoon. It was from one of my team members that had been watching the progress of the exhibit at LACMA. He had just received a call from a friend of his who works in the entertainment industry out of a high rise building on Wilshire Boulevard near the museum. You see the museum fronts Wilshire Boulevard in the heart of West Los Angeles. This corridor is home to most of LA's business boardrooms, large law offices, and executive offices of the entertainment industry. The friend was saying that she had just been asked to leave her building as the fire department HazMat squads were cordoning off a four-block area around the museum. She knew of the Mandala at the museum and was wondering if we knew what was going on. We did not.

A short time later as I was listening to the local news radios station, I began hearing reports of a number of brush fires breaking out in Ventura County, Los Angeles County, San Bernardino County, Riverside County, and Orange County. Having been a fireman for 24 years, my ears perked and I tuned in to hear what was going on.

Later that night several of us heard a report that a prominent pastor of a large church collapsed at the end of his church's Wednesday night prayer service and was taken to the hospital. This pastor was to be taking over leadership of a gathering that was attempting to bring together on a regular basis, pastors from all over the County. He was diagnosed with a brain aneurysm and died a day later.

I don't know that all three of these incidents were related, but I believe so and here is why. On Thursday, several of the team visited the museum and casually spoke to a couple of the museum guards asking what had happened the day before. The story they got was this. The monks had arrived in their full regalia along with the horns, drums and cymbals and done a short ceremony that he believed was the symbolic opening of a gate in the Mandala. As the monks chanted their magic invocation, the guard said that a stench came up out of the ground all around the museum and they had to leave. The HazMat Squads were called and cordoned off the area, but they could not find anything. The team interviewed several other employees of the museum and received a similar report from everyone.

Now in the natural you probably could write off the smell to the fact that the museum is right next to the La Brea Tar Pits, an area where there are several tarry natural petroleum pools on the surface of the ground. These pools had trapped many ancient animals in the tarry waters. A number of skeletons recovered from the pits are displayed in the Museum of Natural History on the same grounds. However, none of the employees could recall anything quite like this happening before, and the area had never before, been cordoned off.

The Gate of Fire is Opened

Our former Buddhist and consultant got together with some of the team and we went through the catalogue to see if it shed any light. We learned that the gate opened on Wednesday afternoon was the Fire Gate. There was a picture of a demon, assigned to this gate, in the catalogue. He is pictured standing in the midst of a semi-circle of mountains all with flames on them. A couple of days later we were able to see a satellite photo of Southern California showing the fires that had started on Wednesday and were spreading across the mountains in a semi-circle all the way around Los Angeles County. We went back to the museum to look at the Mandala again and carefully examined the quarter section devoted to the fire gate. There in great detail around the outer edge of that section were the mountains with flames on them, people walking up the mountains, people on the mountains with flames on them, and above the mountains 21 skeletons. As the fires burned for several weeks in a ring around Los Angeles Country the death toll begin to rise as did the destruction of property. By the time the fires had been contained, there were 21 people dead as a direct result of the fires. The property damage and loss of homes, cars and businesses was in the high millions. Amazingly, there were no homes burned down or loss of life in Los Angeles County where a protective canopy of worship and prayer had been raised over the whole county ten months prior.

What about the stench? We know that demons are invoked into the mandala to populate the gates and to be assigned tasks when they are sent out from the gates. It is my theory and most of the team agree, that stench came out of the abyss as the demons were called forth to spread the fires.

The Pastor

What about the pastor? This is just conjecture. When members of our team shared it with the staff at his church, they absolutely refused to even consider our speculation. They thought that we were trying to say that there was sin or other problems in the pastor's life. That is absolutely not what we were suggesting. It seems to us that this pastor was about to take on a unifying role among churches all over the LA area. Something that had never been accomplished before and yet looked promising at that point. I know some of you are about to jump out of your chair and tell me that this could never happen this way to a man of God who is under God's protection. Hold on and listen a bit more.

It is a well know strategy in war to take out the opposing army's general or top officer, as this causes confusion, is demoralizing and greatly weakens the ability of that army to succeed in the battle. Why would it not be a strategy of the demonic realm, which has been through a lot more wars than any of us humans, to take out a leader who showed the most promise toward bringing unity in the body of Christ across the LA area? Of course a great portion of the church in America today is in denial that the demonic realm even exists any more in spite of what we see going on in the world around us.

Here is another excerpt from the Trimondi book regarding the "Great Fifth," the fifth Dali Lama, after whom the current fourteenth Dali Lama patterns himself.

> The "Great Fifth" is supposed to have performed a "voodoo" ritual for the defeat of the Kagyupa and the Tsang clan in the Ganden monastery temple. He regarded them, "whose spirit has been clouded by *Mara* and their devotion to the Karmapa", as enemies of the faith (Ahmad, 1970, p. 103). In the ritual, a likeness of the Prince of Tsang in the form of a *torma* (dough cake) was employed. Incorporated into the dough figure were the blood of a boy fallen in the battles, human flesh, beer, poison, and so on. 200 years later, when the Tibetans went to war with the Nepalese, the lamas had a substitute made of the commander of the Nepalese army and conducted a destructive ritual with this. The commander died soon after and the enemy army's plans for invasion had to be abandoned (Nebesky-Wojkowitz, 1993, p. 495).[1]

The Lord does not say that no one will lose his or her physical life in the battle; the promise is that "he who overcomes shall not be hurt by the second death."[2] Revelation also says, "And they overcame him because of the blood of the Lamb and because of the word of their testimony, and they did not love their life even to death."[3] We also know that many of the apostles died a martyr's death. Enough said, draw your own conclusion, but I found the circumstances of this young pastor's death "coincidental."

Perhaps again at this point though I need to repeat some of the disclaimer from the introduction:

> "In the interpretation of the centrality of this passage in Daniel for the present time, I will make statements about certain other religious beliefs and practices. Please hear me clearly, I am not doing this out of any animosity and do not wish to create any animosity toward the individuals who hold and practice those beliefs. I make these statements to illustrate the depth of our misunderstanding of the age in which we live, and the reality of a spiritual realm, of which few people in the United States today, are able to conceive. I hate the demons controlling and destroying these human vessels. I pray salvation through the blood of Jesus for the humans involved and affected by them. The fate of the demons they carry, worship and to which they give authority, is already determined. My greatest hope is that the human vessels not suffer the same end."

Our Priestly Function

I am not trying to cause people to rise up in anger against humans who have practiced witchcraft, Tibetan Buddhism, Masonry all their life or any other form religion that does not acknowledge the God of the Bible. Many of these have never known the True God. Scripture tells us there is a veil over their eyes,[4] they are under the dominion of Satan.[5] As a result, they have been led and held in bondage all the days of their life by the fear of death.[6] The scripture tells us that we have been made to be a kingdom and priests to our God. We are not to be condemning the sins of the people; we are to be carrying out our priestly function of making atonement through the blood of Christ for their sins. We are to be bringing Holy Spirit fired worship and prayer into the midst of the plague of this world.[7]

After the opening of the fire gate and the devastation caused by that release of destruction, we began looking much more closely at the Mandala and the three remaining gates. The four gates, according to reference material we were finding, represented Fire, Water, Earth, and Air in that order clockwise around the Mandala. However, we had not yet found anything that showed us which direction around the Mandala the gates would be opened or anything about the timing of the ritual. All we could do is observe closely, keep praying, asking the Lord, and wait.

Weather Watch and Worship

By Friday November 7, there was a large storm system moving South through the San Joaquin Valley of central California. The TV weather guys were saying this is a big one and people were scrambling all over the fire burned areas of Southern California to sand bag and cover hillsides to prevent flooding and landslides. Some were cheering the rain as needed to put out the last of the lingering fires and urging us not to be concerned as this was the fulfillment of a prophetic word given by Chuck Pierce at a conference in West Covina, California in September 2003.[8] That word had said, "Don't resist the floods or reject the floods for they are signs of what I am doing in your midst. They are signs of how the heavens are beginning to open and the atmosphere is beginning to change." But again, having been a fire fighter, all I could see this storm doing was causing more death and destruction.

Saturday morning as the clouds grew darker over Los Angeles, I had called some intercessors and worshippers to meet me out at Hancock Park behind the museum at 3p.m. Eight people showed up including a talented young man with a guitar. We found a small stage like area off the path through the park. For the next two hours we just worshipped free form. We sang hymns, we sang in tongues, we sang scripture and we danced. I did not feel that we were resisting the floods or rejecting them. We were just drawing near to God and resisting Satan as James instructs us.[9] We were not there to entertain and made no attempt to talk with or direct our attention toward those passing by, but some came and sat on the steps and rested. Others played with their children on the lawn around where we were.

Shortly after we started worshiping a small patch of blue opened up in the center of the sky. An hour and forty-five minutes later there was not a cloud in sight and the sky was clear from horizon to horizon.

I got home that evening just in time to hear the television weatherman say, "Folks, I don't know what to tell you, this storm just petered out." Well, I knew better, it didn't peter out, it Jesus'd out!

Monday night I was at home getting ready to head up to San Jose the next morning for business. Late in the evening, an intercessor called me and said, "Have you charted out the locations of all of the mandalas that are currently being done in Los Angeles and Orange County?" I said that, "no I had not, but I would take a look at this and call her back." I don't know that we even knew the location of all of the mandalas being done concurrently in these two counties, but we were aware of a number of them so I drew them on a map and then drew connecting lines to see if there was any pattern. There was. Lines between the mandalas intersected at two distinct points. One was in the City of Commerce, which is an industrial area south of central Los Angeles, and the other in Compton, which is just north of Long Beach. I called the intercessor back and relayed the information so others could be praying about what to do with that information.

The Water Gate Floods Contained

The next morning I drove up to San Jose about 350 miles north. I spent the night in a motel and when I awoke in the morning I turned the television on while I was shaving and dressing. The big news that morning was about a huge storm that had dropped 5 inches of rain and 18 inches of hail on the City of South Gate. I groaned. Why had I not seen it? South Gate lies right between Commerce and Compton and The Water Gate of the Mandala was the South Gate of the Mandala!

In any case there was very little damage done as there are major river flood control channels in that area and as a result very little flooding. Was the Lord trying to tell us that it would be the South Gate, The Water Gate that would be the next to be opened, or did our worship and the intercession over that area contain this storm to where it would do very little damage?

The LA Times the next day would describe this storm that on Saturday had broken up and drifted out to sea. There it gathered an "inordinate" amount of moisture, slowly drifted back over the LA area and in a storm of "Biblical Proportions" dumped the 5 inches of rain and 18 inches of hail only in South Gate.

21 Days and Counting

We now knew the direction of the opening of the gates and knew the timing of the ritual because we also had just found a series of 21's in the Mandala and in the description found in the catalogue. In addition, it had been 21 days since the opening of the Fire Gate. The next gate to be opened would be the land gate and we were expecting that to happen on December 3.

During this time, a number of the intercessors were starting to hear from the Lord what the overall strategy of this Mandala might be. Remember in the last chapter I talked about the purpose of the Chakrasamvara Mandala being to alter the law of the world by initiating the world rule of the Chakravartin. What we were seeing in the natural was that the monks who built the Mandala were spending a lot of time building relationships with influential people in the business and entertainment worlds. The Mandala was created to release four major destructions, the last of which, according to the prophets we had heard from in the spring, was a dirty nuclear weapon to be released in the LA and Long Beach harbors. Through these two harbors passes 34 percent of this nations commerce. An event such as a dirty nuclear weapon would shut down the harbors for years and would devastate the economy of the entire nation. Such an event would not likely cause much damage in the rest of LA though.

Taking Care of Business Before the Earth Gate

Nevertheless, before the Air Gate, we still had to deal with the Earth Gate, which was looking more and more like it might be the release of an earthquake that would take care of doing damage to the rest of LA! What the intercessors were hearing, was that these combined disasters in such a short time, would utterly bring this country to its knees. Into this chaos, as a result of all of the influential relationships being built, would come the monks who would morn the losses, blame the damage of the harbor on terrorists and suggest, "Isn't it time that we bring the Dalai Lama, the Prince of Peace on earth, into a position of authority so that he can bring order to this Chaos?" Mind you, this borders on speculation on our part, but this seemed to be the set up that the Lord was revealing to us.

It seemed that we might have had some influence in altering the intended outcome of the opening of The Water Gate. There was no devastating storm, it was first disbursed through the worship on Saturday and when it re-gathered, the downpour was contained to South Gate.

So what could we do to contain the opening of the Earth Gate, which we were all sure would result in a large earthquake? A group of us met for a day of prayer to ask the Lord what to do. It seemed logical and we were hearing from the Lord, that this might involve a prophetic act of reconciliation over defilement of the land. A pastor from El Monte on the East side of Los Angeles had been working on just such an act with other pastors from that city.

Healing for Defiled Land

In 1771, Father Junipero Serra had founded the San Gabriel mission in a location along a river in an area that is now called the Whittier Narrows Recreation Area. It is a large regional park and surrounded by protected wild land. At the founding of the mission, Father Serra's group was protected by a small contingent of soldiers. The story goes that the leader of the soldiers kidnapped and raped the wife of the then

Tongva Chief. The Chief heard about this and came to confront the soldier who shot and killed the Chief. This was the first spilling of native blood by a European in the area we now call California. Since this issue had never been dealt with in a Biblical manner and the scripture tells us that blood defiles the land, this group of elders and pastors in El Monte, the nearest city, had decided that it was their responsibility to follow the Biblical pattern in Deuteronomy to deal with it.[10] They had been waiting to find a Tongva representative to participate in this act to remove the bloodguilt from the land. There was a Christian Tongva descendant on our team so we arranged a date and time before the opening of the Earth Gate to carry out this prophetic act.

There also was an issue over the land because of the worship by the Tongva of a god other that the God of Abraham, Isaac and Jacob. Therefore, we took a team and a Tongva representative to the site of the Village of Pavugna down in Long Beach to repent of following false gods and defiling the land through practices very similar to Tibetan Buddhism.

The third issue involved the spilling of blood on the land. A major reconciliation and identificational repentance ceremony was held in Chino Hills to deal with this.

These were the only three things that the Lord gave us, so we believed it was sufficient.

On the day of December 3, we were all watching our watches and listening to the news channels as we were going about our day. Nothing happened except an apartment house fire down in Anaheim near Disneyland.

By this time, several of our team had caught the attention of prayer leaders and some pastors throughout California. Someone heard from the Lord that we needed to guard the central artery of California, Interstate 5 as it runs all the way from the Mexican Border to the Oregon border. On the Saturday following the opening of the Earth Gate, teams from all over California, prayed on overpasses over the 5 from the Mexican Border to the Oregon Border.

One is Not Enough

On that same Saturday however, the Tibetan monks brought in a team of 13 Nepalese monks and they constructed another mandala on Wilshire Boulevard two blocks West in another part of the museum. This one was not open to the public. I think they were trying to figure out why their Earth Gate opening had misfired and trying to remedy the problem with another secret mandala. This was a one day project and the sand was taken out to the Malibu Lagoon to pour into the water. I Don't know what the significance of that place is to them, but the Lord had us put one of the poles to the canopy over Los Angeles County in that location 11 months prior.

Now we believed it was time to deal with the harbors preemptively. The Lord instructed us to build a canopy of worship and prayer over the harbor. We took a team of fifteen dedicated warriors and worshippers out to the harbor with four points on the corners and a center pole on Terminal Island where the prophet had seen a cargo container with this bomb. On Terminal Island there is only one cargo container pier. The rest of the piers are oil and gas terminals and storage. What a mess a bomb would make there right under the Vincent Thomas Bridge across the harbor and at the throat of both harbors.

As we simultaneously began to worship in our five locations, a number of our team saw in their spirit large golden ropes link the five poles and then a pure white canopy unfurl over the harbor. The thing that struck me is the harbor is a noisy place, but a noticeable hush came over the whole harbor as the canopy unfurled. Others would comment on this also as we gathered later in the day. One of the teams on a hill overlooking the harbor at the Northeast corner saw red stripes of blood coming down the canopy giving it a festive appearance.

A couple of days later in what was perhaps a misfire from the second mandala, a significant earthquake did occur in California off the coast at San Simeon about 200 miles North of Los Angeles. Some damage occurred at the Hearst Castle overlooking the very small town of San Simeon, but the majority of the shock wave went under the coastal mountains and erupted in the parking lot of the Paso Robles City Hall and Library. This opened a 40 foot deep and very wide chasm in the parking lot. Sulfur laden mud began flowing out of the hole. On the other side of the City Hall there is a park square, and on the opposite corner of the park an old building with a clock tower. The clock tower collapsed and killed two women walking by. Remember that the base ritual system in Tibetan Buddhism is the Kalachakra Tantra. The time god! I am just speculating but I think that the collapse of the clock tower was significant as was the death of just two. I just don't know that I can fully voice that significance right now.

Fencing the Coastline

During that week, an intercessor in Oakland up near the San Francisco Bay, heard from the Lord that we needed as a state to erect a fence or barrier along the entire West coastline of California. This was to be done by teams of people driving specified segments of the coastline and placing stakes with scripture on them every fifty miles along the coast. I got a call early Friday morning December 19 informing me that the team leader who was supposed to organize teams for Southern California from Oxnard to the Mexican Border, had received news of a death in the family and had to fly out to the East Coast. I was asked if I could put together teams to cover this very long section of the coastline on Saturday. I found four intercessors and another warrior who believed that the Lord would have them to do this even though these intercessors normally did not venture far from their prayer closets. We formed two teams with Corona Del Mar being our join up point. This beach area whose name means "Crown of the Sea" is the area where Calvary Chapel for years baptized new Christians in the ocean."

I took two intercessors with me and we went all the way to the fence at the Mexican Border where it goes out into the ocean. We found a dirt road that got us to within a mile of the location. We walked the rest of the way. It was a wonderful day of worshipping and praying our way up the coastline ending in Corona del Mar at about 10p.m.

The other team coming down from Oxnard did not have quite as nice a day as they battled traffic through the Los Angeles coastal area and came under severe demonic attack as they attempted to go around the Palos Verdes Peninsula. That would result in another group of warriors doing several prophetic acts on the Peninsula some months later.

The final result on Saturday the 20th of December was that, in one day the entire coastline of California was prayed and worshipped over and scriptural proclamations were pounded into the ground every fifty miles.

Something is in the Air

The next cycle of 21 days would now come on Christmas Eve December 24. Our team gathered all day on Monday the 22 to pray and ask the Lord if there was anything else we needed to do. The answer was no.

Over the weekend, one of the team members who had worked with intercessors in Washington, D.C. received a call warning us that government agencies had mobilized teams into Los Angeles, looking for dirty nuclear weapons! The countries threat alert was raised on Monday, and on Wednesday the 24th a number of airliners were denied entry into the United States being turned around in the air. I don't know what that was all about, but somebody in the Government felt that there was a credible threat to the West Coast on December 24. The Lord had told us this more than 6 months prior, and He had also told us exactly what to do, where to do it and when to do it. Nothing happened! Remember my story about changing the oil in your car in the introduction to this book. The Christian walk is one of faith. All these things were done by faith in obedience to our Lord.

There was one more issue to be dealt with, the deconstruction ceremony scheduled for January 4, 2004 with the pouring out of the sand that afternoon.

Deliverance at the Deconstruction

We still had not heard or seen anything about where the monks were intending to pour out the sand, which is a defiling act. However, since the Lord had shown me in a dream 6 months prior that it was going to be at the Santa Monica Pier, I went ahead planned what He had showed me to do. I had put out a general notice to my email list inviting people to join me for worship out at the end of the pier at 7a.m. We were going to enthrone the Lord on our praises and establish His dominion over the pier and the waters around it.

January 4th was on a Sunday and the ceremony was planned for late morning, somebody probably thinking that all of the Christians that could have any influence over the outcome of the ceremony would be in church.

The night before, one of our team was spending the evening with a relative and they went walking out on the pier as did hundreds of other people on a nice Southern California January evening. As they got out to a place over the water where there is a little alcove in the railing for fishermen, here were two of the senior monks from the Mandala with two other men in business suits. It was obvious from their actions that they were looking over the rails to make sure that the sand would go into the water. Immediately the team member called several of us to relay this information.

On Sunday morning, after the 7a.m. worship time on the pier, there were 6 of our team that showed up at the museum, but there were also several other teams of intercessors that we knew and recognized in the crowd. There was limited space in the room where the Mandala was, so we got there early and took up positions inside the room around the outside of the crowd so that we could see everyone but not have people behind our back. The Lord gave each of us different assignments to carry out when the chanting began for the purpose of invoking the demons back into the Mandala.

One of the team was behind the monks praying over them. Another was on the opposite side of the room from the monks and was just worshipping silently. I was led to command each of the demons to the feet of Jesus as they would come into the room. Another person was led to create a disturbance among those around him so that they could not focus their meditation. Another team member was down in front next to a group of children who were sitting on the floor directly in front the Mandala.

I have to say I was pretty nervous about being in that room that day. I do not particularly like dealing with deliverance and demons, and there were supposed to be 62 of them to deal with. But I just silently prayed and worshipped, and the Lord calmed my heart.

When the ceremony started, the monks did a guttural chant, played the drums, cymbals, and occasionally blew the long horn. Within less than a minute, I sensed the arrival of the first demon and I just quietly said something like, "demon number one I command you to attention and send you to the feet of Jesus for Him to deal with you." Then the presence I had felt left and another showed up. "Demon number two, I command you to attention and send you to the feet of Jesus for Him to deal with you." That one left. So it went on for 62 demons. Meanwhile the team member down by the kids was trying to calm them down. When the first demon had come into the room, they started getting sick to their stomachs. The team member very quietly told them that it was just because a demon had showed up but they would be gone soon. One little child began to cry and said, "My parents didn't tell me there were going to be demons here." He prayed protection over the children and calmed them.

Like the Prophets of Baal

This part of the ceremony was supposed to last less than 15 minutes. But when the monks finished the chant, I could see in their faces that something was not working as they all looked at one another and whispered something. One of them reached under his chair and pulled out what must have been a chant book. He flipped rapidly through the book and finally showed the others something. They started another chant. This one was a bit more frantic than the first with increased clanging of cymbals and beating on the drum. I did not sense any more demons arriving. Apparently, this didn't work either as after this they again flipped through the book, nodded at each other, and started an even more frantic rendition. I could not help comparing what I was seeing and hearing to the description of the prophets of Baal up on Mt. Carmel with Elijah as they were trying to "wake up their gods."[11] After these three attempts that had taken almost 45 minutes, they all looked at each other again, whispered some more and the senior monk got up to proceed with the ceremony minus the demons. I was envisioning the demons all cowering at the feet of Jesus.

The senior monk used a spoon tied to a stick to lift out carefully each of the 62 seeds that were supposed to symbolize each of the demons that were not there. When he was done, the sand was swept up and put into a vase with the seeds. The ceremony was over. I casually asked one of the monks where the sand was to be poured out, he claimed he was not sure, but I said that I had heard Santa Monica Pier. He looked at me strange and then said, yes I think that is where they said.

We left and went back down to the pier and set up a surveillance team all around the pier and also sent some teams driving up to Malibu and Paradise Cove, both places with piers in case they did a last minute switch. Other teams went south to watch over the Venice Pier and Marina Del Ray.

The Dominion Had Changed

Sure enough at around 4p.m. the monks showed up in full regalia at the entrance to the pier. They were in a marching formation, abreast of each other. From the entrance arch of the pier there is a road that comes down a hill before it joins the actual pier structure. They walked down the hill and stopped where the road joins the pier. They stopped and just stood there for at least 15 minutes. It appeared that they could not set foot on the pier. That had to be God's dominion over the pier established as of 7a.m. that morning and now they could not enter onto it. Finally, they turned around and went back up the hill to where there is a staircase down to the sand of the beach. They went down and walked out to the water's edge on the North side of the pier. One of our team went ahead of them and actually went out into the water with a video camera to tape what happened. One of the monks with the vase tried to run out between the waves and dump the vase at the waters ebb, but when he poured out the sand, a strong off shore wind blew it all back in their faces. The monks turned to leave and talk with some television camera crews that had just showed up.

It appeared that we had won this three-month long battle, but I knew this war was not yet over. This exhibit was moving on to Columbus, Ohio. I also knew that there were many other mandalas being done all over the country as well as, the Awake Project, the Peace Vase Project, the Lord Maitreya Project and the Sacred Heart Relic Tour. At least for the minute, it looked like we had a little time to put the pieces of this puzzle together and ask the Lord what the final picture looked like.

What it looked like was Daniel 7:21-26. So lets you and I look at the whole picture in the next chapter so you can talk to the Lord and draw your own conclusions.

AUTHORS NOTE: As I was finishing this chapter, I was prompted by the Lord to go look into an old archived e-mail box that I have not used since early 2004. There I found an e-mail I had sent out on November 5, 2003, which would eventually become the basis for this book. In that e-mail, I had also included two prophetic words that were given by Chuck Pierce and Cindy Jacobs at a conference in the Los Angeles area in September 2003. I did not see or hear of these words until November when several who had been at the conference were scolding us that we should not try to stop any destruction that might come from the opening of The Water Gate of the Mandala.

As I read the prophecies, I did not see it that way. What I saw was a call to arise and take possession of the Kingdom. I was seeing that it was not that we should not stand in the gap to prevent widespread destruction being released through the Mandala, but that we should not resist or stop the shifting and flooding over the spirit of Gods people to cause them to wake up. Since most of what we were doing was simply setting feet to the land, and worshipping the Lord in those places so that He would be enthroned on the praise of His people and His dominion would be established in that place, I did not see that we were in anyway "resisting or rejecting" what the Lord was doing.

Realizing how pertinent these prophecies from September were to the events of fall 2003 and the battle we were waging with the demonic forces being released from the gates of the abyss, I decided to include these two prophetic words in full as APPENDIX C to this book. I do not feel led to go into detailed explanation of how I feel they apply or interrelate to the events I was a part of, as I was not even fully aware of the existence of these prophecies until the middle of the fall. I was much too involved with just doing what the Lord was telling me to do. I was not able to spend time trying to figure out how what He had told these two prophetic voices related to what we were doing until after the fact. Thank you Cindy and Chuck for your continued obedience to speak what you are hearing from the Lord.

Endnotes

1. http://www.trimondi.de/SDLE/Part-2-08.htm Sub-heading entitled: **"Voodoo magic"**
2. Revelation 2:11
3. Revelation 12:11
4. 2 Corinthians 4:3
5. Acts 26:18
6. Hebrews 2:14-15
7. Numbers 16:46-50
8. Words given by Cindy Jacob and Chuck Pierce at that conference foretold fires, rain, flooding, moving of the earth and changes in the atmosphere in California for the time period of November 2003 through January 2004. See the full text of their prophecies in Appendix C. Permission for use of quotes in this book of these 2003 prophetic words over California granted by Dr. Chuck Pierce-https://gloryofzion.org/ and Cindy Jacobs-https://www.generals.org/
9. James 4:7-10
10. Deuteronomy 21:1-9
11. 1 Kings 18:25-29

CHAPTER 21

A FOURTH KINGDOM WAGES WAR WITH THE SAINTS

The fall 2003 exhibit at the Los Angeles County Museum of Art was called "Circle of Bliss: Buddhist Meditational Art." It was publicized as an educational, cultural and art event. What the publicists left out, was that this was also a political, military, religious, pornographic and occult event if you want to cover the full circle of this "bliss." Let's talk about each one of these categories.

Educational: Yes, this event certainly was educational. If we look at the last half of the title "Buddhist Meditational Art," you would think that the emphasis is on the word "art." However, according to the 800-page catalog of the event, the emphasis was on the word "meditational." According to the catalogue, the purpose of the exhibit is to teach the art of Buddhist (and in this case particularly Tibetan Buddhist) meditation. If you study Tibetan Buddhist history and the purpose of the meditational portion of this religious based culture, the whole purpose of meditation is to draw into ones' self, certain demons/deities to empower you to overthrow other demons/deities and eventually escape this life all together by reaching Nirvana. It is the testimony of several former Dali Lamas and of Aleister Crowley that once you have allowed some of these demons in, they cannot be removed and they can be pretty nasty.

Here's some education for you. Nirvana, regardless of current blissful definitions you may find on Wikipedia, has traditionally been defined as escape into utter nothingness or more completely as "Extinguishing of the flame of the candle of the soul into utter blackness." On the other hand, as a Christian you might equate this to the description found in the Bible as separation from God for all eternity and the place of the "outer darkness" where Jesus says the sons of the Kingdom who have not believed, and the worthless servants will be cast, a place of weeping and gnashing of teeth.[1]

Another part of the educational aspect of this "art" exhibit, and for which bus loads of elementary, junior and high school students were brought to be educated, is the pornographic nature of the artistic representations of many of the idols and paintings of these "deities" and "demons." Take for example the picture of the god Chakrasamvara who is the central principality or deity of the Chakrasamvara Mandala that was done at LACMA. The picture of this deity that was sitting on a small table right next to the picture of the Dalai Lama, at kid height, shows Chakrasamvara in a pose of sexual penetration of his consort Vajravahari with genitalia exposed. This particular depiction of the god Chakrasamvara is just one of 64 different manifestations for which there are paintings, all of which include this pose of sexual penetration. Many of the other fabric, stone and bronze idol depictions of various gods and demons of Tibetan Buddhism also show sexual poses or other forms of nudity. This is because sexuality and sexual magic is at the core of Tibetan Buddhism.

This is very similar to the practices of sexual magic by Aleister Crowley, Jack Parsons and L. Ron Hubbard that was central in the 1946 ritual to "birth the moonchild." It is centered on subjugation of the female for the purpose of absorbing from her the life energies. Aleister Crowley learned these practices and incorporated them into the OTO as a result of the dictation and information he was taught by a demonic entity that appeared to him in 1903 and identified its self as an "Ascended Tibetan Master."

Cultural: Yes again this was an exhibit of a culture that is totally foreign to us. It is a culture that is primarily centered upon conquering and subjugating deities and demons in order to draw that power into self to elevate ones' self along the path to enlightenment. One of the central teachings of Buddhism and a practice to which the Dali Lama adheres, is the "doctrine of Expedient Means or skill in means." The closest equivalent to an understanding of this doctrine we have in our culture is "the end justifies the means." "The implication is that even if a technique, view, etc., is not ultimately "true" in the highest sense, it may still be an *expedient* practice to perform or view to hold; i.e., it may bring the practitioner closer to true realization anyway. The exercise of skill to which it refers, the ability to adapt one's message to the audience, is of enormous importance in the Pali Canon."[2] It is the use of this cultural doctrine by which the Dalai Lama has been able to constantly adapt his message to whatever audience he is speaking to, thereby gaining their attention and agreement, while all the while still holding to his ultimate intention to proselytize the world into a Buddhist empire.

This is an aspect of exposure to this culture of which the average American is oblivious when they are drawn to and mesmerized by the colorful, skillfully constructed mandalas being constructed all over the world. They do not understand the Tibetan Buddhist culture that creates the mandala and summons the demons into it for the purpose of subjugating a region and the people within that region.

Art: Yes, this was an art exhibit and you cannot deny the skill of the artist in the creation of the many pieces that were on display including the Mandala. Some might also include as beautiful art works, the ritual knives that are used for ritual human sacrifice, the girdles made of human bones, the skull cups made of human skulls and used in ritual to drink fluids that you and I would consider disgusting and defiling. As mentioned above, many of these art works would also be considered pornographic by the standards that once existed in this country (Not sure that there is any standard any longer).

Political: The Merriam-Webster Online Dictionary defines politics as: 1a: the art or science of government b: the art or science concerned with guiding or influencing governmental policy c: the art or science

IN FAVOR OF THE SAINTS

concerned with winning and holding control over government.[3] The title given to a Dalai Lama when he is installed in that office is "god and king of Tibet." He is the head figure in the Government of Tibet, at least until it became a government in exile in 1959. However, most of the governments of the world cannot recognize him as a head of state, as this would anger the Chinese who claim dominance over that territory. Therefore, the Dalai Lamas diplomatic credentials instead identify him as the religious head of Tibetan Buddhism. This is a minor inconvenience however and has in no way limited his access to presidents, prime ministers, and other heads of state all over the world for purely political purposes. Well not quite purely political purposes.

When the Chinese invaded Tibet in 1951, they recognized that it was through spiritual means by which Tibet has been able to maintain its sovereignty throughout the centuries. Tibet has never had a large or strong physical army; they have always used diplomacy and magic (witchcraft) to hold political power.

One of the issues troubling the Dalai Lama the most in recent years about the Chinese occupation of Tibet is that the Chinese government took the Panchen Lama into "protective custody" and substituted a Panchen Lama of their own choosing. Who is the Panchen Lama you might say? The Panchen Lama is considered number two in the Tibetan governmental hierarchy and is a lama personally selected by the current Dalai Lama as the one who will discern and select the reincarnation in the person who will become the next Dalai Lama, god and king of Tibet. Let me put this to you a little clearer. It is the job of the Panchen Lama to search for and find a human who is possessed by the same deity (demon) as the previous human Dalai Lama in order to continue movement toward the Shambhala Buddhist Empire, or bringing the Chakravartin into his ultimate political position as "king of kings" the "ruler of the world."

Since the physical body of the Dalai Lama is human and will die a physical death, it is essential to the demonic political establishment of Tibetan Buddhism to have control over this selection process for the next Dalai Lama. It is for this reason that the art and science of politics is employed at all levels to influence business leaders, celebrities and politicians for the affecting of governmental policy around the world and "free Tibet."

Military: I used the term military above because you and I usually think of the overthrow or overpowering of a government in military terms. Very seldom in the world have we seen a government simply hand over control to an opposing form of government or force without there being some military involvement to enforce the issue at hand. Here is what the Kalachakra Tantra teaches about the takeover of the world by the Chakravartin. "...the *Chakravartin* possesses exclusively peaceful characteristics. All his "conquests", reports the scholar Vasubandhu (fourth or fifth century C.E.), are nonviolent. The potentates of the world voluntarily and unresistingly subject themselves on the basis of his receptive radiation. They bow down before him and say: "Welcome, O mighty king. Everything belongs to you, O mighty king!" (quoted by Armelin, n.d., p. 21). He is mostly incarnated as an *avatar*, as the reincarnation of a divine savior, who should lead humanity out of its earthly misery and into paradise." "A Buddhist world ruler grasps the "wheel of command", symbol of his absolute force of command. In the older texts the stress is primarily on his military functions. He is the supreme commander of his superbly armed forces. As "king and politician", the *Chakravartin* is a sovereign who reigns over all the states on earth. The leaders of the tribes and nations are subordinate to him. His epithet is "one who rules with his own will, even the kingdoms of other kings" (quoted by Armelin, n.d., p. 8). He is thus also known as the "king of kings". His aegis extends not just over humanity, but likewise over Buddhas, Bodhisattvas, wrathful kings, gods, demons, *nagas* (snake gods), masculine and feminine deities, animals and spirits. Of his followers he demands passionate devotion to the point of ecstasy."[4]

Occult: Again, to quote the The Merriam-Webster Online Dictionary, occult means: "matters regarded as involving the action or influence of supernatural or supernormal powers or some secret knowledge of them." "Secret" is one of the key words in this definition. In fact, the Spanish word for worship or religion is "culto" or the

English word cult. Worship and all religions generally involve some acknowledgement of supernatural or supernormal powers including Christianity. However, what differentiates Christianity as a cult from being occult is the "secret" aspect of the knowledge used in the practice of calling upon supernatural or supernormal powers. The Tibetan Buddhists do not introduce this understanding to monks until they have already completed their preliminary training. And they certainly are keeping secret the actions they are taking through the building of a mandala to release the influence of these supernatural powers (demons) over the region and the people within it. Another term now used more commonly for secret understanding is "esoteric."

The book of revelation tells us: "And there was war in heaven, Michael and his angels waging war with the dragon. And the dragon and his angels waged war, and they were not strong enough, and there was no longer a place found for them in heaven. And the great dragon was thrown down, the serpent of old who is called the devil and Satan, who deceives the whole world; he was thrown down to the earth, and his angels were thrown down with him."[5] "Woe to the earth and the sea, because the devil has come down to you, having great wrath, knowing that he has only a short time."[6] Perhaps this is why the Tibetans call many of their deities "wrathful deities." Jesus calls Satan or the devil that was cast down the ruler of this current world or age.[7] Paul refers to him as the "god of this world" when he explains, "And even if our gospel is veiled, it is veiled to those who are perishing, in whose case the god of this world has blinded the minds of the unbelieving, that they might not see the light of the gospel of the glory of Christ, who is the image of God."[8]

When the Iron Bird Flies

Let me give you some perspective on all of this. An ancient Tibetan prophecy from about A.D. 745 states, "When the Iron Bird flies to the land of the red man, the dharma will come to the West."[9] Dharma, "is an Indian spiritual and religious term, that means one's righteous duty or any virtuous path in the common sense of the term."[10] According to the teachings of the Kalachakra Tantra, it is the duty of the Dalai Lama to pursue dharma in the West in fulfillment of this prophesy and as progress along the path to enlightenment in the form of the Chakravartin. He is to alter the times (Kalachakra the time god) and shift the law of the world by changing the rule of the world or should I say changing the worlds understanding of who the "true" ruler is.

Ascended Tibetan Masters

Here is a little more background on how this is being played out over the last one hundred plus years.

In 1918, Forest Bailey left his position as U.S. General Secretary of the Theosophical Society. This organization was formed in 1875 by Helen Blavatsky in Germany. This organization, which has been called "New Age Buddhism," greatly influenced German Masonic and as an esoteric religion included revelation, which was supposedly, given by spiritual entities which identified themselves as "Ascended Tibetan Masters." Some of the revelation that was included in Madam Blavatsky's writings stated that "the Christians were very uninformed and weak minded and that they worshipped Satan while the enlightened members of the society worshipped the true gods." Further reference was made to the fact that the Christians would eventually become a problem that would have to be dealt with!

The Lucifer Publishing Company

When Forest Bailey left the Theosophical Society, he took with him a young woman Alice who would eventually become his wife. Together the two of them moved to New York City and established the Lucifer Publishing Company. This name was too obvious for the times and was soon changed to the Lucis Trust Publishing Company. This publishing house would eventually become a publisher for the United Nations and today they have offices on Wall Street in New York and are the focal point for the formation of a one-world religion based on the principles of Tibetan Buddhism.

The basis for the teachings of the Lucis Trust and their daughter organization World Goodwill are the 24 volumes of writings by Alice Bailey, which were dictated to her during the 1920's and 1930's by a spiritual entity that appeared to her and identified itself as an "Ascended Tibetan Master." Alice also addresses in her writings at one point that the Christians are a problem that will have to be eliminated some time in the future. Her writings or should we say the doctrines of demons which she wrote down and taught from have been gradually modified over the last several years to come more in line with a subtle appearance of being Christian teachings. Even the web site is using the terms the Christ, the Kingdom of God and other Christian terms to mask the previous use of the Buddhist terms Lord Maitreya, the Avatar and the Shambhala Kingdom.

It is quite evident in having watched the metamorphosis of this site for the last several years that the deception is growing, "so as to deceive even the elect if possible." However, certain parts of the Lucis Trust website are becoming much more transparent. I downloaded this statement from that website today:

> There are comments on the World Wide Web claiming that the Lucis Trust was once called the Lucifer Trust. Such was never the case. However, for a brief period of two or three years in the early 1920's, when Alice and Foster Bailey were beginning to publish the books published under her name, they named their fledgling publishing company "Lucifer Publishing Company". By 1925 the name was changed to Lucis Publishing Company and has remained so ever since. Both "Lucifer" and "Lucis" come from the same word root, *lucis* being the Latin generative case meaning *of light*. The Baileys' reasons for choosing the original name are not known to us, but we can only surmise that they, like the great teacher H.P. Blavatsky, for whom they had enormous

respect, sought to elicit a deeper understanding of the sacrifice made by Lucifer. Alice and Foster Bailey were serious students and teachers of Theosophy, a spiritual tradition which views Lucifer as one of the solar Angels, those advanced Beings Who Theosophy says descended (thus "the fall") from Venus to our planet eons ago to bring the principle of mind to what was then animal-man. In the theosophical perspective, the descent of these solar Angels was not a fall into sin or disgrace but rather an act of great sacrifice, as is suggested in the name "Lucifer" which means *light-bearer*.[11]

So As To Deceive Even the Elect

This deception of the "elect" is becoming very evident through events such as what occurred one weekend in 2004 at the First Presbyterian Church of Santa Monica in California. The pastor who was there at the time and who has a Dr. of Theology from Fuller Seminary stated to the face of two of our team that he did not see any issue with allowing the Buddhist Heart Shrine Relic Tour to use their facility on Second Street in Santa Monica. This location is one block from where ten people were killed in what we strongly believe to have been a witchcraft conjured spilling of innocent blood and one block in the opposite direction from a statue which is a spiritual gateway or portal as identified by a former practitioner of witchcraft as the place where he used to come to contact his demons and cast spells on the entertainment and business community of Hollywood. The Heart Shrine Relic Tour is a collection of body parts and residue of cremation of the Buddha and a number of other Buddhist monks. Seeing and being in the presence of these body parts is supposed to impart energy through meditation on them and worship of them.

Make an Image

In the video that was handed out at this site, scenes are shown where these relics are held over the heads of "Christian" pastors to bless and energize (demonize) them. This collection of body parts and residue after it has been toured all over the world to attract the hearts and gain the worship of all peoples is then to be placed in the 500 foot high Lord Maitreya statue that is being built in India in order to "energize or bring to life" that statue. Does that sound anything like the "image to the beast" that those who dwell on the earth are told to make as spoken of in Revelation?[12] If you are waiting for some future appearance of the antichrist, or to be raptured out of this world before the events foretold occur, you perhaps need to reconsider your theology and make certain it is actually based upon the bible and the revelations of Christ through the Holy Spirit and not on novels written by men in recent years. But then that is another whole discussion.

Christians would do well to understand the teachings of the bible concerning the kingdom of which, "we have been made to be," according to Revelation 5:10.

Daniel tells us of the visions he was given about the kingdoms of the world and of a last kingdom which will rise up in the last days. This kingdom according to Daniel 7:23 will be different from all the other kingdoms. Could it be that all of the previous kingdoms that can be identified as military and political kingdoms of the past, will have been different in that this is a spiritual kingdom which will devour the whole earth, tread it down, and crush it. Which will, according to verse 24, subdue three kings and verse 25, will speak out against the Most High and wear down the saints of the Highest One.

All of these things we are seeing come about as the Dali Lama and Buddhism in general have been more and more blatant in speaking out against Christianity and Judaism, painting them as hateful and divisive because they make claims of exclusivity for salvation. Even at this writing, this influence on government policy has put a bill through congress that will criminalize "hate speech." This bill is so broad that even teaching some of what the Bible teaches as truth from God will become a criminal act.

Further evidence of the connection of Tibetan Buddhism and this last kingdom that is raised up, is in the statements of Verse 25, "and he will intend to make alterations in times and in law". The ritual system of this Dali Lama, whose title is god and king of Tibet, is the Kalachakra Tantra. Kalachakra is the time god. The Kalachakra rituals are intended to shift the age out of the age of Pices into the age of Aquarius. Out of the Christian age into the Aquarian age. The witchcraft instruction manuals I have reviewed in the past also refer to the Christians as being of the age of Pices. The Lucis Trust web site also explained this understanding a couple of years ago, but it is constantly morphing and shifting and the reference URL that I had for this is no longer available.

Disguised as an Angel of Light

So we see that the intent of the Dalai Lama to alter time as is described in these last several chapters, could be one of the marks of this last kingdom that is raised up which will wear down the saints and overwhelm them. Verse 25 says that he will intend to alter law also. This was evident in the events of the fall of 2003 when the Chakrasamvara Mandala and ritual was done at the Los Angeles County Museum of Art. The Chakrasamvara Mandala is intended to invoke a world ruler and as such is called the "Law Mandala," for when you change the ruler of the world, you alter the law of the world. So it is that we see this kingdom of Tibetan Buddhism disguising itself in the world as "an angel of light" with all of its talk of peace, harmony and love, but in the same breath pointing at the Christians that stand in opposition as being the problem in the world.

It is not just the Christians, Tibetan Buddhism also has a significant problem with Islam and Judaism. The Awake Project was an initiative within the inner circles of Tibetan Buddhism, to by spiritual means, cause Christianity, Islam and Judaism to destroy one another or at least cause the rest of the world to work toward eliminating these three sources of "hate mongering."

How Can This Happen?

How is all this happening? Two ways:

First, through the doctrine of Expedient Means that I mentioned above. The Dalai Lama is using his charm and humor to gain the admiration and respect of world political leaders, world religious leaders, influential leaders in the business and entertainment world and many just plain ordinary folk. He is also using spiritual means or "signs and wonders" to bring healing and restoration to people.

Secondly, on a larger scale the many monks and Lamas within Tibetan Buddhism are systematically taking dominion over the world through "The Peace Vase Project" and the building of mandalas.

In Chapter 19, I talked about how the Buddhists used geomancy, witchcraft over the land, to take spiritual authority over the land and thus political control of the country also. This exact same process is now being used to bring forth the Shambhala Buddhist Empire. In Tibet, the Buddhists consulted the oracles (demon-possessed monks) and were instructed to locate spiritual power points throughout the nation, build altars there, and make offerings to local gods on mountain peaks, valleys, rivers and lakes. The Peace Vase Project consists of the construction of 10,000 vases containing offerings (actually defiling substances) that are being distributed and buried on mountain peaks, in forests, rivers and lakes all over the world. It is my understanding that over 7,000 of these vases have already been buried throughout the United States. Many of the spiritual power points across the world were established in previous centuries by Masonic surveyors and city planners. These power points include universities, capitols cities, libraries, and museums, to which Tibetan Buddhist monks are now going and building their mandala altars to gain spiritual dominion.

Give that God a Metal, and Meddle with the God of this Land

In the Congress of the United States, at the request of several prominent members of congress who are ardent followers of the Dalai Lama, he was honored and given the highest metal that can be given to a citizen. At the same time that the congressional ceremony was going on, a mandala was being constructed in the National Cathedral on a hill overlooking Washington, D.C.

As I said, I will let you draw your own conclusions from all of this. But let me mention one other passage from Daniel.

> "And in the latter period of their rule, When the transgressors have run their course, A king will arise Insolent and skilled in intrigue. "And his power will be mighty, but not by his own power, And he will destroy to an extraordinary degree And prosper and perform his will; He will destroy mighty men and the holy people. "And through his shrewdness he will cause deceit to succeed by his influence; And he will magnify himself in his heart, And he will destroy many while they are at ease. He will even oppose the Prince of princes, But he will be broken without human agency. "And the vision of the evenings and mornings Which has been told is true; But keep the vision secret, For it pertains to many days in the future."[13]

Endnotes

1. Matthew 8:12, 22:13, 25:30
2. http://en.wikipedia.org/wiki/Upaya
3. http://www.merriam-webster.com/dictionary/politics
4. http://www.trimondi.de/SDLE/Part-1-09.htm   Sub-heading entitled: **"The world ruler: The sociopolitical exercise of power by the ADI Buddha"**
5. Revelation 12:7-9
6. Revelation 12:12b
7. John 12:31, 14:30, 16:11
8. 2 Corinthians 4:3-4
9. Enroth, Ronald. <u>A Guide to New Religious Movements</u>. Downers Grove, IL: InterVarsity Press, 2005, P.123
10. http://en.wikipedia.org/wiki/Dharma
11. http://www.lucistrust.org/en/arcane_school/talks_and_articles/the_esoteric_meaning_of_lucifer
12. Revelation 13:14-15
13. Daniel 8:23-26

CHAPTER 22

WHEN THE SAINTS HAVE BEGUN TO TAKE POSSESSION OF THE KINGDOM

It is my prayer that through the true stories I have shared throughout this book, you can see and understand that there are plenty of humans led by the demonic realm that have established authority structures of the dominion of Satan all over the world. When these authority structures of Satan are in place, individual demons attached to the immorality, woundedness, worship from, or invitation of humans, are able to flourish and be empowered. I know and I hope you now know that these dominions of Satan can be displaced.

The saints can draw near to God in those locations and Satan will flee. God will be enthroned on the praises of His people and His Kingdom will draw near to you.[1]

Many of the humans on this earth, because of their lack of knowledge of the true God, call on these demon gods in order to gain personal power and protection, but the cost may be the loss of their own soul, which delights Satan at having separated another soul from the Love of God.

We know that when Jesus sacrificed His life on the cross, the spilling of His righteous blood defeated the second death and released from bondage those who through the fear of death had been held in bondage all the days of their life.[2] We know that for anyone who believes in Him with their heart, it is counted as righteousness and their confession or repentance with the mouth results in salvation.[3] We also know that many are perishing in the world because the "god of this world" has put a veil over their eyes so that they cannot see the light of the glory of Christ and so that the image of God cannot fall on their mind.[4]

You heard Paul tell how the Lord appointed him as an officer under authority and as a witness of not only what he had seen, but of the things that the Lord was still to reveal to him. And then how the Lord was going to protect him in that authority as he was sending him to both the Jews and Gentiles, to get their eyes open, get them out of the darkness into the light and out from the authority structures of Satan to God, so that they could repent.[5]

We must realize that in spite of our best efforts in simply telling people to repent, believe in Jesus and you will have eternal life, many are so blinded and deafened by the god of this world that they cannot see or hear our kind intentions. They are held in fear and bondage by a dominion that they do not understand or are afraid to move toward what is unfamiliar to them under the threats of the one who is holding them captive.

No Power No Credibility

As we look at the world around us, our message is losing credibility, because it has not carried the power with it to cause change and open their eyes. Many are losing hope as the economy, the immorality, and the mocking of our society, is battering those who call themselves Christians, from every direction. A few minutes rest and protection every Sunday is the only glimmer of relief from this constant barrage by the world all around us. Even that rest is now being threatened by legislation and courts ruling unjustly.

For years we have thought that if we get out and protest, if we make our voices heard, the politicians would rule in our favor. But we failed to recognize that many of the human politicians who we were looking to for protection were also blinded by the god of this world and have only legislated further oppression, injustice and immorality. We have thought that if we got enough believing Christians elected to office they could protect us, but we failed to change the spiritual dominion over the places where these men and women had to operate and as a result they too became corrupted by darkness surrounding them.

We have prayed in solemn assemblies for God to do something but sometimes been disappointed as the prayers seemed unanswered or we have blamed those who did not get out and do something to make the prayer happen.

Many are hoping and praying today that the earth might open up and swallow the evil and rebellion like happened to Korah, Dathan and Abiram.[6] Others are crying out to God, "get me out of here, where is the rapture." But I don't think that the Lord is done with us yet, and I don't think that we have carried out all of the responsibility He left us to do. As bleak as things look right now, and as dark as things look like they could get, I can see the little cloud the size of a man's fist that Elijah saw and I am going to keep doing what the Lord tells me to do until the rain falls. If we don't change the spiritual atmosphere over our Country soon we will lose the freedoms we have. If the Enemy is not stopped, he will attempt to silence those who worship the One True God. If we do not like Moses step up to the responsibility given to us, and act to send the priestly anointing into the midst of the "plague," how many will be destroyed?

All Authority Means All Authority

Jesus stood on the mount of ascension and proclaimed, "All authority has been given to me in heaven and on earth, go therefore." Back in seminary, I can remember one of the professors teaching us to always ask what is the "therefore" there for. In this case it's there because the Lord has been given all authority. I used to puzzle as to why if the Lord was given all of the authority and He split the scene right after telling me He had it, where was it that I was supposed to go and why? Then I began to understand the concept of delegation. When someone is in charge they have authority to accomplish a task. However, if they delegate that task to someone else, they still have the overall authority, but the one to whom they have delegated the task also is given the authority to carry out that task.

When Jesus appointed Paul as a minister (officer under authority charged with enforcing the authority of Jesus) Paul was sent under the protection of that authority to go to the Jews and the Gentiles to open their eyes, get them out from under darkness into the light, and to remove them from the dominion or authority structure of Satan to God, His Kingdom, His authority structure. This short story tells us several things.

First, Jesus was not expecting us to try to figure out how to lead people to him or how to get them to repent of their sins knowing that they could not see or hear what we were trying to tell them. What He was telling us is that you have to get their eyes open first, you've got to get the darkness that is blinding off first. You have to get them out of the place where the god of this world has authority and control over them.

Secondly, Jesus knew that it was only His authority that could make this happen, because He is the One who won the battle over death and judgment and the One to whom Satan and his demons must listen. But Jesus delegated that authority to us as officers in His Kingdom to rescue those who are still being held in captivity and in prisoner of war camps.

When all authority was given to Him, the title document to this whole earth passed into His Kingdom, but Hebrews 2:8, tells us "we do not now see everything subjected to Him." We look around and see that there is a lot of the Kingdom that is not subjected to Him and we are curious for a short while, but then quickly move into the safety of a part of the Kingdom that does seem to be subject to Him. We might wonder why that part of the Kingdom over there is occupied by people that seem to be under Satan's authority, but it never occurs to us that we have been delegated authority to enforce the Kings title throughout the entire Kingdom.

Remember the parable of the master who went away and left his servants in charge. The two servants that were diligent to be about their master's work and doubled what the master had left with them were rewarded upon the master's return. But the servant who simply buried what he had been given because he was afraid of the master, even though he returned all of what he was given, hears the master call him a wicked, lazy slave, what was given to him was taken away and given to the faithful servant who had produced the most gain and then he was cast as worthless, into the outer darkness.[7]

Teaching All That I Commanded

When the title documents were given that gave Him all authority on earth and in heaven, He said, "Go therefore and make disciples of all the nations, baptizing them in the name of the Father and the Son and the Holy Spirit, teaching them to observe all that I commanded you; and lo, I am with you always, even to the end of the age."[8] Each and every one of us as we have come to receive the Lord and an inheritance among those who are being sanctified by faith in Him, become a disciple and are to be taught to observe all that He commanded the original disciples. Part of what He first exampled for his disciples and then sent them out to do, we find in Matthew chapter four and chapter nine where it tells us:

> "And Jesus was going about in all Galilee, teaching in their synagogues, and proclaiming the gospel of the kingdom, and healing every kind of disease and every kind of sickness among the people."[9]
>
> And from chapter nine, "And Jesus was going about all the cities and the villages, teaching in their synagogues, and proclaiming the gospel of the kingdom, and healing every kind of disease and every kind of sickness."[10]

Note that in both of these instances that it was the "gospel (or good news) of the Kingdom" that Jesus was proclaiming. He was telling them that they had been under the dominion of Satan, but now the Kingdom, the dominion, the authority structure of God had come near to them and this was good news. Because of that change in the dominion that was now over them (there's a new sheriff in town) they were being healed of every kind of disease and sickness.

When Jesus looked out and saw how many people there were out there that were suffering under the bondage of the dominion of Satan, He felt compassion and compared them to a bunch of sheep that are stuck on their backs, feet up in the air, in a rut in the ground, having no shepherd to put them back on their feet. He then tells His disciples, "The harvest is plentiful, but the workers are few, therefore beseech the Lord of the harvest to send out workers into His harvest."[11] I think that this was a subtle hint that they did not catch or act upon because in the next verse at the start of chapter 10 it tells us: "And having summoned His twelve disciples, He gave them authority over unclean spirits, to cast them out, and to heal every kind of disease and every kind of sickness."[12]

He showed them what the Kingdom was about and the power of the authority He had over those who were being oppressed by the dominion of Satan, and now He delegates that authority. He appoints the disciples as His deputies to enforce the authority He has. He then sends them out with specific instructions: "And as you go, preach, saying, 'The kingdom of heaven is at hand.' "Heal the sick, raise the dead, cleanse the lepers, cast out demons; freely you received, freely give."[13]

Luke tells us, "And departing, they began going about among the villages, preaching the gospel (*of the kingdom*), and healing everywhere."[14]

Are We Missing Something Here?

Somewhere along the path of the history of the world since those events two thousand years ago, not everything Jesus commanded has been taught to everyone that has become a disciple since. We see glimpses within the walls of the church of people being healed and delivered of the demons who have oppressed them. There are occasional recorded instances of some neighbor or co-worker who was under the dominion of Satan having their eyes opened, and being taken out of the dominion of Satan to God so that they can repent of their sin. Overall though, I don't see many deputies around anymore who are enforcing the authority of Jesus and bringing the Kingdom near. Ephesians tells us:

> "And He gave some as apostles, and some as prophets, and some as evangelists, and some as pastors and teachers, for the equipping of the saints for the work of service, to the building up of the body of Christ"[15]

But some of the some He gave, seem to have forgotten that it is their job to equip the saints for the work. Another subtle hint, as those "some" complain about the vast multitudes and their inability to meet all the needs. Delegate!

Jesus delegated the authority to get people's eyes open, to get them out of the darkness into the light, out of the dominion of Satan, to God, so that by repentance of sin they might have an inheritance (in the Kingdom) among those being sanctified by faith in Him.[16]

The longer we neglect that delegated task, the more overrun by usurpers and thieves the Kingdom is becoming.

Overpowered Overwhelmed and Worn Down

Well folks, the Kingdom is being overrun. The enemy is prevailing. We've been overpowered, overwhelmed, worn down and the enemy is pounding on the castle walls and gates where we are all holed up. Are we going to just cower in fear, wait for the rescue helicopter and hope it arrives in time, or are we going to put on our armor, start listening to the Lords battle plans and get out there, begin to take back possession of the whole Kingdom and occupy it until He comes?

Just today, I received a phone call and email from a pastor in Columbus Ohio. This pastor sent me an email of a mandala that had been constructed in Ohio this past week. They were taking a team out this afternoon to deal with it, to bring the Kingdom near, but they had never seen this mandala before and were asking if I knew anything about it. As I looked at the picture, I had not seen this one before either.

IN FAVOR OF THE SAINTS

What I saw in the Mandala was the symbols of the Chakavartin as ruler of the world. It looks to me like this is the seal of the Shambhala Buddhist Empire. It seems that the Tibetan Buddhists believe that they have won the war, and they are now producing mandalas all over the "heartland of America" proclaiming the victory over the gods of this nation.

I don't believe the war is over yet, I've read the "book" and I know how the story comes out. But I also believe that before the Ancient of Days passes judgment in favor of the saints, that the saints need to be taking up the authority they have been given to possess and occupy the Kingdom, all of it, not just the inside of our churches.

We Must Change Our Tactics

This is not a battle that can be won through our words and protests. This is not a battle that can be won in the human courts. This is not a battle that can be won in the legislatures. This is a battle "not by might, nor by power, but by my spirit says the Lord." You could just cry out for God to step in and destroy the whole mess, but when God told Moses and Aaron to step aside, they fell with their faces to the ground. Moses knew he had been assigned responsibility over God's people and the authority to carry out that responsibility. It was time to step up to the plate. So he called to Aaron to get up and carry out the priestly function he had been anointed for.

You have been made to be this kingdom and a priest to our God. The Lord has said you shall have widespread influence and prevail.[17] Right now the enemy is having wide spread influence and prevailing. The blows of the battle are getting heavier. However, I have just showed you in over 300 pages that you can prevail. You can carry out your anointing as a priest. You can take Holy Spirit fired worship and prayer into the midst of the plague that is destroying. You can stand between the living and the dead and not condemn the sins of the people, but in your priestly role bring the blood of Jesus over them as the atonement for their sins.[18]

You can lay hands on the sick, see them healed and tell them that the Kingdom has drawn near to them this day (That will open their eyes!). You can walk into a scene of utter chaos at your place of work, in a city council meeting or at your neighbor's house, quietly or silently pray and worship the Lord as you watch His Kingdom destroy the authority that was causing chaos in that place. In fact, you can do anything that the Lord tells you to do and for which you have faith to obey him. Will You?

The Lords primary instruction to me in recent years is to keep my eyes open to see the places that He will show me, where the dominion of Satan has been established. I am then to obey Him when he shows me how to establish His dominion in that place. I am to be putting my "shalom shoes" on daily so that every place I set the sole of my feet, I will be destroying the authority in that place that is establishing chaos.

The Lord may have a different assignment for you as there are many roles in the army of the Kingdom. You need to listen to Him very carefully and do exactly what He is telling you to do. Don't be afraid to ask questions to clarify, He is not offended.

Don't Copy What the Lord Told Me

Absolutely <u>do not</u> decide to just go out without hearing clearly from the Lord and do something because you read about it in this book and thought it sounded like a good thing to do. Believe me, in this day if you do that, you will get beat up.

Maybe you cannot say right now that you have ever clearly heard the Lord or felt his direction. I would urge you to get out your Bible start reading and start asking Him questions about what you are reading. If you read something that expresses your heart toward the Lord like a Psalm, pray and speak it aloud to Him or sing it. There are many times when I have not felt like praying that I have just opened the word and had conversations with the Lord about what I was reading or just sang to Him.

Maybe you are sitting there right now and you are so overwhelmed by all that you have just read that you do not even know where to start. Hear me, I have been there too! So come on, lets you and I talk to Him together, He understands.

> Lord, I am overwhelmed, I don't know what to do, sometimes I am not even sure that You are still there anymore, but I am going to take a step of faith and believe that You are listening to me right now. Help me Lord. Help me to open my eyes to see the world around me as You see it. I am tired of seeing it the way I do. Lord, open my ears to hear the cry of those who are caught in the midst of the destruction and plague all around us and forgive me for all the times I have tried not to listen. Lord, train my ears to hear Your voice, and forgive me for all the times I have ignored or chosen not to listen.
>
> I have filled my world with busyness, entertainment and inattention. Forgive me. Can I give You my appointment book? I want to make myself available for the divine appointments You have been trying to schedule in my life. Lord teach me to recognize the things You are doing all around me and make me sensitive to come into agreement with the things I see You are doing. Lord, when someone asks me to pray for them, remind me to stop right then, ask You what to pray and then do it with them, right then, not just make a promise that I don't intend to keep. Lord, also don't let me tell someone I am praying for them and not do it. Teach me not to just pray my good intentions and the things that come to my mind, but I want to learn to tune my own self down and really listen to what You are doing for the person in front of me. I want to be the free flowing conduit through which all of Your power can flow into their life.

Teach me how to effectively put on the armor, to cover my family, our pets, our property, our finances, our vehicles and more. Teach me to be able to stand in the midst of this evil day, and not just stand, but to be used to take possession of the Kingdom and occupy it in the places You have assigned and appointed me. I know I cannot do this in my own power, and I cannot do it in my own strength. I must hear you clearly Lord and I will keep asking until I do. Help me to take up my priestly function, to stop just complaining about and condemning the sins of others around me, but to instead start bringing Your blood, shed for them as an atonement for their sins.

Lord, send others who will join with me in this battle and with whom I can join. Teach us what we are to do and grant us the grace to be obedient.

To You oh Lord, be all the glory, power, and dominion forever and ever. Amen

You Must Hear the Lord Yourself

If you are not sure you can clearly hear the Lord, I urge you to go back and read Chapters 3 and 4, but mostly focus on asking the Lord to train your senses so you will know the Shepherd's voice. At the same time determine that you will spend time in the Word, particularly the parts you are not very familiar with, while asking Him to give you understanding. Don't give up until you know Him. Do be careful though that it is the shepherd's voice you are hearing until you become more familiar with it. Perhaps there is a friend or pastor who you know hears the Lord that will be willing to help you with this step.

I urge everyone who reads this book to spend time practicing putting on the armor over and over until it becomes second nature and you can do it in the black of night or in the midst of a surprise attack. Understand what each piece is for and how it protects you so that when something slips or a spear point penetrates, you will know how to adjust. Don't forget about armor bearers, especially if you are a person who is regularly in front of groups where you do not know everyone present. That goes for you too pastors! Except in the very smallest of settings, you seldom know if there may be someone in the group who is carrying out an enemy spy raid and sabotage attack inside the fortress.

Confession and Forgiveness Before Battle

If you are new to all of this, I am going to tell you that the first place you need to start is to examine if there is any un-confessed or ongoing sin in your life that you have not dealt with. This includes covenants, verbal contracts, curses you may have spoken and vows that you may have made rashly. The Lord already knows about it and I guarantee that the enemy will use it against you if you try to go into battle with it. Just talk to the Lord about it, he is looking for your willingness to obey Him.

You may be tempted by the mercy that the Lord has extended to you, to just go out and confess to the person you have wronged. Be very careful about this unless and until you clearly hear from the Lord this is what you are to do. If that person is under the influence of the dominion of Satan, your confession to them may not be received with grace, mercy or forgiveness, and the consequences of your heartfelt confession to them could be far greater than you might expect.

In my own life years ago, I was convicted by the Lord and confessed to another person how I had misused some of their funds. It was not anything that I had done intentionally but nonetheless what I did was not right. I confessed it to them and led by the Lord fully restored with interest the money that I had breached their trust in using the way I did. Though the person was hurt by what I had done, they forgave me and accepted the restitution. I learned a lesson that has helped me to try to avoid any appearance of evil since.

However, another person I told about this confession, who was not even the wronged party, treated my confession as though this was an ongoing sin issue in my life and continued for years to use my confession

WHEN THE SAINTS HAVE BEGUN TO TAKE POSSESSION OF THE KINGDOM

about this one thing as evidence that I could not be trusted. This was used against me not only in my handling of funds but over every other part of the relationship as well. Whatever degree of respect (which I now realize was not much) this person had held for me before that point vanished and was never recovered. So again, be quick to keep short accounts with the Lord, but be careful to listen to Him on your dealing with others.

Here is a reminder of John's teaching on confession:

> God is light, and in Him there is no darkness at all. If we say that we have fellowship with Him and yet walk in the darkness, we lie and do not practice the truth; but if we walk in the light as He Himself is in the light, we have fellowship with one another, and the blood of Jesus His Son cleanses us from all sin. If we say that we have no sin, we are deceiving ourselves, and the truth is not in us. If we confess our sins, He is faithful and righteous to forgive us our sins and to cleanse us from all unrighteousness. If we say that we have not sinned, we make Him a liar, and His word is not in us.[19]

Unforgiveness is another biggie. This seems to be a major weapon in the hand of the enemy for all kinds of destruction. Unforgiveness, like confession of sin (because it is sin) is an issue of your heart, not necessarily the heart of another person. God will look at your willingness to forgive as a matter of obedience and is not likely to trust you with other assignments if you can't deal with this one. As I mentioned above with confession, this is about you, your attitude and your obedience. Going to someone and simply saying, "I forgive you," may have very unexpected results if that person is under the influence of the dominion of Satan. Be sure you are hearing from the Lord what you are to do.

I observed this experience with a close relative. A daughter then in her fifties, went to her mother and simply said "I forgive you for the things I did not understand when I was younger." This simple "I forgive you" which was an expression of a change in the daughters heart, was misunderstood by the mother. This caused years of broken relationship, anger and bitterness on behalf of the mother who now felt judged by the daughter and refused to acknowledge that there was anything she possibly could have done for which she needed forgiveness. Believe me, the enemy will twist your words and use them against you if he has the opportunity.

Start In Your Own House

Now if you have your armor on, and you are all ready to start taking possession of the Kingdom, I suggest you start with your own house, and your own property. Spend some time walking your house with your shalom shoes on and worshiping the Lord. Acknowledge that all around you is really His as you acknowledge His dominion over it all. I have at times gone so far as to drive stakes into the ground at the corners of my property line with verses acknowledging that the property is dedicated and consecrated to the Lord. You may want to go around your home and hold various things that you consider precious to you and offer them to the Lord. I have also asked the Lord to assign His angels to guard over and keep watch over His property that He is letting me use and take care of. Be sure that you have secured the gates to your own castle before you venture out to save the city.

If you have already done this, then try going into a city council meeting, sitting quietly in the back of the room, worshipping silently and praying for each of the council persons and the issues that are brought up. Pay attention to the spiritual atmosphere in the room. Is there contention? Is there chaos? Or is there order and peace? Dialog with the Lord and ask Him what you are to do. Don't go in there with your Jesus Saves tee shirt on, carrying your big Bible, or commanding the demons. Those distractions and markers could cause you to be a target of someone else's intentions. You are there to enthrone the Lord in that place and change the spiritual dominion influencing what is going on, not advertise yourself.

Changing the Dominion Over Your Place of Work

In the same way, if you get to work and find that things are utterly chaotic as my wife did the other day, take a few minutes to silently walk the work space enthroning the Lord on your praises of Him. Or better yet do it every time you go to work, taking possession of the Kingdom and continuing to occupy it. Consider also spending time outside of your scheduled work hours praying for each of those you work with. Be sensitive to the divine appointments that the Lord will make for you to touch the lives of others. The book "*The Adversary*," by Pastor Mark Bubeck, is an excellent source of prayers to get you started. Find the one in his book that applies and modify it for your particular situation, substituting in the name of the person you are praying for. I found the prayers on pages 106-113 particularly helpful for this. Then pray out loud if you can. For years I used Mark's book as a starting point for putting on the armor when I would first wake up in the morning. Sometimes I would be groggy or find my attention wandering as I was reading the prayer, so I would force myself to go back to the beginning and concentrate on making it my prayer. There were mornings I would have to start over 4 or 5 times until I knew I was paying attention and was actually praying the prayer all the way through to the end.

I mentioned above about not wearing your Jesus Saves tee shirt or waving a big Bible. Be careful about how you appear in public. Much of the world already thinks we are a bunch of religious freaks and kooks, don't reinforce the image. What you wear and say on the outside is not what will change people's hearts and the spiritual atmosphere around them. It is the power and authority of His Kingdom. As I said earlier in this book, we can aim and fire the weapons, but unless those bullets, artillery shells and bombs are filled with His powder (power) they are useless. Remember, Paul tells us:

> "For our struggle is not against flesh and blood, but against the rulers, against the powers, against the world forces of this darkness, against the spiritual forces of wickedness in the heavenly places. Therefore, take up

the full armor of God that you may be able to resist in the evil day, and having done everything, to stand firm."[20]

Seldom has the Lord had me do more in actually speaking to a demon than commanding the demon to go to the feet of Jesus for Him to deal with them. Mostly the Lord has had me draw near to Him in worship and prayer, yes resisting Satan or the demons present, but when Jesus shows up they flee.[21]

I firmly believe at this point, if we will begin now to do as Moses did and instructed Aaron, get up from our place with our face to the ground, take priestly responsibility to pour coals of Holy Spirit fire into the censer and lay on the incense of worship and prayer, not just inside your church, but running into the midst of the plagues of this world, standing between the living in Christ and those dead in their sins, bringing the atoning blood of Jesus over the sins of the people, we will be beginning to take possession of and occupying the Kingdom. It is then that I believe that the Ancient of Days will come and pass judgment "In Favor of the Saints."

Endnotes

1. James 4:7
2. Hebrews 2:15
3. Romans 10:10
4. 2 Corinthians 4:4
5. Acts 26:16-18
6. Numbers 16:1-35
7. Matthew 25:14-30
8. Matthew 28:19-20
9. Matthew 4:23
10. Matthew 9:35
11. Matthew 9:37-38
12. Matthew 10:1
13. Matthew 10:7-8
14. Luke 9:6
15. Ephesians 4:11-12
16. Acts 26:18
17. Revelation 5:10
18. Numbers 16:44-48
19. 1 John 1:5b-10
20. Ephesians 6:12-13
21. James 4:7

APPENDIX A

DEFINITIONS

I use the term "ley line" a number of times in this book so I now provide here the definition found in *Wikipedia*, the free online encyclopedia.

Ley lines are alignments of a number of places of geographical interest, such as ancient megaliths. Their existence was first suggested in 1921 by the amateur archaeologist Alfred Watkins, whose book *The Old Straight Track* first brought the phenomenon to the attention of the wider public.

The existence of these apparently remarkable alignments between sites is easily demonstrated. However, the causes of these alignments are disputed. There are three major schools of thought:

- *Anthropological:* According to proponents of some ley line theories, the early inhabitants of Britain determined the placement of Stonehenge and various other megalith structures, buildings, monuments, or mounds according to a system of these lines, which often pass through, or near, several such structures. Some of these theories believe leys to have had some astronomical significance, or to relate to traditional religious beliefs associated with these sites. Others simply see leys as marking trade routes.
- *New Age:* Some have claimed that these points resonate a special psychic energy named earth radiation. These theories often include elements such as geomancy, dowsing or UFOs.

- *Skeptical:* Skeptics of these ley line theories believe that they belong in the realms of pseudoscience. Most skeptics believe that ley lines can be explained completely by chance alignments of random points that appear intuitively unlikely, but can be demonstrated to be unsurprising coincidences. Some skeptics are investigating if these points have electrical or magnetic forces associated with them.

The *Wikipedia* full article is available at "http://en.wikipedia.org/wiki/Ley_line," for your review and the drawing of your own conclusions. For the purposes of this book, I have used the term, because the Lord pointed out the geographical "coincidences" to me, and this is the term used by spiritual mappers to describe lines between spiritual gateways used in a number of forms of occultic practice.

Gateways – I am writing my own definition of gateways here though some in the occult and witchcraft may have specific definitions. I have come to understand that these are specific locations that lay at the intersections of Ley Lines.

These points are spiritual entry points to "astral" pathways that operate in more than one dimension. I am not going to try to explain that statement in much more depth other than to say that in the realm of this world, those using witchcraft to cast remote spells, practicing "path working," and or astral projection all use pathways that interconnect at various gateways and must petition the gatekeeper, "demonic/angelic being," at that gate in order to proceed past and on to another interconnecting path.

In Tibetan Buddhism, the mandalas consist of a palace with a number of gates each protected by a particular demonic "deity." As the mandala is empowered and inhabited through ritual chanting, the demons enter the palace through the gateways and are given assignments related to the type of mandala that has been constructed and the principal deity of the mandala. In the ritual, the gates are then opened in a particular sequence and specific deities go out to perform their tasks.

APPENDIX B

THE REVELATION OF THE SEAL OF THE CITY OF PASADENA, CALIFORNIA

The following is an attempt to summarize information that was revealed to me over a two week period in February 2002. This happened as I was seeking and praying to understand the significance of spiritual influences over Pasadena during the past 125 years. I do not wish to bring to your attention the hundreds of pages of documents that the Lord brought to my attention during this several weeks to give me understanding of what I was reading and seeing, but I will fill in a few details to show the basis for believing that the City seal has the significance of evoking and giving authority to the spirit of Babylon in this city.

This study started with seeking to understand the influence, if any, of the actions of Jack Parsons and L. Ron Hubbard in a ritual that they carried out during the winter of 1946 which had the express intention to birth into the material realm a woman who would be the physical manifestation of the spirit of Babylon. In Jack Parsons' own words, he sought to do this because:

> "The present age is under the influence of the force called, in magical terminology, Horus. This force relates to fire, Mars, and the sun, that is, to power, violence, and energy. It also relates to a child, being innocent (i.e. undifferentiated). Its manifestations may be noted in the

destruction of old institutions and ideas, the discovery and liberation of new energies, and the trend towards power governments, war, homosexuality, infantilism, and schizoprenia."

"This force is completely blind, depending upon the men and women in whom it manifests and who guide it. Obviously, its guidance now tends towards catastrophy."

"The catastrophic trend is due to our lack of understanding of our own natures. The hidden lusts, fears, and hatreds resulting from the warping of the love urge, which underly the natures of all Western peoples, have taken a homicidal and suicidal direction."

"This impasse is broken by the incarnation of another sort of force, called BABALON. The nature of this force relates to love, understanding, and dionysian freedom, and is the necessary counterbalance or correspondence to the manifestation of Horus."

During some of the prayer walking times in January and February several others and I had specifically prayed at locations associated with Jack Parsons (Cal Tech, the 1000 block of South Orange Grove, Jet Propulsion Laboratories, and the Arroyo above Devil's Gate Dam)

As I was studying the journals of Jack Parsons one particular writing, entitled Liber 49 is a document that Parsons claims was dictated to him by the manifested spirit of Babylon that appeared to him on February 28, 1946. This document is also given significance as the fourth book of the Law, referring to the first three books of the law dictated to Aleister Crowley by the spirit master Aiwaz in Cairo Egypt in April 1903. Jack Parsons became associated with Aleister Crowley (who was the self proclaimed anti-christ) through the California chapter (The Agape Lodge) of an organization taken over by Crowley in about 1916 called the OTO or Ordo Templi Orientis. This organization originally came out of the upper levels of the Masonic Order in Germany in the first decade of the 20th century. There is some indication that it existed under other names prior to that, but I have not been able to prove this. Parsons ends up taking over the Agape Lodge after moving it to his home at 1003 South Orange Grove. In about 1944, he forms a business partnership with L. Ron Hubbard a science fiction writer and later in the year 1951, the founder of Scientology.

In the beginning of January of 1946, Parsons and Hubbard begin a series of rituals, which would later be called the "Babylon Working" (the term working is used in circles of practitioners of Magick and witchcraft to designate a ritual performed for a purpose). The first part of the ritual was to bring forth an "elemental" a woman that would participate in the sexual portions of the ritual. Upon returning home after this portion of the ritual, they found at the door a woman Marjorie Cameron who fit the description. Most of the Babylon Working, which went on throughout January, February and March of 1946, was done jointly with these three persons. On several occasions there were physical manifestations of wind, objects being smashed, persons being hit by unseen entities and by noises in the night. A guest at Parsons' house during this time refused to go to the second floor because of the manifestations there.

On February 28, Parsons went alone, while Hubbard was out of town, out to the Mojave Desert to evoke Babylon and experienced the manifestation that is described in his diary and became the Liber 49 document.

Here is a small portion of that book to give you a flavor for what was going on:

> "Yea, it is I, BABALON. And this is my book, that is the fourth chapter of the Book of the Law, He completing the Name, for I am out of NUIT by HORUS, the incestuous sister of RA-HOOR-KHUIT.
>
> It is BABALON. TIME IS. Ye fools.
>
> Thou hast called me, oh accursed and beloved fool.
>
> Now know that I, BABALON, would take flesh and come among men.
>
> And gather my children unto me, for THE TIME is at hand.

And this is the way of my incarnation. Heed!

Thou shalt offer all thou art and all thou hast at my altar, withholding nothing. And thou shalt be smitten full sore and thereafter thou shalt be outcast and accursed, a lonely wanderer in abominable places.

Ye Dare. I have asked of none other, nor have they asked. Else is vain. But thou hast willed it."

This book goes on to describe how Babalon will lead Parsons through the ritual and how she will guide the woman who is to be her physical manifestation.

The point here is that Parsons, Hubbard and Cameron were working in the practice of Magick, a particular form of witchcraft refined by Crowley and having its roots in the Gnostic Mass, Rosecruscian and Knights Templar, and making use of the Cabalah, Tarot and astrology. Crowley had been a part of another organization called the Golden Dawn, which came about in about 1875 the same time period in which Helen Blavinsky in Germany was forming the basis of what is called the Theosophical Society. The Theosophical Society also has many of these elements in it.

To get back to Parsons, on March 1, 2 and 3 of 1946 the ritual was completed in Pasadena with Hubbard describing a vision he had of a savage and beautiful woman riding naked on a great cat-like beast. (Ishtar or Babylon is often pictured standing on the back of a lion). They felt they had accomplished their purpose and had the full expectation that there would be a physical birth of a woman who would be indwelt by the spirit of BABALON (this is the spelling that the witchcraft people say is the correct spelling).

Later that year Hubbard runs off with Parsons' girl friend, the sister of Parsons' first wife, who ran off with the former head of the Agape Lodge. Hubbard takes Parsons for a great portion of his wealth through a series of business deals. Parsons focuses for the next several years on his work with the U.S. Government for which JPL was founded. He also is consulting with the newly formed Israel and with Mexico. This causes him some problems though, as the Government accuses him of sharing secret information with Israel and revokes his security clearance.

During this time Aleister Crowley dies in 1947, the Roswell sightings occur in 1947, Israel is founded in 1947 as well as a number of other significant events that are cited by various occult groups.

On October 31,1948, Parsons is again visited by the manifestation of the spirit Babalon and this time she takes him into the under world and leads him through rituals of the "Black Pilgrimage." Here are Parsons' words; "Now it came to pass even as BABALON told me, for after receiving Her Book I fell away from Magick, and put away Her Book and all pertaining thereto. And I was stripped of my fortune (the sum of about $50,000) and my house, and all I Possessed."

"Then for a period of two years I worked in the world, recouping my fortune somewhat. But that was also taken from me, and my reputation, and my good name in my worldly work, that was in science."

"And on the 31st of October, 1948, BABALON called on me again, and I began the last work, that was the work of the wand. And I worked for 17 days, until BABALON called me in a dream, and instructed me on an astral working. Then I reconstructed the temple, and began the Black Pilgrimage, as She instructed."

At one point in this process, Parsons says, "And thereafter I returned and swore the Oath of the Abyss, having only the choice between madness, suicide, and that oath. But the Oath in no wise ameliorated that terror, and I continued in the madness and horror of the abyss for a season. But having passed the ordeal of 40 days I took the oath of a Magister of Templi, even the Oath of Antichrist before Frater 132, the Unknown God."

"And thus Was I Antichrist loosed in the world; and to this I am pledged, that the work of the Beast 666 shall be fulfilled, and the way for the coming of BABALON be made open and I shall not cease or rest until these things are accomplished. And to this end I have issued this my Manifesto."

The Manifesto document was written in 1949 in which Parsons proclaims himself as the Antichrist. Several references are made to the motto of the OTO and many associated brotherhoods which is, "Do what thou wilt shall be the whole of the law" (This is also called The Law of Thelema).

Parsons goes on to say in this document, "And within seven years of this time, BABALON, THE SCARLET WOMAN HILARION will manifest among ye, and bring this my work to its fruition....

An end to conscription, compulsion, regimentation, and the tyranny of false laws.

And within nine years a nation shall accept the Law of the BEAST 666 in my name, and that nation will be the first nation of the earth."

Though I do not believe that the spirit of BABALON was manifest in one woman as I think Parsons believed would happen, we do see that within seven years of 1949, Playboy Magazine is published and starts a series of legal battles that opened the publishing industry and the movie industry to tolerate and legalize publishing of more and more nudity, and other lessening of the standards of morality which had been in place. Not that the immorality was not going on in the background of the movie industry, government, business and elsewhere before than, but starting in 1953 the laws which had banned publication and held standards for the motion picture industry and even language on radio began to be challenged. Within nine years we are building bomb shelters, the U.S. is getting involved in Viet Nam. The manifestation of the immorality of the woman who represents both love and war is pouring out the cup of her immoralities over the peoples and nations.

As a side note, in June 1952, Parsons is killed in an explosion in his garage at 1003 South Orange Grove. The official story is that he dropped a vile of highly explosive material.

In 1951, the Theosophical Society moves its international headquarters to Pasadena. Its original U.S. headquarters had been in a building that is now the administration building of the Point Loma College, which moved from the campus here in Pasadena in 1973! 1951 was also the year that L. Ron Hubbard laid the groundwork for Scientology and published Dianetics.

The study of all of this later working, I believe has its roots in Pasadena from earlier invitations of the BABALON spirit. As I was reading much of the material behind the OTO, Aleister Crowley, Jack

Parsons, the Theosophical Society and the Masonic roots of Pasadena, I kept running across references to the ritual of the Rosy Cross. This ritual was specifically having to do with the sexual union between the Sun God and the Moon God for the purpose of birthing the Moon Child. Low and behold, the Moon Child is none other than the Queen of Heaven and what ever other name you want to call her, but is specifically centered around the names, Ishtar, Babalon, and Venus. These are the primary names throughout a long history that are considered synonymous with Nuit, Inanna, Isis, Dianna in terms of all referring to the same spiritual entity.

I would like to point out at this time, that I believe it is incorrect to refer to this as the "Jezebel Spirit" as Jezebel was simply a human woman who manifested the spirit of this other entity. No one outside of a small segment of the Christian community is referring to, calling on or worshipping Jezebel.

There are hundreds of thousands of references on the internet to groups today that are worshipping or calling upon Ishtar, Babalon, Inanna or Venus.

The local witch coven in Pasadena additionally, identifies with the Virgin of Guadelupe as associated with these other Goddess manifestations. I would suggest that to talk about the spirit of Jezebel would be to point to the material rather than the actual spiritual authority behind the actions of the human person. It would be the same as saying that something was accomplished by the spirit of Don Upham rather than by the Spirit of Christ that was being manifest through Don Upham. I think to keep talking about the spirit of Jezebel is a smoke screen of the enemy to avoid revealing of the true identity of the authority behind Jezebel who was a worshipper of Bael. Though this is my opinion, I feel it is confirmed by the hundreds of pages of documentation contained on hundreds of web sites and published works that the Lord led me to during this time of study and prayer.

Specifically in this city and in Hollywood (Hollywood being not a city, but the motion picture and television industry in general as having been birthed in the greater Los Angeles area), Babalon is continually called upon and made reference to. Hollywood has identified with Babalon since 1916, when during the filming of his silent feature length movie "Intolerance," D.W. Griffith enthroned Ishtar.

This enthroning was done on the largest set ever built in Hollywood and was constructed to be the gates of Babylon. The set sat at the corner of Hollywood and Sunset for 20 years with Ishtar enthroned at the high place of the set. Griffith had not had the money to tear it down so it sat until the Government tore it down in 1936. In the year 2001, the Gate of Babylon has again been constructed in Hollywood in the form of the Babylon Court, part of the Kodak, Academy Awards Theater project at the corner of Hollywood Blvd., and Highland Avenue in Downtown Hollywood.

To get back to the ritual of the Rosy Cross and how this relates to the seal and founding of the City of Pasadena, I had my senses stirred by the description in this ritual of the woman Babalon dancing amid flames and settling into a blood red rose of 7 times 7 petals, a rose of 49 petals representing the number of Babalon. Over this rose is the cross which represents the Sun God, and below the cross the disk of the sun and hexagram.

Knowing that the official flower of Pasadena is the Rose and it is of a dark red color, I began to wonder if there was any connection. I did more than wonder as I also heard a brief segment on NPR, KPCC talking about how the rose was the symbol of secrecy. It was used in Roman and Greek periods as a sign that conversations and actions occurring in a party or dinner where a rose was present, were considered confidential, or secret, and were not to be spoken of outside of that location. This led to the rose design in the metal work of ceilings in some restaurants. Conversations "under the rose" were to remain in confidence. I checked this out in the encyclopedia and found that to be true.

The rose is also the flower of Venus and of Babalon.

Armed with this information I began looking at the illustration of the rose in Pasadena and seeking to see if there was anything relating to the 49 petals. I asked my son who is a design student at the Art Center, if he had run across anything during a project working with the City of Pasadena on their image and logos during this last fall. He said he was not aware of anything about a rose of 49 or 7x7 petals, but a few minutes later he brought up the copy of the original and still official seal of the city. He pointed out to me that the top of the crown has seven elements on either side. I pondered this for a while that evening, my head swimming with an overload of occult and cultic information that the Lord had been revealing. I could see that there were elements present in the Crown that were very similar to a number of things that I had run across in relationship to the Gnostic Mass, the rosecrucian rituals, and the practice of Magick. I prayed and went to bed.

At 2:30 in the morning, the Lord awoke me with the phrase repeating repeatedly, "The Key Is in the Crown." I got out of bed and went to work at my desk. I gasped in surprise over and over during the next several hours and days as the Lord showed me that every detail of every element in the city seal relates to various aspects of these rituals and "Secret Understandings."

Here is a breakdown; (refer to the three drawings on pages 12-14)

The two larger openings in the crown represent the eyes of Horus which were the right being the sun god and the left the moon goddess. Egyptian mythology has it that the left eye was ripped out by the jealous brother of Horus, SET or Seth. This is a long story, but the eye is returned to Horus, but rather that being returned to the eye socket, it is used in a ritual to reincarnate Osiris, who was killed by Seth. It is set on a pyramid gateway to the underworld and became the all seeing eye on the back of our one dollar bill. This left eye again represents the moon goddess who is identified with Isis, Innana, Ishtar, and Babalon.

The Key represents the authority to unlock. In relationship to the left eye of Horus it is the key of authority to unlock the under world given to the Moon Goddess. Thus, we see the key in the eye of the Moon goddess, the left eye. The cloverleaf design of the top of the Key is an ancient symbol of authority. On a newer version of the city seal, the bottom of the key is a letter "E" which represents the East, which is great significance with the higher levels of Masonic and with Tibetan Buddhism.

The five larger openings or stones in the bottom rim of the crown represent the 5 elementals of all life. Various groups make reference to the five senses, the five aspects of the mind, the five basic genomes of man, the five elements of the spiritual realm and many other elemental 5's. Five is a significant number in many of these rituals as it also relates to earth, wind, fire, water and spirit.

On the right side as you look at the bottom of the crown is three series of four dots. This represents both the four elements of earth, wind, fire and water, but also 3x4, which is 12, which represents the 12 astrological signs, and also relates to the Tarot.

The cross on top of the crown is not just any cross but a cross of five elements. This is as described in the ritual of the rosy cross, where this cross again represents not only the Sun God, but also the four elements of earth, wind, fire, water and the fifth of the spirit.

The particular design of the cross is very similar to a specific pentacle, which is very much different from every other pentacle or pentagram. In general, the pentagram is based on a mathematical dividing of a circle by pointing to each of the 12 signs of the Zodiac. Rituals involving these pentacles are used to call up or evoke various angelic beings to receive instruction from them. With all of the other pentacles, Bael is called upon in the ritual. This pentacle of the cross instead is related to the Sun and is used to evoke an entity which appears for the purpose of telling you how to break your mental bonds and be free, free of the mental bonds of guilt associated with sin, so that "There is no law beyond Do What Thou Wilt."

Below the cross is a circle that is spoken of as the disk of the Sun.

The two parting parts below the cross and disk I believe represent entry into the sexual organ of the woman, but I do not have specific reference for this other that the highly sexual nature of the rituals involved and the whole recurring concept of the birth of the moon child, which is the physical manifestation in the material world of the spirit of Babalon. This is exactly what Jack Parsons set out to accomplish. In Astrology, the moon child is Venus, or Babalon.

I believe the 7 elements on either side of the top of crown represent the 7x7 or the number of Babalon, 49. Overall, the top of the crown represents the union of the Sun and Moon sexually to birth Babalon to which authority is given by the key to open the underworld. This relates to the ancient legend of Astarte, one of the wives of Seth who became trapped in the underworld and eventually bargained with her farmer, and thus not too smart husband, to take her place in the underworld for part of the year. Inanna, Ishtar, and Babalon are later incarnations of this same story.

The first circle is like a chain and consists of 64 elements. This is pretty obscure, but it has to do with the number 31 which is a key to the "Tree of Life" (not in anyway to be confused with Christ as the tree of life). This "Tree of Life" is a very complicated figure that forms the basis for the Tarot, for Astral Projection and reaching other astral planes. 31 is the number of a pathway to understanding the "Tree of Life." I have yet to check this out, as I have not been back to Washington, D.C. since discovering this, but I believe the design in the plaza of the layout of the city is in the design of this tree of life. Anyway, 31 + 31 is 62, which is 2x31 so 2 is added to 62 to equal 64. The 31st Path of the "Tree of Life" is called Perpetual Intelligence. The number 2 represents Love and unity. I am not going any further into this other than to say that 64 is significant in this design.

The outer circle is like a rope and as such is a circle that is meant to bind in. This circle as a rope has 96 twists. Here we go with 31 again. 3x31 is 93. 93 represents the beast, the law of Thelema which was Aleister Crowley's whole spiritual premise, it represents Agape, and also Aiwaz which was the spirit being that dictated this whole thing to Crowley in 1903. The number 3 represents 0 or nothing because it is made up of 3 and 1, which in numerology reduces to 0. Here we have a play on words, which in the Cabalah is a play on the 1st first and 13th letters of the Hebrew alphabet, Aleph and Lamed. All the vowels are dropped and the word play becomes AL and LA or 31 and 13. This word play is further explained as God and Not God. This is where reference to Islam comes in, as ALLA is God – Not God. The A and L are also part of the Masonic symbol of the compass and the square. The compass represents the letter A and the Square the letter L. 96 represents 3x31 or 31+31+31+3. In the newer versions of the seal (date of origin still undetermined) the inner circle has 69 elements. 69 is the number that represents the union of the Sun and the Moon. It also the reverse of the number 96. This is where the ying and yang come from as the balance between the forces of good and of evil. Perhaps also what Jack Parsons was trying to get at.

When I got to this point, the Lord gave me four scriptures. Numbers Chapter 7, Revelation Chapter 17, Revelation Chapter 20 and Revelation Chapter 22. Chapter 20 was the first chapter given. It talks about an angel coming down from heaven with a key and a chain and that the angel binds up the beast and locks it in the abyss for a thousand years. Rope is used for binding, we have a rope to bind in the outer circle, a chain in the inner circle, and the key pointed down to the abyss. Is this just coincidence that the Lord would give me those specific verses at this immediate time of my seeking wisdom about what I was looking at.

Next, I was counting up all of the elements in the two circles and the sun disk and the 7x7.

This comes to 96+64+1+49=210. I was wondering if this had anything to do with the numbering of the 210 freeway as having started in Pasadena and stretched in two axes out from the center of the city. The freeway is both North and South and East and West in the City. 210 is also the number of Jack Parsons' name according to one source. At this point, the Lord gave me Numbers 7. This passage is the offerings given at the consecration of the Tabernacle in the wilderness. Basically, 12 offerings were given by a priest of one of the tribes on each of 12 days. The offering given was identical each day, only the priest and the tribe represented was different each day.

Here is the offering, a silver plate of 130 shekels of silver, a bowl of 70 shekels of silver and a gold pan of 10 shekels of Gold. As I wrote these numbers in the margin of my bible, I noted that this adds up to 210 shekels of precious metals. Isn't that a coincidence? If it has no significance, why did the Lord show this to me specifically in relationship to the seal of the city and the number of 210 that keeps showing up in relationship to the city of Pasadena. The offerings in the silver were to be of flour and oil and were mixed for a grain offering. The offering in the gold pan was an incense offering. I believe that the Lord was showing me that this has something to do with healing and nurture represented by the grain offering, worship, and prayer as represented by the incense offering. Why the silver plate and silver bowl and a gold pan, why 210 shekels of precious metals, I don't know yet, but I believe there is significance here that relates to Pasadena.

The next offering was one bull, one ram and one male lamb one year old for a burnt offering and one male goat as a sin offering. These numbers in the margin are 111 and 1.

Why three animals as a burnt offering and one as a sin offering. I believe this has something to do with holding back the celestial beings from entering into the affairs of man. Since the Goat in the occult is the representation of Satan. Perhaps the goat is the source of the sin so it also is the offering sacrifice to counter the effects of sin. If you want to get weird with numbers that also may relate to Pasadena. 111 as the number one hundred eleven has the number one subtracted and we get 110, the number of the first freeway built in the United States, here in Pasadena. Therefore, we have both the numbers 110 and 210 contained in Numbers Chapter 7 offerings to consecrate the Tabernacle in the wilderness. Again, I believe all of this has to do with life as it was intended by the observance of the Lord's commands for nurture and healing and worship and prayer. Burnt offerings to that may have something to do with holding back some spiritual force affected by celestial beings and the recognition that sin would need to be dealt with.

The next offering is a peace offering of two oxen, five rams, five male goats and five male lambs. This number in the margin was 2555. If you divide 2555 by 7 it is 365. So this number could represent 7 years. But there is another number here by just adding 2+5+5+5=17. Now the Lord gave me chapter 17 of revelation. The center of this chapter, verses 9 through 13 deals with the beast of 7 heads and 10 horns (17 elements). These are said to represent kings and kingdoms with which the woman Babalon has committed immorality. It seems entirely possible to me that the 17 peace offerings in Numbers 7 relate to offerings of peace in relationship of the kings of the world toward God. Again, I think God was trying to tell the Israelites something about their responsibilities and authority through the offerings and the effects that maintaining them would have on the future.

I pondered how in fact all of this relates to the seal of the City of Pasadena, to an invitation of the spirit of BABALON into the city. I next thought I would need to find evidence that there may have been people in the city and involved in the formation of the city who were likely to have had knowledge of these rituals and therefore may have acted with some purpose in the design of the city seal.

What I found is that during the 1800's there was a stirring up of old things and ancient religions. In particular, the upper levels of the Masonic order were dedicating themselves to retain the old knowledge and continue the workings of the cabala, the tarot, and of the previous organizations of the Rosicrucian's and the knights Templar. Were these organizations in Pasadena in 1886? Yes! An Order of the Good Templars was formed in 1879 and was made up of nearly every one living in the area at the time. The Masonic lodge was chartered in 1884 and was very involved in the city. In 1885, a committee of five was sent to the Board of Supervisors of Los Angeles County to request incorporation of the city. The head of that committee was the Grand Master of the Masonic Lodge. On June 5, 1886, an election was held for trustees and officers of the city. Four out of the seven original officers were charter members of either The Order of Good Templars or of the Masonic Lodge. The first meeting held of the officers was on June 28 and one of the orders of business for that day was to adopt as the fourth ordinance the seal of the city that was described in the ordinance. When they met that day they already had a city seal design, which I believe was influenced by whatever perverted understanding existed in the upper levels of these two organizations. I believe that there was a purposeful evocation of the union of the sun and the moon and the authority to be given to Babylon to be over the city.

What can be done about this now? I think Chuck Pierce gave some clues. He gave dates of September 18 as the start of war. February 18 to March 18 as a time of open window and that things would be set in place or in motion by April 10. What is the significance of these dates to occult world. September 18-19 was Rosh Hashanah and September

27 Yom Kippur. Right in between is September 23 the beginning of the zodiac sign of Libra, which is the sign of Venus, the goddess of love and war. It is also the fall equinox, also of significance to witchcraft.

February 19 – March 20 is Pieces, which is said to be the sign of the Christians.

Meanwhile among the followers of the Gnostic mass and Aleister Crowley, March 19 and 20 marks the feast of the supreme ritual celebrating the evocation of Aiwaz and the opening of a new aeon the day before the March equinox of the Gods. April 8, 9, and 10 is the Feast for the Three Days of the Writing of The Book of the Law with observance at high noon on each day. The local Witch Coven is holding a workshop on drumming on Sunday April 21 here in Pasadena.

As for the seal, I believe this represents a "root iniquity" by the founding fathers of the City of Pasadena. There is also a window of opportunity for the seal to be changed. I have verified that an official of the city has been working with the Art Center College of Design to consider up dating the city's image. He was to be going back to the Art Center during this month to discuss this further. He stated that there had actually been complaints about the seal, as some people do not feel this seal is appropriate for the city. I suspect that this is based on a misunderstanding and belief that the cross on top of the crown represents Christ and His Reign. City officials brushed this off though simply by saying, we have had this seal from the beginning and we will keep what we have had from the beginning. The whole city hall is representing Babalon as there are eight torches on each tower and the crown and key of three sides of each tower. Eight is the number derived for Babalon under the Magick of Aleister Crowley and the OTO.

I believe "Identificational Repentance" is the first order of business here, as that root iniquity has opened the door for this city to be a birth place of both good and evil. It is the influence and money from this city that founded Hollywood and the movie industry, such that "those who dwell on the earth were made drunk with the wine of her immorality."

The Lord gave me a prayer which I begin praying immediately and I have even been praying this regularly in all kinds of places and at all kinds of times.

It is my belief that there will be an opportunity to approach officials from the city to show this material and those city officials will also do an act of identificational repentance to break the root iniquity.

The following two pages are of the City Seal, annotated to point out elements identified in this paper. The third page following is from a book on Magick that is meant to be a textbook for the beginning witch to learn the tools of the craft. The witch craft taught in this book is of the line of Aleister Crowley. This page is part of the teaching on the meanings of various pentagrams and how they are used to evoke different entities for specific purposes of instruction. This particular pentacle is different from all of the others and has a different incantation than the others.

The last page is my suggested prayer of identificational repentance as given to me by the Lord on the day following the discovery of the meaning of the Seal.

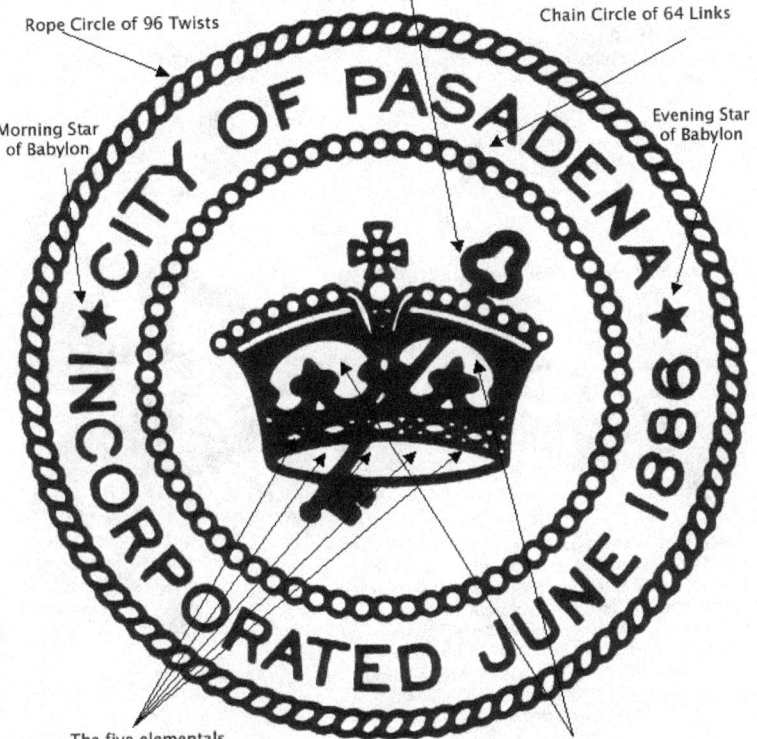

The ritual of the Rosey Cross describes the union of the sun god and the moon goddess (a sexual union) the ritual describes the sun god as represented by a cross of five elements and with the disk of the sun below

See next page for more info on this design of cross representing sun god

This design shows the sun god sexually entering the moon goddess. A later design of the seal has this opening closed up

Unseen or visable in this design is a hexagram or 6 pointed star which is described in the ritual

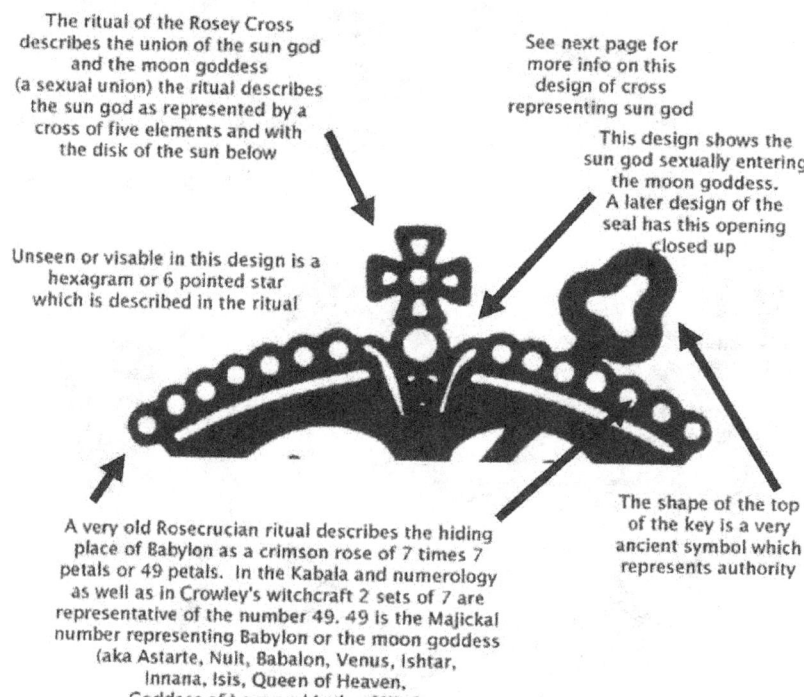

A very old Rosecrucian ritual describes the hiding place of Babylon as a crimson rose of 7 times 7 petals or 49 petals. In the Kabala and numerology as well as in Crowley's witchcraft 2 sets of 7 are representative of the number 49. 49 is the Majickal number representing Babylon or the moon goddess (aka Astarte, Nuit, Babalon, Venus, Ishtar, Innana, Isis, Queen of Heaven, Goddess of Love and Lady of War)

The shape of the top of the key is a very ancient symbol which represents authority

Lesson Nine / 405

In the Greater Key we are again confronted with a puzzle to our understanding, a puzzle obviously created to fool those without training. Between Books One and Two of the Greater Key is a section filled with "pentacles" and how they can "bring" you various powers and abilities. This seems to imply that they are actually talismans. However, if you go through Book One and actually study the evocations, you will see that the magician is told to show the pentacles to the Spirit which appears and "demand all that he shall wish from the King of Spirits." As you can see, implying that these symbolic figures are talismans is a cover to prevent their true potential from falling into the hands of the untrained and unprepared.

Below is a Pentacle associated with the Sun. Its purpose is to free you from thought patterns which keep you from achieving your desires. The evocation should be done on the day and in the hour of the Sun. If so done, the entity which appears will tell you how to break your (mental) bonds and be free. In your evocation, use the term "Lord Yud-Heh-Vahv-Heh" instead of "Spirit Bael."

The Gnostic Mass which is still used among witches and practicioners of Majick as refined by Aliester Crowley was timed to invoke the sun god at the hourof noon

Free of the guilt of sin

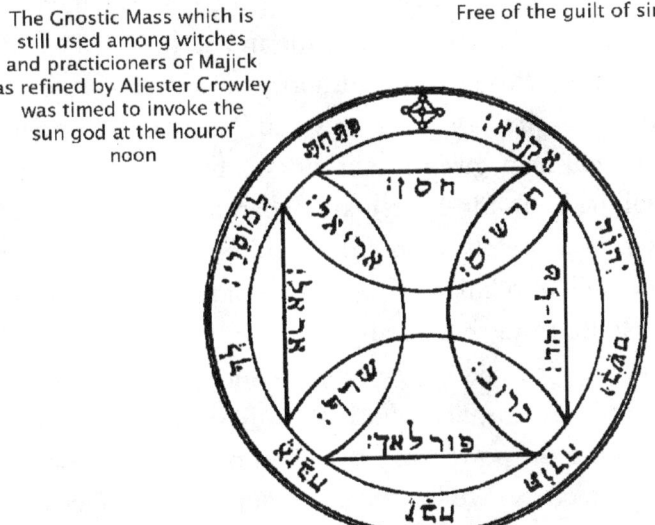

This penticle though I do not understand or desire to understand every element is based on the 12 astrological signs and the Hebrew Kabala which is a form of numerology used to create symbols of the names of angels and also to give numerical significance to words.

This page is from a handbook for begining practicioners of Crowley witchcraft

Identificational Repentance for the Root Iniquity in Pasadena

Lord Jesus and to our Father the Lord God Almighty, I repent on behalf of the men and women who acted to evoke this great evil and who have continued to give authority to babalon in this city. I repent on behalf of the men and women who have and continue up to this time to evoke the sun god to break their mental bonds and be free to sin. I repent on behalf of the men and women who have and continue to seek out babalon in order to shake off and free themselves of limitations and the covering, protection and signpost of the commandments you have given Lord God Almighty. Lord I repent on behalf of the further work of Jack Parson, L. Ron Hubbard and Marjorie Cameron as they foolishly acted to loose babalon into the material realm.

To the most high God, to the Lord God almighty, and in the name of our Lord Jesus the Christ who is our advocate, we petition you almighty Father that the celestial and angelic beings which have empowered the opening of this city to the rule and authority of babalon be rebuked. Further since you gave all authority on earth and in heaven to our Lord and savior, the Lamb that was slain before the foundation of the world, and you have given us authority such that whatever we bind on earth will be bound in heaven and whatever we loose in earth will be loosed in heaven, we therefore this day bind up the beings given authority and invited into this city by the founders and trustees of this city, and we loose from those beings the keys to hades and death, and ask that they be returned to the rightful authority. We bind the workings of all those in this city who have sought to use the stele of Osiris to further bring the powers of the underworld into this city and create a wall of protection. We loose them from the bondages of the fear of death that they have brought upon themselves and others in the city. Lord we bind the working of any other person or group that has called upon, evoked or sought to use the power of beings banished from Heaven and we instead loose Your Kingdom almighty God and Your Holy Spirit to enter their lives, demolish the strongholds and blindness and turn their eyes and hearts to you.

We ask that your warring angels and messenger angels be sent to the men and women in authority in this city as they make decisions about the seal and identity of this city in the next months. We pray that the eyes of their understanding would be opened to remove this ritual and invitation of babalon to reign over this territory. We pray that your holy spirit would lead them to place this city solely under the authority of Jesus Christ and the reign of the Kingdom of God.

We bow before you Lord Jesus only and ask that you would further reveal the mysteries that have been hidden under the rose so that all men, women and children in this city might come to the knowledge of salvation, repent, be healed of the iniquities of the fathers of this city and be delivered the resulting physical, mental and spiritual sickness in this land. We thank you Lord that we know this work is already accomplished in you.

APPENDIX C

PROPHETIC WORDS

(Given at the International Congress on Power Ministries in West Covina, CA; sponsored by Global Harvest Ministries, September 19, 2003.)

WORD FOR CALIFORNIA
Prophetic Word from Chuck Pierce (September 2003)

I would say to you, "The wind will come from the west.
    The wind will come from the west. You're beginning a new season. It's a season that will shake things throughout this nation. New wine is found in the cluster and I am about to cluster together those that are co-laboring throughout this state and I am going to form a new wineskin. What was and what even began but never got completed, I would release the wineskin in this state that would bring to completion that which was thwarted by the enemy. There will be a mega-fold anointing that will come. I would say to this state - you are hanging in the balance. You are hanging in the balance but I will send a wind to the west. This wind will begin to blow from November (2003) though January (2004). And how you grab and how you catch the wind is how not only this state will begin to turn toward Me, but this nation will begin to turn.
    There will be an adverse wind. The wind will bring great rain and there will be floods. Don't resist the floods or reject the floods for they

are signs of what I am doing in your midst. They are signs of how the heavens are beginning to open and the atmosphere is beginning to change. For the enemy has held this cosmic atmosphere in his hand to control a nation and even to control the Pacific realm. But I am changing this atmosphere, the west wind is coming, rain is coming. There will be slides and shiftings because it is going to be a sign of shifting things into place in this region.

IF YOU REJECT WHAT I AM DOING AT THIS TIME, I say the drought will get worse. As the drought gets worse locusts will come and darkness will overtake the area.

So I say, watch for the winds that will begin in November (2003). Let them blow through January (2004) and let Me blow you into a whole new place where it is known that My glory is moving in the midst of this state. And then what never has been completed and brought to fullness will rise up. Be filled by My Spirit, My Pneuma - and it will be known that My glory has come to California."

Prophetic Word from Cindy Jacobs (September 2003)

The Lord says to California, "Not only will there be shaking, there will be a fire. But when you see this fire in a place and you know it's judgment, particularly against the pornographic industry — you are going to know I am getting ready to bring a fire of the Holy Spirit. For I am coming with My visitation. I am coming. Stir yourself up today and begin to understand that I am starting to move you in a new realm. You choose, you choose what you will believe. You choose what you will stand for. You will see surely. I will use you to help change and shift to transformation."

Shake off that apathy. Just shake it off. Shake it off. Wake up! Wake up! Father, in the name of Jesus, I bind and break off that spirit of religion and that apathetic spirit, that slothful spirit - I bind it in Jesus' name. I say to you, like Deborah said to Barak, Arise! Arise and take your land. No one else is going to shake it off for you. You've got to make a decision. You have got to decide - if no one else is going to see transformation, I will see it. If no one breaks through - if I have to fast, if I have to pray, if I have to get on my face and close myself off with God. I'm telling you what, this nation will not be changed unless we break that apathetic spirit. It will not change, it will not shift. California will not shift - that spirit of entertainment that we are in the middle of - that spirit of entertainment. But I tell you God says, "I Am the great I AM - you just shake it off. You shake it off! You've got to make a decision tonight!"

And the Lord Says, "California arise! For you are coming to a place that you have never been before. Satan has tried to abort your destiny many times. But this time I am mingling the anointings from the generations together. I am beginning to marry those anointings. Look and see what I am going to do. For eye has not seen neither ear heard neither has entered in the heart of a man the things I have in store for you. Though the enemy has come in like a flood, know this, you are in your day of breakthrough. You are in your day of turning. You are in your day of going to a place that you have longed for, for many days. Grab hold of the governmental anointing that I am loosing. For I am going to put the government upon My shoulders. Look and see, for I am going to deal with the state legislature of California. I am going to deal with their wickedness. Look and see because I am going to go from one legislator to another, to another. Do not think I do not see that they are going against the will of the people. This day watch the state legislature shift. And don't think I don't see what the 9th Circuit Court of Appeals has done. For I am getting ready to judge the 9th Circuit Court of Appeals. The court of Heaven has declared and decreed: 'Enough is enough!'"

CPSIA information can be obtained
at www.ICGtesting.com
Printed in the USA
BVHW080327090722
641409BV00002B/6